Transforming
the Canadian History Classroom

Transforming the Canadian History Classroom
Imagining a New "We"

SAMANTHA CUTRARA

UBCPress · Vancouver · Toronto

© UBC Press 2020

All rights reserved. No part of this publication may be reproduced, stored in a retrieval system, or transmitted, in any form or by any means, without prior written permission of the publisher, or, in Canada, in the case of photocopying or other reprographic copying, a licence from Access Copyright, www.accesscopyright.ca.

29 28 27 26 25 24 23 22 21 20   5 4 3 2 1

Printed in Canada on FSC-certified ancient-forest-free paper (100% post-consumer recycled) that is processed chlorine- and acid-free.

Library and Archives Canada Cataloguing in Publication

Title: Transforming the Canadian history classroom : imagining a new "we" / Samantha Cutrara.

Names: Cutrara, Samantha, author.

Description: Includes bibliographical references and index.

Identifiers: Canadiana (print) 20200211293 | Canadiana (ebook) 20200211439 | ISBN 9780774862837 (softcover) | ISBN 9780774862844 (PDF) | ISBN 9780774862851 (EPUB) | ISBN 9780774862868 (Kindle)

Subjects: LCSH: Canada – History – Study and teaching. | LCSH: Classroom environment – Canada.

Classification: LCC FC155 .C88 2020 | DDC 971.0071—dc23

Canada

UBC Press gratefully acknowledges the financial support for our publishing program of the Government of Canada (through the Canada Book Fund), the Canada Council for the Arts, and the British Columbia Arts Council.

Printed and bound in Canada by Friesens
Set in Zurich, Univers, and Minion by Artegraphica Design Co. Ltd.
Cover designer: Will Brown

UBC Press
The University of British Columbia
2029 West Mall
Vancouver, BC V6T 1Z2
www.ubcpress.ca

To the students I have taught and learned from.
May this book do justice
to the experiences you've shared with me.

Contents

Acknowledgments / ix

1 Meaningful Learning: Imagining a New "We" / 3

2 The Present of Today's Past: Current Trends and Curriculum / 42

3 Students Speak: A Desire for Connected, Complex Canadian History / 65

4 Teaching the Others in the Room: Limiting Connection, Removing Complexity / 101

5 Meaningful Sites of Teaching: The Need for Time, Space, and Place / 145

6 Historic Space: Meaningful Learning in Canadian History / 166

Notes / 203

Works Cited / 207

Index / 240

Acknowledgments

I want to begin by acknowledging that this research was completed and this manuscript was written on the traditional territory of many Indigenous Nations. The area known as *Tkaronto* has been caretaken by the Anishinabek Nation, the Haudenosaunee Confederacy, the Wendat, and the Métis. The current treaty holders are the Mississaugas of the New Credit First Nation and this territory is subject to the Dish with One Spoon Wampum Belt Covenant, an agreement to peaceably share and care for the Great Lakes region. This land remains home to many Indigenous Peoples and, as a settler within Canada, I am continuously trying to understand how to best fulfill my commitment to the Indigeneity of this place in my teaching, research, and writing.

In 2015, almost four years since finishing research I conducted while at York University (Toronto), I felt that it was time to go back. I had made a commitment to the students with whom I worked to ensure that their voices would be heard and would have an impact on how we teach and learn Canadian history. I felt this was the moment to fulfill that commitment. I also felt enough time had passed to enable me to feel less angry and confused about situations I had encountered during my research. With the passage of time, I began to understand these feelings as important rather than as simply reactionary. I also knew that what I wanted to say was crucial to the conversation about Canadian history and identity – even though this was not so clear in the context of the multiple aims of my research. And so I returned. I left a comfortable job in my field to fulfill a commitment I had made to a group of fifteen-year-old students.

This book is that commitment fulfilled.

Thus, I first want to thank the students and teachers I worked with during my research for sharing their work, experiences, hopes, and fears. I want to thank the principals who allowed me into the schools as well as the school board for recognizing the importance of conducting this research in their schools. I hope I have done them all proud.

I also want to thank UBC Press, my editors at UBC Press, Darcy Cullen and Ann Macklem, for supporting this work and allowing me to speak with a voice that was authentic to my experience.

I want to acknowledge the financial support of MSA during the manuscript process.

I want to thank and acknowledge the communities of support at York University, the Ontario Institute for Studies in Education at the University of Toronto, and the Institute for Women's Studies and Gender Studies at the University of Toronto. I also want to thank the History Education Network (THEN/HiER), which played a valuable role in fostering community and discussion among history educators across Canada during a key time in my research. Among these institutions and communities, I especially want to thank Barrie Bennet, Susan Dion, Roger Simon, Alice Pitt, Alison Griffith, Cecilia Morgan, Ruth Sandwell, Linzi Manicom, Michelle Murphy, Carla Peck, Jan Haskings-Winner, and Penny Clark.

Friends and family have heard about this project for years and I thank them for their continued love and support, especially Michael, Yvette, and Cosette Cutrara, Emma Lind, Tarah Brookfield, Susana Miranda, Taunya Trembley, Mary Chaktsiris, and many others: thank you.

I am also indebted to the many teachers, educators, historians, archivists, and museum interpreters I have worked with and learned from over the last twenty years, especially those from Black Creek Pioneer Village, Gibson House Historical Museum, and the Archives of Ontario.

I also thank the students at Seneca College and the University of Toronto, who have taught me to be a better writer.

Finally, I want to acknowledge the commitment, love, and humility to engage in this work. Also, always G.

Transforming
the Canadian History Classroom

1

Meaningful Learning
Imagining a New "We"

Who do we imagine when we imagine Canada? What do we imagine? Who and what make up Canada's past? Who and what define Canada's future?

We can answer these questions from a variety of perspectives, but, as cliché as it sounds, you have to look to the past to understand the future. Perhaps this is why there is so much debate about what and who should be part of the national history curriculum. Formal history education provides a structured basis for imagining a national community, grounded in the past with growth toward the future. "This is who and what Canada is," curricula seem to assert. "Use this knowledge to invest in our strengths and rectify our weaknesses," it encourages. When we look at the history of history curriculum in Canada, we can see an evolution in the stories we tell – from allegiance to the British Crown to a critical acknowledgment of our mistakes in the past (Osborne 2000, 2002) – but Canada as a good place, a peaceable place, a place with respect for government and a tolerance for difference, remains a strong metanarrative snaking its way through the learning objectives and expectations across the provinces.

Yet, with a rapidly changing Canadian population and the impetus to answer the calls to action made by the Truth and Reconciliation Commission, Canada is rethinking the stories it tells about itself – the heroes we worship and the events we commemorate – because who and what Canada is is also changing. The 2011 census highlighted that Canadians represent two hundred different ethnicities and that 19 percent of Canadians identify themselves as a visible minority (Statistics Canada 2013). As a nation growing through immigration (Statistics Canada 2017c), one in five Canadians is foreign born, with over 2 million immigrants making Canada their home since the year 2000. Statistics Canada projects that, by 2031, 30 percent of Canadians will be a visible minority with a mother tongue other than English or French and that 55 percent of these people will be immigrants or the Canadian-born children of immigrants residing in urban centres (Statistics Canada 2010). Visible minority and immigrant populations are generally younger than the population as a whole, with almost 34 percent of the immigrant population between 2006 and 2011 under the age of twenty-four and 19 percent under the age of fourteen (Statistics Canada 2013). Aboriginal populations in Canada are also growing – the fastest-growing population in Canada – due to high birth rates and a greater claim to Aboriginal identity. Aboriginal populations are also young and metropolitan. One-third of Aboriginal people are under the age of fourteen and over half live in metropolitan centres (Statistics Canada 2017a).

These demographics suggest that, following our sesquicentennial, Canadian classrooms, especially in urban centres, will be host to young transnational and (post/neo)colonial populations in ways that could never have been imagined at Canada's Confederation (Statistics Canada 2017b).[1] These youth will have Canadian identities layered with experiences and histories from all over the world. They will come to experience ethnic and cultural diversity as a normal part of being Canadian and will see Canada in the same way they see their own lives – as multilayered, global, networked, and in need of justice. While the vision and enactment of an idealized multicultural Canadian identity is rarely, if ever, perfect, research shows that Canadian youth recognize and take pride in their diverse enactments of Canadian identity. And so, as these youth mature, this pride will challenge the ways concepts and enactments of citizenship, nationality, and belonging in Canada are neither as straightforward nor as connected as they once were imagined to be (Ahmad Ali 2008; Grant 2016; Ostashewski, Frey, and Johnson 2018; Tastsoglou and Petrinioti 2011; Wenshya Lee and Hébert 2006). Our job in our history classrooms, I venture, is to help students make sense of these experiences and concepts as part of being a *Canadian* – a twenty-first-century transnational and (post/neo)colonial

Canadian – who will work toward greater justice for people on this land and around the world.

However, history and citizenship education in North America has been notorious for promoting a one-dimensional understanding of national belonging that is far from the realities and stories of most young people today (An 2009; Ong 1996; Salinas and Alarcón 2016; Vickery 2016). Canadian history education often reaffirms a vision of Canada as a nation developed through European settlement and commercial trade, with growth based on making progress through the wilderness, gaining independence and freedom through military involvement, and developing a tolerance for multiculturalism. This version of Canada leaves out the violent history of colonialism, the state's perpetuation of continuous racial injustice, and the desire (and actions taken) to make, and keep, Canada white. This version of history fails to complicate stories of colonialism, settlement, and/or migration; it fails to question and complicate the ways gender and sexuality have acted and interacted to frame and define respectability and class; it fails to trace the development of the nation as the development of neo/colonial capitalist expansion; it fundamentally fails to reflect the complex history of the complex world Canadian students are living in. The absence of these histories in how we teach Canadian history means that these stories of colonialism, migration, race, gender, and capitalism fail to be invited in and explored in our classrooms as having a lasting legacy on the present. But it is these stories, these complex and intersectional stories, that frame the lives young people lead today, and, as this book will show, are the stories that young people want taught in schools.

The lack of recognition of how the complexities of the past affect the realities of the present has lasting ramifications for how young people understand their place in the past and future of Canada. Students who do not see their experiences reflected in history have a limited understanding of their self and a sense of disconnectedness with the nation and their peers (Dei 1997; T. Epstein 1998; Létourneau 2004; Levstik 2000). George Dei (1997) found that the absence of Black people in the Canadian narrative contributed "to Black students' sense of invisibility and lack of status as Canadians," which directly correlated to the choices Black students made to continue or not continue schooling. As one of Dei's research participants said: "It's like you're learning about somebody else's history ... It started to take a toll on me after a while" (138).

At the post-secondary level, Tony Waters (2005) found that students repeatedly stated that the history they learned in their undergraduate history courses was "real" because it discussed conflict and struggle, while the history they learned in high school was "fake" because it was overly patriotic and positive. Waters's experience indicated that students felt that they had to choose between these two narratives: they were either for or against the national story – they could not be both. In his research with ethnic Estonians recollecting Estonia's entry into the Soviet Union in 1940, James Wertsch (2000) found that people could carry du(a)el(ling) national histories: the official narrative of the state and the personal narrative that reflected their experiences. People could easily recite the official version of the national story, but Wertsch found that they *believed* the other one, the personal one, the one that aligned with their lived experiences. This finding led Wertsch to question whether it was possible to teach beliefs, as well as knowledge, about history.

While teachers often want to avoid conflict and division in the classroom (Pomson and Ron 1998), these findings suggest that teaching an official and sanitized version of the national story does not actually lead to greater cohesion in the classroom. The dualities of national history – real versus fake, official versus personal – indicate that many histories can be present in the history classroom at the same time and that these histories can be at odds with one another. Not acknowledging the multiplicity of histories that we carry around with us can separate more than bring together and fail to demonstrate how the congruence of narratives that make up the past are the very stories that tell who "we" are in the present. As Jamaican Canadian dub poet D'bi Young (2016) stated at Historica Canada's 2016 event, An Evening Celebrating Black Women in Canada, "issues around racism and sexism and classism and ageism and ableism and homophobia and all of those things, are really about a lack of self-knowledge" – a lack of awareness about who and what have come before and the lack of understanding we may have about the connections we all share. Seeing these connections, understanding these connections, *appreciating* these connections brings us closer to breaking down an "us" versus "them" mentality and getting to a greater sense of "we" that can take into account multiple stories and lived experiences as being simultaneously part of the nation.

Yet, as Kent den Heyer and Laurence Abbott (2011, 630) found, for many history educators, the concepts of "we" and "they" in history education "are assumed rather than taken up as the starting points for historical work across the disciplines." Teacher candidates do not recognize that a grand narrative of Canada exists to homogenize and define "Canadian" by stipulating who and what is part of our national identity and who and what are Other. Because they fail to begin with the grand narrative, teachers also fail to problematize it and thus even solidify it, exacerbating who is "us" and who is "them" in the Canadian nation (den Heyer and Abbott 2011; Létourneau and Moisan 2004). However, it is the very concepts of "we" and "they" embedded in the grand Canadian narrative that need to be interrogated in our transnational and (post/neo)colonial Canada, especially for the transnational and (post/neo)colonial youth in our classrooms today.

When young people look at the world around them, they see populist politics, climate injustice, public health crises, war, displacement, and other structural effects of a world that will provide them with less stability than it did previous generations. We are beginning to see that youth are fighting back and demanding that world leaders be more accountable for the racial, gendered, economic, and environmental inequities that shape our world today (Earl, Maher, and Elliott 2017; Pinter 2018; Pires 2018; Teotonio 2018; Vandermaas-Peeler et al. 2018). These activities will not be confined by national walls but will be networked, digital, and global (Middaugh, Clark, and Ballard 2017). These youth are preparing for this world – these youth *are* this world – and to be successful they need to stand on a solid historical foundation that brings together more than separates. A solid historical foundation that reflects the world students see around them. Not a series of stories that fail to hold weight for the connections and complexities young people embody today.

So I ask: How can Canadian history education better take its place in this conversation? How do we teach Canadian history in ways that prepare today's youth for enacting change in this world? How do we teach Canadian history in ways that allow transnational and (post/neo)colonial experiences to be understood within Canada? How can we imagine a Canadian identity in the Canadian history classroom that ensures that the world outside the classroom is contextualized inside the classroom? How can we bring these stories together to speak for a Canadian "we" that comes together to fight against and dismantle national and global systems of inequity? How can we transform the Canadian history classroom to imagine a new "we" that holds space for the multiple ways one can be a Canadian? These are the central questions we, as history educators in the twenty-first century, must answer in both our pedagogies and our classroom practices.

To move forward in Canada, to develop a historically grounded sense of "we" in our history classrooms, to transform who we could be and what we could do in our history education, we need to be in a better position to understand Canada as a multilayered and complex narrative of colonialism, migration, inequity, and resistance. This does not just mean ensuring that a diversity of perspectives is heard, but rather capturing how the *structures* of our nation enable some stories to define how we understand the nation and other stories to be superfluous, or peripheral, to these understandings. The findings of the Truth and Reconciliation Commission of Canada (TRC 2015a), for example, have resulted in more Indigenous content in Canadian classrooms, but the Commission was very clear that content inclusion alone will not lead to reconciliation. Rather, reconciliation needs to be understood as the development and ongoing maintenance of relationships between Indigenous and non-Indigenous peoples based on respect for the land and for the people whose epistemologies, cosmologies, and experiences have been grounded in that land for thousands of years. It is a change in the structure of Canadian knowing, committing, and relating to each other and the land that the Commission has advocated for, but the stories that support this change are the ones settlers have been trained not to hear or rather to "evidence" away (Cutrara 2018; Seixas 2012).

The history classroom seems like an ideal place to develop the fodder for a new "we" in Canada, a place to deconstruct the stories we have been told and to find new ways to put them back together again. A place where stories can grow and change, shrink and be replaced, augment and develop who Canada is now and who it could be in the future. A place to put stories back together again in ways that acknowledge how injustice in the past has led to structural exclusion in the present. To put stories back together again in ways that decentre the voices and aims of our country's founders who tried to legislate away the very cultural and ethnic diversity Canada is known for today. To put the stories of Canada back together again in ways that provide a foundation for greater social action. To put the stories of Canada back together again in ways that demonstrate how the past is visceral, and present, and courts both the inequity and the resistance we see around us. This is not an impractical and idealistic imagining of Canadian history education, but a transformative one designed for the *student* – not for the nation, or for the history, or for the discipline. To transform the Canadian history classroom is to see history education as being able, and willing, to do something different, to do something radical, for the young people in the room and the ways they can be in this country together.

However, so often when we talk about history education, we focus on *teaching* – on better methods, greater resources, more professional development. This is important – we need to ensure teachers are equipped to do this difficult work in their classrooms – but when we *only* talk about teaching, when we *only* focus on teaching, we fail to focus on *learning*. We fail to focus on students: who they are, what they know, and what they need for the future. When we only focus on the work of the teacher, not on the experience and needs of the student, we can inadvertently slip into what Paulo Freire (2006) calls the "banking" model of education, whereby teachers "deposit" content into students' heads, as if students were nothing but empty vessels. Another way to think of this is as education for transmission, not transformation (Miller and Seller 1990). Where education is designed to be repeated by the student, not activated into something new.

When we make the explicit effort to think about *learning* rather than teaching, we can be reminded that the students in our classrooms are people before they are students. They are young Canadians who will inherit the world we are creating. They are not empty vessels waiting to be told the rules of Canadian legitimacy. They are young people interested in understanding the rules of the society they see around them. They are interested in understanding why those rules do not always make sense, how those rules can seem to challenge their own lived experience, and how those rules are not neutral or unchanging. They may also be interested in seeing how those rules can be challenged, sublimated, subverted, rewritten, and radicalized. How people like them are in a position to seize these rules, "invert their meaning, and redirect them against those who had initially imposed them," to quote Michel Foucault (1980a, 151).

When we think about learning over teaching in our history classes, we can start seeing how young people are in their history classes waiting to be shown, whether they recognize it or not, that history is possibility, not predetermination (Freire 2004, 59–60), and we, as history educators, can guide them toward this knowledge. If we want our students to be literate in navigating their world, they need to know that their stories, their transnational and (post/neo)colonial stories, are there. And that we recognize the pain in their disavowal. And that these stories are not individual experiences but *national stories,* and to learn them is the work that *all* Canadians have a responsibility to engage in, not just the ones who feel their voices are missing. When we focus on *learning* Canadian history, rather than *teaching* Canadian history, we can provide space for the transformative exploration of the Canadian past to help young people see themselves in the Canadian present and future.

This focus on students and their learning is what I call *meaningful learning* in Canadian history education. Meaningful learning in history education involves history that has significance to students' lives now and in the future, both inside and outside the classroom, framed with interpretations of the past that align with their sense of familial or community history in and for the wider world. This sense of meaningful learning in Canadian history is both affective and political. Ideally, in their learning, students would feel a connection to history and be reaffirmed in their understanding of how complex the world is today. With this knowledge, students can be stirred to make change for a world that has greater justice for themselves and others. This definition draws on Joseph Novak's (2010, 18) definition of meaningful learning as the "constructive integration of thinking, feeling, and acting leading to empowerment for commitment and responsibility." For Novak, meaningful learning requires three things: connection to prior knowledge, meaningful material, and the assent of the learner. He identifies that meaningful learning happens when students have space to negotiate meaning of new, meaningful content in a positive emotional climate (Ausubel, Novak, and Hanesian 1978; Novak 2010), which develops their sense of "I'm okay" and grounds their sense of self in the classroom community (Novak 2010).

While Joseph Novak comes from a learning science background, the idea of "meaningful learning" can also be found in radical and critical approaches to education, specifically in the work of Freire (2006) and bell hooks (2010). Freire writes that an emancipatory approach to education, a "pedagogy of the oppressed," is a problem-posing approach to teaching and learning that makes people and their histories the starting point for education. It is education, he writes, that is imbued with a "profound trust in people and their creative power" (2006, 75). bell hooks (2010) also identified the importance of centring people and their experience in her articulation of an "engaged pedagogy" that involves a mutual and interactive relationship between teacher and student, with ongoing dialogue based on trust, confidence, and a belief in democracy. Taken together, these ideas stress the importance of the learner, what they already know, what they need to know to move forward in a healthful and secure manner, and the importance of material that can be discussed and actively explored while doing so. This approach to teaching and learning decentres a canon and decentres the ego of the teacher in favour of the student and their needs for the present and future.

To learn Canadian history *meaningfully*, then, is to connect the past with what one understands about the present, the complex and diverse present, in ways that will have a positive and lasting impact on one's sense of self. To learn Canadian history *meaningfully* means students come to know themselves in a past that has denied the multiculturalism that is now lauded in the present. To understand what truth and reconciliation means when decolonizing and Indigenizing Canadian culture makes many Canadians, especially many Canadian leaders, uncomfortable. To understand how power and privilege work through present-day remembrance and commemoration practices. A meaningful learning approach to teaching Canadian history means that today's diverse, transnational, and (post/neo)colonial youth are able to see themselves in the future *and* past of Canada, and that their needs for learning history are integrated in the practice and pedagogy of teaching Canadian history. This transformative approach to history education does not rely on inventing new stories about history, but rather demonstrating the connections we have with the complexity of the past and doing so in ways that demonstrate a care for students as whole and complex Canadians.

Nationalist discourses are designed to define "us" in opposition to "them." But transforming the history classroom to develop a sense of "we" is premised on ever-increasing circles of inclusion and connection: the inclusion of the students and histories in the room; the inclusion of controversial and difficult histories as present in our understanding of the past; the inclusion of Indigeneity and ways we have to continue developing relationships of reconciliation; the inclusion of time and space to research and think through what we know and how we know it, along with what we do not know and why we do not know it; the inclusion and care for the Other and acknowledgment of their presence through their structured absence. This transformation is based on an "ethical relationality" that is an "ecological understanding of human relationality that does not deny difference, but rather seeks to understand more deeply how our different histories and experiences position us in relation to each other" (Donald 2012, 535).

A relational and connected approach to teaching and learning Canadian history, however, is not an easy fit in today's curriculum. Over the last decade, Canadian history curricula across Canada have been focused on an approach to teaching and learning history that supports the development of students' "historical consciousness" through the Benchmarks of Historical Thinking. This approach to history curriculum is more transactional than it is transformative, in that it focuses on the development of rational, skills-based problem solving through the discipline, rather than on personal and social change through a collaborative exploration of the ecological, intuitive, and interrelated conceptions of knowledge (Miller and Seller 1990). Rather than focusing on potentially divisive stories, the historical thinking approach focuses on the questions that "everyone" asks about the world around them – questions such as: How did things get to be where they are today? What group do I belong to and how did we come to be? How do we judge actions of the past? Are things getting better or are they getting worse? What stories should I believe? What stories should we tell? What can I do to make the world better? (Seixas 2006b, 15). Understanding how to think through these questions should be the focus of Canadian history education because, according to Canadian educational theorist Peter Seixas (2006b, 21), "there are too many origins, too many heroes, too many stories" in Canadian history for history education to do otherwise.

However, the questions that Seixas identifies that we *all* share about the world around us are very similar to the questions Justice Murray Sinclair said that Indigenous youth in Canada have been unable to answer because of their violent estrangement from their own histories – questions such as: Where do I come from? Where am I going? Why am I here? Who am I? (Sinclair, Wilson, and Littlechild 2015). The idea that teaching Canadian history should start with everyone having the same questions about the world they live in, and that these questions provide a neutral starting ground for engaging in the disciplinary study of the past, glosses over the fact that history does not affect us all equally and that we do not come, we *cannot* come, to learning history with the same questions either. This presumption of an equal starting ground through these questions conceals the politics in the present and past in ways that are not healthful in students working through, or beyond, them in the study of history.

I make this argument early as a way to position my thinking in the larger landscape of history education in Canada. I explore the history of historical thinking in further detail in Chapter 2, and recognize the ways this thinking is embedded in the fabric of contemporary curriculum. However, given that the historical thinking approach to history curriculum had not been integrated in the curriculum when I conducted my research, the critiques I have of historical thinking (Cutrara 2010, 2012, 2016a, 2018b, 2019) are an *implicit* rather than explicit focus of this book. Instead, the current inquiry and primary-source-focused history curriculum used across Canada can be *complemented* by an approach to pedagogy that places students and their meaningful learning at the centre of how teaching and learning is organized. This complement, this radical visioning of history education, is the focus of this book.

The majority of evidence I use in this book draws on research I conducted in four high school history classrooms in Toronto in 2011. Greater details follow, but, in sum, the purpose of this research was to understand the relationships in a history classroom that supported or curtailed the possibilities for meaningful learning. As I discuss throughout, I found that although students were keen to learn history "meaningfully," they were presented with content and instruction in their Canadian history classes that had nothing to do with who they were or what they wanted to know. The

Canada they learned about in school was disconnected from the Canada they saw around them, and so students stated, and acted in ways, that demonstrated a "hatred" of Canadian history and Canadian history education.

But what I also saw and heard in these classrooms, and what I highlight in this book, is that these students represented a diverse group of young people trying to make sense of who they were in this place called Canada. They wanted to learn Canadian history in ways that acknowledged and cared for their complex connections to Canada more so than, or at least alongside with, the mainstream story of Canada. Yet these desires were not always seen, acknowledged, or even recognized as valid for understanding Canadian history. Because of the tension that developed from the denial of students' desires, relationships were not developed in the classroom – between the teacher and the students, the students and the content, the teacher and the content – in ways that could have invited students to learn meaningfully from the Canadian past.

This book focuses on those experiences in order to demonstrate the meaningful possibilities that can be imagined when students' desires to learn history are put first. This is not advocating for curricular change as much as advocating for a pedagogical approach that is more transformative than transactional or transmissive. This work encourages a shift in how a class may engage in their history education so that the focus is less on remembering facts or assessing evidence and more on the meaningful learning that can be engendered when those facts and that evidence are used to develop a greater, more affective engagement in imagining a nation that includes them. This book is a call for a radical imaginative history education practice in Canada, by placing students – and the stories they carry, the stories they want to hear, the histories they desire to be part of – at the centre of what is done, and can be done, in the history classroom, and using that centre to ratify and support a historically grounded vision of who "we" are in Canada today.

Critical Theory for Reading Canadian History
To advocate for a more student-centric, meaningful learning approach to Canadian history education, I situate this work within the traditions of critical theory and critical pedagogy. Our history in Canada is so messy,

so complicated, so violent that we need to approach teaching the Canadian past with critical tools that can tackle how we can currently be one of the most diverse countries in the world and yet have an unreconciled colonial history marked by resistance to this very diversity. To move forward in our understanding of Canada, we need to move past add-and-stir or drag-and-drop methods of teaching diverse stories from our past (Cutrara 2016b) and instead use theoretical tools that can help us understand how difference has been constructed in the past and the lasting ramifications these constructions have on the present. Critical theories such as critical race theory, feminist theory, and poststructuralist theory challenge systems of oppression like white supremacy, patriarchy, and capitalism that structure our society. If we use critical theory(ies) such as these to understand Canadian history, we can open up space for more nuanced, critical, radical, and transformative ways of addressing the continued inequity in the Canadian present.

Reading history through a critical race theory (CRT) lens places the analysis of race and racism at the forefront of understanding society. CRT evolved out of post-civil rights American legal theory and has influenced different disciplines and research methodologies, including those in education (Ladson-Billings and Tate 1995). When viewed together, the work of Derrick Bell (1980, 1987), Cheryl Harris (1993), Kimberlé Crenshaw (1988, 1995), and Richard Delgado (1988, 1989, 1990) defined what is now seen as the three central concepts of CRT. These are:

1 racism is endemic in North American society, it is not "merely an individual pathology ... [but] a vast system that structures our institutions and our relationships" (Vaught and Castagno 2008, 96);
2 liberalism, and the accompanying ideas of neutrality, objectivity, colour blindness, and meritocracy, support white supremacy and maintain the subordinate position of many people of colour;
3 because reality is created and structured through stories, narratives, and interactions, counterstories and experiential knowledge by and about people of colour can challenge what is presented as reality and be used "as sources of critique of the dominant social order which purposely devalues them" (Stovall 2006, 244).

When understood within the context of these three ideas, CRT points to ethno-cultural differences coded as "race" as being dynamic, contextual, and relational. Race, then, is not a fact, but a "system of socially constructed and enforced categories, constantly recreated and modified through human interaction" (Gillborn 1995, 3). This "postmodern" conception of race breaks open a simplistic reading of skin colour and focuses on the power relations woven through cultural interpretations – power relations directly correlated to the type of opportunities and legitimacy one has in society (Ross 2009).

Because race has been shown to have no standing in a scientific framework (Rose and Rose 2005), some have argued that referencing "race" as an aspect of one's social identity continues to categorize and separate people based on their skin colour and, in so doing, supports a white supremacist agenda (Darder and Torres 2003). But there is a "reality of a racialized society and its impact on 'raced' people in their everyday lives" (Ladson-Billings and Tate 1995, 48), and so using CRT as a lens through which to view the world invites us to more critically interrogate these realities and the influences they have on our lives. When we use CRT to think through the past and present, we come to recognize and examine the social and political reality of differences based on "race" and can ask questions about the operation of these racial differences in our lives – questions such as when and how race is used, by whom, and to what ends (C.I. Harris 1993, 1763). Using questions such as these to frame one's engagement of race and racism (past and present) acknowledges that, as a complicated, constructed, and referential category, race is an important predictor of one's lived realities and cannot be ignored simply because it lacks biological merit.

If we use these ideas to help us understand Canadian history, we see how race has operated (and continues to operate) to stratify and ratify society along racial lines in ways that support white European colonialist privilege over the experiences of those who are racialized. With a CRT reading of Canadian history, we come to see that Canada was not a country that intended to be multicultural; rather, it was a country that intended to stay white. As McKittrick (2006, 95) writes, the "'making' of Canada situates a struggle that enmeshes race, whiteness, and the soil as they are attached to the nation's legal, political, and ideological claims of colonial superiority."

The Indian Act, 1876, for example, was an aggressive attempt to enmesh race, whiteness, and land together in ways that attempted to manage and control Indigenous populations. The act defined who was an "Indian" and stripped First Nations populations of legal personhood, the ability to share traditions, and the agency to interact with whom and where they chose (Joseph 2018). The act is not just a "body of laws that for over a century have controlled every aspect of Indian life." Rather, it is a "regulatory regime" that has provided "ways of understanding Native identity, organizing a conceptual framework that has shaped contemporary Native life in ways that are now so familiar as to almost seem 'natural'" (Lawrence 2003, 3).

This act was aggressively enacted as a "regulatory regime" in the 1884 amendment that increased the role of residential and industrial schools in Indigenous life. These government-sponsored religious schools were designed to "emancipate" Indigenous students from their "tribal governments" and facilitate students' "final absorption into the general community" (J.S. Dennis in a memo to Prime Minister John A. MacDonald in 1878, quoted in TRC 2015b, 55). The mandate of these schools was to "kill the Indian in the child" by removing First Nations' children from their homes and forcing them to work and learn under violent white ideologies and practices.[2] Up until 1920, these schools were voluntary, but in 1920, as a response to declining voluntary enrolment, an additional amendment was added to the act that allowed the Canadian government to compel First Nations' children to attend these schools (TRC 2015b, 62). As Bob Joseph (2018, 53) writes, while "other policies were harsh but could be worked around ... when the government took the children from their families, it was unbearable." The violence of, and in, these residential schools tore apart communities, cultures, languages, and senses of self in ways that continue to have lasting effects today. The release of the Truth and Reconciliation Commission's final report in 2015 revealed the extent of the physical, psychological, and sexual abuse in the residential school system that overtly and wilfully attempted cultural and spiritual assimilation for over 150,000 Aboriginal children between 1870 and 1996.

While Canada worked to eliminate racial diversity from *within* Canada, it also tried to prevent racial diversity from *entering* into Canada through immigration policies that privileged white immigrants from Britain, France, the United States, and Germany. In the words of one Member of Parliament in 1903, these were the immigrants who were welcome because they belonged "to the races to which we belong, they are men who tend to the elevation of our population, and to the progress of our country. They are accustomed to our institutions, they are suitable to our climate, and we desire to get them" (Thomas Sproule, quoted in Kelley and Trebilcock 1998, 131). Race was both implicitly and explicitly codified in these immigration policies, and in the 1919 amendment to the Immigration Act, for example, immigrants could be prohibited from entering Canada if they were deemed unsuitable to the "climatic, industrial, social and educational, labour or other conditions or requirements of Canada," because of their "peculiar customs, habits, modes of life and methods of holding property and because of their probable inability to become readily assimilated" ("Immigration Act Amendment, 1919" n.d.). The "peculiar customs" of immigrants or their suitability to the Canadian climate were often overlooked if immigrants fulfilled the need for labour and/or settlement.

Chinese and Taiwanese men, for example, were brought to Canada in the 1880s as "guest labourers" to expand the transcontinental railway. Often given the most dangerous work, such as handling explosives, these labourers experienced poor working conditions, were paid meagre wages, and incurred expenses for which they had to pay out of pocket – unlike the non-Asian workers (Chan 2019). Chinese and Taiwanese workers were met with hostility and were seen at best, as a necessary evil in the development of the country. As Prime Minister John A. MacDonald declared in 1882: "Either you must have labour or you can't have the railway." However, even MacDonald objected to these workers becoming permanent settlers in Canada. He also stated that once the work was completed, he would "join to a reasonable extent in preventing a permanent settlement in this country of Mongolian or Chinese immigrants" (quoted in Kelley and Trebilcock 1998, 94–95). Many of these Chinese and Taiwanese labourers died in lonely, hostile conditions, with legislation like the Chinese Exclusion Act, 1923, making it difficult for those who remained to establish Canadian homes in the decades following the completion of the railway.

Eighty years later, in the 1960s, the West Indian Immigration Scheme encouraged educated single women from the West Indies to temporarily immigrate to Canada as domestic labourers in white households, forgoing both their education and class privilege in their country of origin to better themselves and/or to see another country (Henry 1968). Although "coloured" British subjects were not desirable in the Canadian nation because, according to the Minister of Citizenship and Immigration in 1955, they were not "a tangible asset, and as a result are more or less ostracized [and t]hey do not assimilate readily and pretty much vegetate to a low standard of living" (quoted in Carty 1994, 217), West Indian immigrants could provide cheap labour in Canada, especially when appeals to white domestic immigrants fell flat (Henry 1968). When faced with an unfriendly, ignorant, and prejudiced society (Henry 1968), these women lived in isolation and were called "our loneliest immigrants" in an article for *Maclean's* magazine in 1961 (Lamming 1961).

However, while these brief examples demonstrate Canada's legacy in using and exploiting the labour of racialized immigrants when it suited its needs, diversity in Canada today cannot solely be equated with immigration. Such a view implicitly privileges a vision of a white, colonial "ethnic nationalism that represents the nation in terms of consanguinity" (Montgomery 2005, 314). People of colour have been Canadian for centuries but can still be asked where they are really from (Chapra and Chatterjee 2009; Paragg 2015; Shadd 2001). It is as if, for example, "'Black Canadian' or 'African Canadian' is – in the public perception – a contradiction in terms" (Shadd 2001, 11). It is these beliefs that can result in a denial of belonging for racialized Canadians in the Canadian present. As McKittrick (2006, 99) writes, "the geographies of black Canada also tend to be constructed according to narratives of absence or elsewhere."

Take for example, the community of Africville. Africville was a village outside of Halifax, Nova Scotia, that was settled in the mid-eighteenth century by Black people who were freed slaves, Maroons of Jamaica, or formerly enslaved people who became refugees after the War of 1812. In the 1960s, almost two hundred years after its founding, in the name of urban renewal, the City of Halifax bulldozed the houses and community buildings in Africville, citing "blighted" and "dilapidated" living conditions (Tattrie 2019). However, the living conditions were blighted and dilapidated because the government made them so. Despite being landowners and paying taxes accordingly, residents of Africville did not receive any municipal services such as water, sewer, or garbage removal, and, added to that, in the 1950s a dump was built at the edge of the community, resulting in even more slum-like conditions (Nelson 2009). Africville became a slum because the municipal government viewed the space and its inhabitants as expendable to the Canadian nation. They were not Canadians with the full rights and privileges held by their white neighbours in other Halifax communities.

How do we reconcile these histories in our understanding of our Canadian identity? How can we come to terms with how "the image of the respectable, peaceful, multiculturalism-loving Canadian citizen, descendant of the two founding nations, France and Britain, goes hand in hand with its opposites: the Indigenous 'Indian,' the Black, the immigrant newcomer and the refugee" (Austin 2010, 19)? How do we make sense of the eradication of non-white peoples in Canadian history when multiculturalism has been lauded as a defining Canadian value, and, along with bilingualism, has been a policy since 1971 and enshrined in law since 1988? It is by using the theoretical tools of CRT that we can come to see how these historical visions of Canada are still coded within policies and practices that reference and organize cultural, ethnic, and "racial" differences today. CRT can help us go beyond a celebration of multiculturalism and toward a critical understanding of culture, ethnicity, and race that is needed to fully understand the Canadian past and present.

While multiculturalism is a codified way for us to understand and respect diversity in Canada, it can unwittingly (re)affirm principles that keep ideas about "us" and "them" more stable than we intend. Multiculturalism in Canada does not do what we think it does – bring diverse cultures together. Instead, it manages "a colonial history, an imperialist present, and a convoluted liberal democracy" in ways that "needs and creates 'others'" to subvert demands for anti-racism and political equality (Bannerji 2000, 10, 97). Because the central tenets of multiculturalism come from a liberal, rather than from a radical, understanding of self and society, multiculturalism implicitly affirms an individualistic, progress-focused management of difference for an ordered capitalist democracy. It also obfuscates the acknowledgment of the First Peoples of this land and our need to understand what colonialism is, how it has operated, and how it continues to shape Canadian identity today (Dion 2005; St. Denis 2011).

Multiculturalism thus provides a centre, a white centre, for managing difference in ways that keep, maintain, and celebrate that white centre and the privileges that come with it (Bannerji 2000; Mackey 2005).

Approaching diversity through a belief in a multicultural utopia does not allow us to explore how colonial practices and legislation, exploitative labour policies for immigrants, and restrictive rules related to migration and cultural expression have been built into Canadian law and society, and how just because these politics, policies, and practices are "in the past" does not mean they are not present in our lives today. On the contrary, these ideas and practices are very much woven into the structure of Canada and they have a continued impact on the present in ways that challenge the vision of multiculturalism we may now laud. As Ahmad Ali (2008) writes, young people in Canada may celebrate Canadian multiculturalism, but they will face disappointment when they begin to have greater experiences with the structural racism built into our country.

Racism and the limits of multiculturalism, however, cannot be understood in a vacuum. Black feminist theorist Kimberlé Crenshaw (1995) stressed the importance of intersectionality in understanding social divisions and stratification. That is, race, gender, class, and sexuality cannot be understood as separate from each other; they are interconnected and contingent on the other. Because history "is not simply what happened in the past but, more pointedly, the kinds of *knowledge* about the past that we are *made aware of*" (Burton 1992, 26; emphasis in original), critical race and feminist theories have pushed our histories in new directions, and so we no longer expect to just learn the histories of white men in our classrooms anymore. However, even with the inclusion of people of colour, women, and labourers in our national histories, these histories remain "precarious," they may still be positioned as add-ons, and thus by exploring both the inclusion and exclusion of these histories from our national narratives, we can see how historical narratives can operate to "discursively maintain the invisibility" of how race, gender, and class operate in society (Rooney 2006, 359). This is the difference between including people of colour, women, or labourers in our study of the past as a way to highlight different perspectives, and using the study of the past to explore how differences in race, gender, and class come to be constructed in ways that maintain white supremacist patriarchal capitalism. It is through using history to understand how society is structured that we can better comprehend the ways power and privilege function through the structures we often accept as normal.

To explore these ideas more fully, we can complement CRT and intersectional feminist theories with postmodern and poststructural theories. Postmodern and poststructural theories are about the disbelief in metanarratives and the structures they support and that, in turn, support them (Lyotard 1997). Postmodern and poststructural theories, drawing on literacy analysis, are theories which help us understand how the world is created by patterns, stories, and signs that shape what and how we come to know and believe is possible. These patterns, stories, and signs become the structures, the (meta)narratives, that seem to define the world and how we may operate within it. Working with postmodern and poststructural theories in our study of the past allows for a "new way of analyzing constructions of meaning and relationships of power that call ... unitary, universal categories into question and historicize ... concepts otherwise treated as natural ... or absolute" (Scott 1988, 33).

It is through postmodern and poststructural theories that we can better explore how history is not a canonical narrative of the past, but rather a medium for constantly refashioning, remoulding, and retelling what happened in the past for the purposes of the present (see, for example, Foucault 1980c; Jenkins 1997; Scott 2001). As Iain Chambers (1997, 80) writes, "history comes to us not as raw, bleeding facts but in textual production, in narratives woven by desire (for truth) and a will (for power)." Harvey Wallace (quoted in Kaye 1991, 71) argues that "all history is a production – a deliberate selection, ordering, and evaluation of past events, experiences and processes." Feminist historian Joan Scott (2001, 290) calls history a "fantasy echo," a "fantasized narrative that imposes sequential order on otherwise chaotic and contingent occurrences." It is with postmodern and poststructural theories that we can begin to see the ways in which history provides a lens on "the problems of its own times more fully even than those of the era about which it is supposed to be concerned" (Ferro 2003, xi). By using postmodern and poststructural theories in our study of history, we can begin to see, and thus prepare to challenge, the ubiquity of social structures and narratives that are preventative to full equity and justice for all.

However, students are not introduced to these complexities when they learn history. For most students, the history they learn in school is a collection of simplified national narratives that are fashioned by political whims and presentist desires. Rather than explore the power and privilege embedded in the past, students are presented with a hollow grand narrative that blurs the lines of then and now to present an ordered story of what may, or should have been, rather than the messy experiences of what was. There is a destiny and a certainty to the histories taught in schools and it is only by denying these mythical narratives as the natural and undisputed points of national origin that we can provide more openings for that which is Other in how we teach, learn, and understand the past (Foucault 1980c, 80). This opening for Other is an opening for justice, an opening that is integral for change and transformation.

Contrary to the idea that postmodernism or poststructuralism are not useful for thinking about history or history education because they are a labyrinth with no exit, destruction with no solution, life with no opportunity, an assault on the promise of education (Barton 2006; Seixas 2000), these theories highlight how story and language are systems of knowledge that shape and are shaped by power and privilege. Part of our work in the study of history is to see how precarious these structures are, to crack them open, and to show how they exclude more than they include. Grand narratives are like a house of cards: once built, the house may look stable and solid, but it is hollow and precarious, one quick breath away from collapse. Grand narratives need the empty spaces, the absences, the spaces *between* the cards to inflate their size and stability. But when looking closely, when examining what the house of cards really is, there is more emptiness, more absence to the structure, than substance.

These ideas come via Jacques Derrida who understands meaning as being negatively constituted by what it is not. In his work, Derrida (1978) emphasizes that things like words, concepts, and texts have many voices; voices that are acknowledged, validated, and amplified and voices that are excluded, disavowed, and actively silenced. Because of the multitude of voices within a word, concept, or text, their meanings are never stable, never absolute, they shift and change depending on the context, era, or speaker. They are a "signifier" of something else, something that is bigger than the thing itself. Think of the concept of "fake news" – the words "fake" and "news" came together in the late 2010s to signify a concept that is politically charged in ways beyond their individual word use. It will be very difficult in the next decade, for example, to not think of those politics when the words are used together. Or think of the impossibility of direct language translation. Every language is a reflection of the culture and society which uses it; it is impossible to transpose one set of words onto another set of words and think the meaning will remain the same. Each word, concept, and text is a signifier of a culturally, socially, and historically contingent phenomenon. They are never centres of meaning beyond themselves.

Because words, concepts, and texts are not fixed, because they represent a particular moment of use, Derrida writes that when we do not take their stability for granted, words, concepts, and texts can crack and reveal meaning beyond themselves. When we challenge their supremacy as being the centre of meaning, we can witness words, concepts, and texts being both the need and the attempt to make order from disorder, meaning from chaos, a normalcy from uniqueness. We can watch words, concepts, and texts turn on themselves and *deconstruct* in ways that show the cracks of where logic is illogical. This is not destroying words, concepts, and texts, but *playing* with them, or allowing for the possibility of play, which can then invite the acknowledgment, and perhaps even subversion, of the power within them.

Deconstruction is often understood as the tearing apart of ideas, but deconstruction is about finding the politics and *play* of meaning behind that which is implied and acknowledging an Other that is purposefully absent(ed). In this way, deconstruction is not "a form of critical analysis which aims at tearing apart everything it finds in its way"; rather, it is a way of reading beyond the negativity of critique and toward a positive reconstruction of taken-for-granted knowledge (Biesta 2001, 32). Deconstruction is a way of acknowledging that "the function of this [imaginary] centre [is] not only to orient, balance, and organize the structure ... but above all to make sure that the organizing principle of the structure ... limit[s] what we might call the *play* of the structure" (Derrida 1978, 278 emphasis in original). Deconstruction is not an apolitical critical analysis but an *affirmative* ethico-political attitude that concerns itself with the Other (Egéa-Kuehne and Biesta 2001), with an openness to the Other, with an openness to the unforeseeable coming of the Other, or to what Derrida refers to as "justice" (Biesta 2009). Deconstruction is an *affirmation* of what is excluded and forgotten, not a critical refutation of what is there. "Deconstruction" is about moving the cards around to see the absences, to see the fallibility of the house, and to provide fodder for new forms of "play." When folded into how we teach history, we can think of these ideas organizing our teaching and learning to foreground that there are other stories out there, that those stories narrate a different view of the world, and that we can develop those stories as a way to make sense of the world around us. Foucault (1980a, 151) writes that "the successes of history belong to those who are capable of seizing [the] rules ... [and who can] invert their meaning, and redirect them against those who had initially imposed them." If one were to apply postmodern and poststructuralist ideas to history education, one's students would be invited to question the structure of history and to invert it to think through, and even challenge, the operations of power that work to exclude certain peoples and experiences from being seen in the past as well as in the present. With postmodern and poststructuralist theories, our students, and ourselves, would be invited to "estrange that which seems familiar, comprehensible, and easily readable" and blast "existing narratives open, rupturing their silences and highlighting their detours" (Segall 2013, 478–79). Teaching and learning history using these bodies of theory is a way of bearing witness to the operations of power written into our national narratives, to listen to what is being silenced and to reclaim the spaces within them for our own stories and experiences.

Thus, by taking a postmodern or poststructural approach to history education, we are not just accepting the world that our grand narratives narrate – we are instead rewriting that world by seeing the deconstruction of the stories we have been told and listening for the stories that have been denied to us. A postmodern or poststructural approach to history education, along with CRT and intersectional feminism, allows us to recognize the rules and expectations of the grand narrative, expand our understandings of the past beyond them, and actively challenge, and transform, our understandings of ourselves, our pasts, presents, and futures through our study and exploration of the past.

Critical Pedagogy for Teaching Canadian History

We can use critical theories to understand structural exclusions of peoples and experiences in Canadian history, but, as this book shows, it is in the *practice* of teaching history where the limitations of these stories operate. Transforming the Canadian history classroom does not require that Canadian history teachers know Canadian history in its entirety. However, it does require them to acknowledge that the stories and experiences that students bring into the classroom are structured by intersectional systems of race, gender, and class, and that acknowledging these stories and experiences allows us to think of Canadian history in different, more complex, ways. Transforming the Canadian history classroom starts with a critical understanding of Canadian history, but it also starts with believing that students have the ability and desire to know and understand these histories and, with that knowledge, to work toward a more just and equitable Canadian future.

A teacher should facilitate learning, not just teach well, and this work involves a deep care for students and an understanding of who they are as individuals. However, history teachers teach with a purpose that they defined before becoming a history teacher (van Hover and Yeager 2007) and this purpose can be at odds with the needs of the actual students in the room. While students are drawn to active instruction and histories that explore injustice, teachers have been shown to avoid active teaching methods and teaching "controversial" histories (Ares and Gorrell 2002; Crowley and Smith 2015; Dion 2005; Harris and Haydn 2006; Kinchin 2004; Levstik 2000; Winn 2004). Teachers can even encourage the retention of problematic narratives because keeping these narratives intact is easier and less professionally contentious than challenging them (Létourneau and Moisan 2004). White teachers in particular can employ strategies such as silencing, social disassociation, separation from responsibility, and use of personal stories to distance themselves from embedded racism and its power in the nation (Case and Hemmings 2005; Crowley 2016). However, the tools of critical pedagogy can help us understand and challenge the limiting and oppressive practices within education, and in doing so, help us feel more equipped to engage in the difficult work of transformation in our classrooms.

Critical pedagogy is a body of educational theory that is committed to the "ideal and practice of social justice within schools" as well as to the "transformation of social structures and class conditions within society that thwart the democratic participation of all people" (Darder, Baltodano, and Torres 2017, 2). The aim of education from a critical pedagogical perspective is to ensure education is developed and practised in ways that help to "build more egalitarian power relations, to strengthen the voices of learners, and to inspire critical consciousness, in order to promote social change" (Cho 2012, 1).

Much of the work of critical pedagogy builds on the work of Brazilian educator Paulo Freire, who begins his now classic *Pedagogy of the Oppressed* by saying that dehumanization – one group denying the humanity of another group – contributes to and justifies a stratified system of oppression (Freire 2006, 43–45). For Freire, the intent of education should be to restore humanity to all people by understanding our value as separate from the oppressive reality that serves the interests of the powerful. Freire advocates for a "problem-posing approach" to education, whereby people and their histories are the starting point for engaging in learning. The problem-posing approach is "based on creativity and stimulates true reflection and action" (84). It relies on ongoing dialogue between educator and student whereby each can learn from and with the other. This is a shift away from a "banking model" of education that is designed to deposit information into students' heads, and toward education committed to talking *with* students rather than *at* them (B.D. Schultz and Banks 2011, 51). Freire (2006) argues that the critical literacy garnered through problem-posing in education is based on the cooperation, unity, and cultural synthesis that is the essence of revolutionary action.

Drawing on Freire's work, other scholars – notably Henry Giroux, Peter McLaren, Michael Apple, Roger Simon, and bell hooks – have teased out the ways in which the micropolitics of the classroom, the politics of the curriculum, and the system of schooling can either constrict or transform the educational experience for students. Like Freire, many of these theorists come from a critical literacy background and they advocate for students to both literally and metaphorically read the word *and* the world. According to those who do critical pedagogical work, these commitments can be achieved through educational approaches that include genuine dialogue, love for people, and the courage to confront and resist oppression (Orelus 2014, 2).

bell hooks (2010), in particular, strongly advocates for the importance of love in education designed for freedom and democracy. hooks defines love as the interdependent combination of care, commitment, knowledge, responsibility, respect, and trust that teachers must have for their students. By teaching with love, she argues, teachers get to know students for who they are and to lead them in the passionate pursuit of knowledge (159). For hooks, love makes education fundamentally about the responsibility to serve and to engage freedom for the betterment of democracy. This vision of education breaks with the idea that learning is private, individualistic, and competitive. Critical thinking as part of this education, hooks argues, is a form of *engaged pedagogy* designed to restore students' will to think and respond to knowledge with and for others.

If the goals in critical pedagogy are to "build more egalitarian power relations, to strengthen the voices of learners, and to inspire critical consciousness, in order to promote social change" (Cho 2012, 1), then hooks's (2010) concept of love is important for developing the trust needed for learning in the service of a more democratic and equitable future. However, love of – or care for – students can also be limiting if teachers do not integrate these actions with a critical awareness of the ways that privilege, protection, and disavowal work in our enactments of these relationships.

Nel Noddings's cited work on the ethics of care in education is often cited as foundational to the conceptions of care in education. Noddings (1984, 2005) conceives of care as a reciprocal relation between carer and cared-for that is complete when the cared-for accepts the care that is being extended. However, in this conception, Noddings places too strong an emphasis on the recipients of care in the caring relationship and not enough on the carer. She writes that the caring between teacher/student may not take place if the student, as the cared-for, is "stubborn, insensitive, or just plain difficult" (Noddings 2005, xv). This vision of a "stubborn, insensitive, or difficult" student fails to take into account the context and content of the relationship and the expectations of care, on both sides, that shape what is being defined as "care" but also as "stubborn, insensitive, or difficult."

Critical pedagogues argue that Noddings's conception of care lacks a contextual analysis of gender, race, and class that acknowledges the power dynamics related to the acceptance or denial of care. From this, they contend that her conception of care is based on a trope of white motherhood that not only may fail to respond to or reflect the needs of students of colour, but can also infantilize them (Antrop-González and De Jesús 2006; Beauboeuf-Lafontant 2002, 2005; Pang, Rivera, and Mora 2000; Rolón-Dow 2005). While Noddings does not focus on culture in the caring relationship, "culture counts" (Gay 2010, 8). As Pang, Rivera, and Mora (2000, 27) argue, "because much of caring involves the building of relationships among teachers, students, parents, and other community members, culture must be an integral aspect of the caring framework."

The caring relationship in a classroom is not a reciprocal and straightforward interaction between teacher and student. Rather, because the majority of the power in the classroom lies with the teacher, the caring relationship is "asymmetrical" with the teacher shouldering the "burden of vulnerability" to develop a consistent and unconditional relationship that meets students where they are. "The teacher cannot control exactly how students will relate to them, interpret their actions, or understand the basis for their relationship" (Bullough and Pinnegar 2009, 249), thus it is up to the teacher to demonstrate multiple ways of acknowledging and caring for the student and their cultural communities in ways that support students' comfort and safety in the classroom.

It is important to be attuned to the dynamics of culture and care because, for students to make the choice to learn – really learn and not just memorize – they need to feel safe with the educator and with what is being taught. Students need to believe that accepting what the teacher is offering, be that care or content, will not be *subtractive* to their sense of self and cultural connections outside the classroom (Valenzuela 1999). In his essay "I Won't Learn from You," Herbert Kohl (1994) writes about this safety when he discusses the role of assent in learning. He describes the active and willed process young people go through when they are choosing to learn or not-learn. Kohl begins with his confusion that the Spanish-speaking grandfather of one of his students refused his offer of English lessons. In thinking through this rejection, Kohl reflects on his own experience as a teen who chose not to learn Hebrew. Kohl realized that his choice to not learn Hebrew was an active and willed choice to not isolate his mother who was cut out of conversations held by the Hebrew-speaking members of his father's family. It was not that he did not want the knowledge of the Hebrew language. He did not want to exacerbate the unequal power dynamics he intuited came from speaking this language in his household.

With the reflection on these experiences, Kohl argued that sometimes allowing yourself to learn can turn you into someone you do not want to become. Not-learning can be a statement of who you are, and who you are asserting yourself to be, in that space. In those educational settings where students see no "middle ground" between the self and learning "subtractively" (Valenzuela 1999), students can make the active choice to be wilfull agents who choose not to learn. In making this choice, they are not opting to fail. Rather, they are making the "conscious and chosen refusal to assent to learn" in order to maintain their integrity in the face of a compromise to their sense of self and culture (Kohl 1994, 41).

One of the ways to support students' safety and sense of self in the classroom is by enacting culturally responsive education (Ladson-Billings 1995). Culturally relevant education is not "subtractive" education. It is designed for cultural familiarity that can support students' active choice to learn. Culturally relevant educators prioritize content that connects with students' lives and histories in ways that draw on what students already know and provides depth and context to the world they see around them. If "the most important single factor influencing learning is what the learner already knows" (Ausubel, Novak, and Hanesian 1978, ix), then ensuring that the curriculum and pedagogy are responsive to the students' culture(s) is a way to set up the learning task so that prior knowledge and meaningful material are at the centre of how students enter into learning. This focus on the student and the development and articulation of students' prior knowledge invites education to be the "key to a student unlocking the mysteries of their existence and provid[ing] the road map to creating their own knowledge" (R. Brock 2014, 290).

In developing my own educational style – in creating a classroom environment in which I hope that students feel safe to learn from and with me, and where they are willing to share their prior knowledge and what is meaningful to them – I draw on the aforementioned concepts of critical pedagogy and meaningful learning; but I also draw on Purkey and Novak's (1984) theory of *invitational education*. Purkey and Novak (no relation to Joseph Novak) argue that schools need to be *inviting* places for students to learn. An *invitational* education can "promote positive relationships and encourage human potential" by offering multiple, and constant, verbal and non-verbal cues that *invite* students into the learning process as valuable and responsible individuals (Purkey and Novak 1984, 2). An "inviting message is a 'doing with' rather than 'doing to' process. It is an effort to establish cooperative interactions" among teachers, students, administration, and staff in schools (Purkey and Novak 1984, 4). When they feel safe, students can take up the invitation to learn at multiple points and spaces in their day. This then creates an "unconditional" atmosphere for learning (Kohn 2005), an atmosphere in which students do not have to feel that they have to make the choice to learn in ways that would be "subtractive" to their culture and sense of self (Valenzuela 1999).

Bearing these ideas in mind, I think of the act of teaching as a series of invitations I provide to my students. As a white, very normative-looking middle-class woman teaching in one of the most ethno-culturally diverse cities in the world, I recognize that when students enter my classroom they will make assumptions about who I am and who they could be when learning. Many students will not see the potential similarities that I may share with them, such as having a past that involves frequent international migration, living in places with deep roots to slavery, or being a racial and linguistic minority in the schools I have attended. However, they do not need to know these things about me in order for us to learn together. In fact, forcing these stories onto them as a way to legitimize my presence in the classroom may well delegitimize the connections we share. Instead, as an educator, I understand my role as demonstrating an understanding of our similarities and a respect for our differences through providing students with unconditional invitations to bring their full selves to class. I do this by bringing my full self to class. I highlight what I know, what I do not know, and what I am interested in learning with the students. The invitations they take up are the ones with which I am most successful. When they do not take the invitation – when they are misbehaving or resistant, when they are on their phones or talking to their friends – I see that as a failed invitation and will try again. Thinking of my work in the classroom as providing a series of invitations that I want my students to accept with me is a way for me to constantly check the waters: Am I developing a classroom that enhances my students' learning or have I set up the classroom to privilege what I feel comfortable teaching? This is a constant reflection of who I am in the classroom and how my teaching can better align with the findings of what makes a critically caring and culturally responsive educator.

The Experiences of Teachers and Students

The experiences, stories, and observations found in this book come from my fifteen years as a history educator in traditional and non-traditional sites of education. More specifically, this book draws upon classroom research I conducted in 2011 following a 2007 pilot test with individual students.

While working in a living history museum in 2004, I theorized a way of understanding history I've called *Historic Space*. Historic Space is a poststructuralist approach to understanding history that encourages students to *map, expand,* and then *challenge* historic periods, or historic spaces (see Chapter 6 for a detailed discussion of this approach). In 2007, using concept learning strategies to apply these ideas in practice, I considered whether Historic Space aligned with how students understood history – something my experience working in museums had gestured to – and whether harnessing this way of understanding history could provide more opportunities for students to think through the inclusions and exclusions that are part of the grand narrative. The results of this research indicated that learning history through Historic Space allowed students to learn more about the period than they had previously known; prioritize and expand on this knowledge based on their own interests and histories; connect with the material in active and affective ways; and confront and address controversial histories in ways they had not done before. I found that through Historic Space, students developed a more meaningful and inclusive understanding of Canadian history while covering the same curriculum and using the same textbooks as they had in their previous Canadian history classes. With their maps they created of their *historic spaces,* I found that students were able to take control of the historic narrative, their learning, and the meanings they took from past events in ways that were potentially transformative in how they understood the world (Cutrara 2007, 2010). With these promising results, I expanded this research to explore what this strategy would look like in a classroom.

In the winter of 2010–11, I gained approval from my institution and from a school board in Toronto to conduct research with teachers and students. I reached out to teacher networks for recruitment and cold-called specific teachers whom I thought might be interested in participating in this research project. While I wanted to see what Historic Space would look like in a classroom, I was interested in the broader questions about meaningful learning in history education – the student-centric learning that I felt Historic Space could achieve. In this research, I was interested in coming to understand the ways in which relationships in a history classroom supported or curtailed the type of meaningful history education that could prioritize students' active, involved, and radical meaning making in the study of the past.

Over the 2011 winter/spring term, I conducted research in four secondary school classrooms across three schools, working closely with both teachers and students to understand how teaching and learning functioned to support the possibilities for meaningful learning in history education. All the schools in which I worked were part of the same school board and all the teachers had backgrounds in history and an interest in making it engaging for their students. While I had hoped to recruit teachers who taught the mandatory Grade 10 Ontario course, "Canadian History since World War I" (CHC2D/P) at mainstream schools, only two of the four teachers I recruited fit that criteria. The other two taught at alternative schools: one taught the Grade 12 The West and the World course (CHY4U) and the other Grade 11 Politics (CPC3O).

The alternative schools I worked in were not independent schools, but alternative public schools that covered provincial curricula and were bound by school board mandates. Most public school boards have alternative schools that are designed to assist students who are at risk of not completing their schooling in a mainstream environment. For the teachers who work at these schools, the precariousness of students' lives is ever-present. I have found that teachers were often drawn to teaching in these schools because they understood teaching as enacting a holism in teaching, learning, and connecting with students that they felt was best represented in alternative learning environments.

For a comparison of the four research sites, see Table 1.

All four teachers were similar in that they strove to be "good teachers" who demonstrated care for their students and articulated a desire for students to leave the classroom able to think critically about the world around them. However, what this meant for each teacher was contingent upon the environment in which she taught. For the teachers at the alternative schools, good teaching and learning practices involved responding to the unique and potentially challenging aspects of students' lives. For the teachers at the mainstream school, however, there was a much greater emphasis on institutionalized discourses of teaching and learning. Things like learning styles, assessment techniques, and student success were all readily-used concepts that framed good teaching and classroom practices. Teachers who worked within these mainstream contexts often got swept up in these discourses – discourses that created and maintained "curricular roles" within which teachers and students were to interact (Cutrara 2017). Thus, while all four teachers were "good" in their own right, they were not "good" in the same way. For this research, I found that the diversity of ways in which one could be a "good" teacher – and the correlated relationships that came from this – was instructive in shaping the contours of what student-centric, meaningful history education could look like.

To respond to the different contexts of research, I used a design-based research (DBR) methodology to explore the "buzzing, blooming confusion" of a classroom while investigating an innovation in practice (Barab and Squire 2004, 4).[3] DBR is a research methodology that combines participatory action research (PAR), ethnography, and grounded theory to explore a teaching and learning intervention in situ. As a mixed-methods "living methodology" (Steffe and Thompson 2000, 273), DBR is used "with the intent of producing new theories, artifacts, and practices that account for and potentially impact learning and teaching in naturalistic settings" (Barab and Squire 2004, 2). With DBR, I could bring an "intervention" like Historic Space to a classroom, observe teaching pre- and post-intervention, collaborate with teachers and students on its operation to shape lessons, and from these experiences develop theory related to the possibilities of innovation and transformative change in teaching and learning practice.

TABLE 1
Summary of research sites

	Mainstream			Alternative
Type of school	Site 1	Site 2	Site 3	Site 4
Grade	10	10	12	11
Course	Canadian History since World War I, Academic (CHC2D)	Canadian History since World War I, Academic (CHC2D)	The West & The World, University Preparation (CHY4U)	Politics, Open (CPC3O)
Time period covered during research intervention	Post–World War II (1945–70)	Post–World War II (1945–70)	French Revolution	Nineteenth- and twentieth-century colonialism/ postcolonialism
Unique content "challenges"	West Indian Domestic Scheme, Africville	West Indian Domestic Scheme, Africville	Théroigne de Méricourt, Toussaint Louverture	Postcolonial readings of British colonialism and imperialism
Teacher demographics	"Erin"[1] Permanent, full-time teacher. White woman. Teaching for 9 years.	Permanent, full-time teacher. White woman. Teaching for less than a year.	Permanent, full-time teacher. White woman. Teaching for 7 years.	Permanent, full-time teacher. White woman. Teaching for 3 years.

1 Erin is discussed at length in Chapter 4.

With DBR as a framework, I was in each research site for three research phases: phase one was observation, phase two was intervention, and the third phase was a wrap-up and reflection. During the intervention phase, Historic Space was used to shape the teaching and learning practices of one unit. The units were not chosen for content, but rather for timing – when the best time was for teachers to have me in their classroom.

Because of my interest in classroom relationships, during all three phases of the research I generated data from teachers and students, and, along with my observations, these data sets were used to develop theory grounded in real-life teaching and learning practice (Charmaz 2006; Glaser and Strauss 1967; Strauss and Corbin 1997). During the research I conducted semi-structured interviews with teachers and group interviews with students. Teachers also had the option of completing one-sentence journals and students were given surveys and journal prompts at various points across the three phases. I was a participant-observer-educator in every class and wrote field notes for the lessons. When I was absent from classes, lessons were video recorded, with the students taking the lead in setting up and taking down the video equipment. These video cameras were donated to the teachers following the research.

With a methodology like DBR that invites adaptation and responsiveness during the research period (Barab and Squire 2004), I came to each classroom with a teaching and learning plan to share with the teachers, but these plans morphed according to discussions with the teachers, my observations of the students, and the data I was collecting at each site. For example, if a teacher found that her students responded better to flexible teaching strategies than to a deliberate and structured strategy, and if those same students corroborated the teacher's observation in their interviews and behaviour in class, then the teacher and I privileged instruction that encouraged flexibility. If I brought in material I thought the students wanted to learn, but the students asked for different material, then the teacher and I would collaboratively identify what would better respond to students' needs. If a teacher was uncomfortable with new instruction or was unable to teach one day, I would teach the class and gain greater insight into the daily performative work of teaching. The idea was that I would participate as a member of the class community and do so following the teacher's lead with the students' interests in mind. In this role I feel that I was successful: students treated me like another teacher in the class and the teacher would defer to me with regard to the more technical aspects of the research. The responsiveness engendered by DBR ensured that the research reflected the living context of the classroom, the realities of teachers' work, and the ever-changing needs of students.

This research structure was important for answering my research question: What are the relationships in a history classroom that support or curtail the possibilities of meaningful learning? However, one research site – a mainstream Grade 10 Canadian history class taught by a mid-career, award-winning teacher – troubled my notions of meaningful learning in ways that did not easily align with my other research findings. In spite of content and instruction that was designed to engender meaningful learning opportunities in the classroom, students in this class still indicated on their exit surveys that they did not learn history meaningfully. I was not surprised by the students' responses – I was in the class with them and saw their continued resistance to history education – but I still questioned why little meaningful learning took place when we did so much that aligned with how students said they wanted to learn. These questions stayed with me after the research was over and through the next stages of my career.

In that class, I felt particularly conflicted by working with a history teacher who, to all intents and purposes, was "good" – she had been awarded and celebrated as an ideal, student-centric teacher – but who I could see was curtailing the opportunities for her students, her racialized students, to learn history in ways that were meaningful. As a young researcher and a non-classroom teacher, I thought perhaps it was just me. Perhaps the teacher and I just did not fit well together and I was being unduly harsh about her practice. Perhaps I could not fully appreciate how difficult it was to teach Canadian history in a formal classroom.

But in the years since, in my work developing a province-wide education and exhibition program and in providing nationwide educational consulting to teachers and other educators, I have come to realize that the tension I witnessed in this class is part of a broader tension that educators face when teaching a version of the Canadian past that does not align with the Canadian present. I have also come to observe that the teaching practices that develop from this tension can both isolate and reject students whose experiences are outside the standard narrative we have about Canada. This troubling tension is the primary focus of my analysis.

While I had multiple data sources across the four sites, I have now triangulated particular data sets to explore and make sense of the tension I have witnessed between teaching Canadian history and the needs of students learning Canadian history. To demonstrate students' wants and needs in the classroom, I have used the survey results, journal prompts, and group interview transcripts from students across all four schools. I use the teacher who troubled my perceptions of good teaching and meaningful learning as a case study of how practice can undermine philosophy when one is teaching material that challenges one's perception of self and world. I use the transcripts from the formal interviews I conducted with this teacher during the research period as well as the field notes I wrote following the informal conversations we had in and out of class. I then look at the larger context of teaching by using the three interviews with each of the four teachers in my research sample to highlight the ways in which an institutional context must support meaningful *teaching* if it is to support meaningful learning. Finally, in my discussion of Historic Space, I use these same data from all four sites but augment them with video recordings, copies of student work, shared lectures, and pedagogical notes, as well as data from my 2007 research. The focus on these diverse data sources has resulted in a robust exploration of teaching and learning practices meant to respect, as well as to reverently challenge, teachers' practices in Canadian history classrooms.

Chapter Breakdown

Over the next decades of the twenty-first century, Canada will undergo dramatic changes to its identity and population in ways that will forever alter who and what the nation understands itself to be. As a settler colony and a Commonwealth country with an ongoing sibling rivalry with its closest neighbour, that dramatic change is part of a historical legacy that has (re)developed Canadian identity over centuries of settlement. Young people deserve to know this. Young people deserve to know about the ebb and flow of national identification, the movements of bodies across borders, and the systems of oppression that have thrived under colonialism. With a focus on "we" in the history classroom – a relational, affective, and politicized "we" – Canadian educators and historians can transform the Canadian history classroom into one that addresses the current context of the Canadian nation and can bring us, meaningfully, into the twenty-first century.

This book is divided into six chapters. Following the introduction provided in this chapter, in Chapter 2 I discuss popular and curricular conversations about heritage and history curriculum in Canada. During the first decade and a half of the 2000s, Canadian culture and identity have been oscillating between conservative commemoration, multicultural celebration, and (post/neo)colonial reconciliation. Canada and its peoples have not fully reconciled these three dimensions of the past and present, and yet they haunt our interactions and plans for the future. When understanding this context we begin to see the transnational and (post/neo)colonial lives young people are living in Canada today, and how, or if, history and social studies curricula have responded to them. It is in this chapter where I discuss the limitations of the current historical thinking approach to history education by arguing that historical thinking fails to hold room for the relational, affective, and political knowledge that can lead to meaningful learning.

In Chapter 3, I use the voices of students to articulate young peoples' needs for Canadian history education. It is easy to brush off students' explicit hatred of the textbook and their preferences for learning "interesting" history over "boring" history as the superficial demands of teens. Arguably, these pronouncements do seem one-dimensional and cliché; however, I pair students' words with their behaviour and interpret their demands for history education to be more than what they appear. Students are looking for history education that is invested with connection, complexity, and care. This triad of connection, complexity, and care is especially relevant for racialized students who have a hard, if not impossible, time reconciling their experiences as Canadians with a learning history that denies these experiences as being insufficiently "Canadian." I argue that, through the triad of connection, complexity, and care, we can support a Canadian "we" that invites students to understand themselves in the Canada of the past, present, and future.

In Chapter 4, I use one teacher as a case study of someone who had the desire and materials to teach with connection, complexity, and care but who continuously undermined the possibilities of meaningful learning in her history class by limiting connections and removing complexity from the Canadian story. By pathologizing her students as Others who could not make connections to Canadian history, and by keeping a tight rein on the Canadian story by appealing to chronology and an understanding of "facts," this teacher centred her own personal vision of Canadian history, a version that left the histories and experiences of racialized people, including those of her students, on the sidelines. This case study serves as an example of how, even if the pedagogy is sound, students' meaningful learning in the Canadian history classroom can be undermined through teaching practice.

Although teachers have considerable power to direct the content and instruction in their classrooms, it is important to remember that they do not work in a vacuum but, rather, in an institutional context that influences the possibilities of their work. Thus, in Chapter 5, I move to the institutional context of formal schooling to argue that, if schools are not places that can encourage meaningful teaching for teachers, then it is difficult for teachers to imagine creating an environment of meaningful learning for students. Except in explicitly alternative learning environments, school structures rarely provide teachers with the time, space, or place to develop the connection, complexity, and care necessary for students to learn meaningfully with historical narratives. Consequently, teachers can enter a classroom without any sense of needing, or wanting, to build relationships. This lack of relationality between teachers and students that the school structure can engender has direct ramifications for the possibilities of teaching and learning in individual classrooms. Thus, being clear about these limitations can help educators develop strategies to circumvent them, to find the time, space, and places they need to prioritize their own meaningful teaching in the history classroom.

In Chapter 6, I conclude this book by demonstrating how a method of inquiry based on a student-centric and poststructuralist approach to history education can practically and meaningfully help frame teaching and learning Canadian history. The idea of *Historic Space* is based on a poststructuralist understanding of history and is interpreted through concept learning focused on students' active construction of meaning.

Historic Space provides an opportunity for students to construct, deconstruct, and reconstruct historical narratives in ways that invite them to explore the operations of power and privilege in the past and present. It also invites students to challenge traditional narratives with counterstories that trouble our understanding of "truth" (Delgado 1989). It is a model that privileges learning over teaching and that, in doing so, develops meaningful learning and a sense of "we" with, and in, the Canadian story.

"History," "the past," "the nation," "teaching," and "learning" are all concepts fraught with complexities regarding what they mean and how they can be enacted. However, as this book shows, by keeping students as the focus of our conversations about Canadian history education, by believing in their inherent desire to learn national history, by believing in their contributions to birth a new, more just, and radical version of "we" in the Canadian nation, we can mould our practices and pedagogies to have greater resonance for students' futures and transform the Canadian history classroom to imagine a new "we."

2

The Present of Today's Past
Current Trends and Curriculum

What is the purpose of learning history? Are we doomed to repeat it? Do we lose grounding? Are we stranded without space or place? Does history provide us with the skills for understanding evidence or the content for narrating experience? As adults, as educators, as historians, we can answer these questions with a blend of cliché and seriousness, never completely getting at the reason we sense history's importance but never completely abandoning the dime-store clichés that frame our popular engagement with the past either. The moral panic that accompanies these questions is often directed toward youth, as if the frivolity of adolescence will somehow erase the past and the lessons it can provide for the future.

It is with this fear that history and social studies are racked with so much public debate about what, how, and why they should be taught. Education historian Ken Osborne (2000, 2002, 2003, 2011) has shown that these conversations have been happening in Canada for over a hundred years, with the pendulum shifting to a new fad every generation. These debates are often sparked by a panic about the decline of national identity and are used as a rallying call for educational reform by those who want straight facts, those who want historical redemption, and those who want more transferable skills. While this chapter does not rewrite the history of those debates, it does provide a snapshot of contemporary discussions and the curricular trends of history education that attend to those concerns.

With the context provided in this chapter, I will explore what lies underneath the impetus for educators to (re)frame Canadian history education in ways that better respond to the needs of today's Canadian youth. I do this by giving an overview of the current climate of national history as discussed in popular media as well as the current trends, outcomes, and possibilities of provincial history and social studies curricula.

Current Climate

It is often said that Canada is a young country, but exactly what is meant by this is unclear. The statement suggests that, as a country that was formally established by Confederation in 1867, or with its distinctive participation in World War I, or with its first Union Jack–free flag in 1965, Canada does not have a past that is deep enough to unequivocally define who and what it is. By saying that Canada is a young country, there is an implicit assumption that Canada has an identity so fragile, so precarious, that winds of change from individuals, governments, and global forces could be enough to wipe clean the identity that has been shaped so far.

Canada's crisis of national identity is not as unique as it may seem. All nations have identities that are in flux, and Canada is no different. Nations are "imagined communities" (B. Anderson 2003), invented by traditions (Hobsbawm 1992) and the labours of intellectuals (Eley 2000). Whether developing the national identity of an "old" or a "new" country, maintaining a stable national identity is the basis of all national rhetoric. Drawing on the past to define the future is central to nation-building discourses. Often these nationalist conceptions are gendered, with the feminine representing tradition and the masculine representing progress and change (Wenk 2000). To remain salient, national rhetoric must inform the private as much as the public, with these ideologies becoming entrenched in how one conceptualizes and enacts national identification at home and in the community (Eley 2000). However, even though it does have similarities with other nations, Canada also has unique challenges.

In Canada today, there is a disconnect between the vision and enactment of Canadian identity that has been created by official means, by those on the ground, and by those that haunt our past. As recent debates over monuments and naming in Canada have shown, who and what is celebrated as historically significant changes and shifts over time. These debates are often rooted in demographic fear of change and are symptomatic of popular and cultural transformation rather than the cause of it. While a "History War" was fought (rhetorically) in the 1990s between historians who wanted more political and economic history and less social and cultural history,[1] the first two decades of the 2000s have been marked by the creeping conservative rhetoric of populism and nationalism, on one hand, and the evolving enactment of Canadian identity in Canada's transnational and (post/neo)colonial cities, towns, and reserves, on the other. While the beginning of the 2000s saw the federal government under Stephen Harper (2006–15) using commemorative moments to rationalize a vision of a conservative militarized future, ordinary Canadians have regularly attempted to understand and reconcile their place in a country that currently lauds the multiculturalism it previously resisted or attempted to eradicate. This tension is still in play as we move into the 2020s, and it could become even more pronounced with the rise of populist politics at home and abroad. It is thus important to understand the ways in which a shift in Canadian identity was culturally imagined under Harper's Conservative government and the ways that that imagining shaped, and continues to shape, the landscape of Canadian history and heritage during the first decades of the twenty-first century.

When it came to heritage and identity development, Harper was keen to entrench his vision of Canada in the Canadian past by developing a legacy of militaristic conservatism through implementing seemingly innocuous, yet significant, changes to Canadian identity. Getting rid of the long-form census, returning the title of "Royal" to the Canadian armed forces, and reinstalling a portrait of the reigning monarch in Canadian embassies around the world all made slight, but key, changes to the way Canada was conceptualized and the way belonging was understood. While peacekeeping had been courted as a core component of Canadian identity through the second half of the twentieth century, Canada's continuous involvement in military actions since 2001 made this identity incongruous with its current status.[2] Rudyard Griffiths argues that, in prioritizing Canadian interests over Canadian values, Harper reset the peacekeeping pillar of Canadian identity and left Canadians wondering how to reconcile a national identity that no longer espoused a vision of peace (Carlson 2012). During their time in power, Conservatives attempted to fill this gap with the celebration and commemoration of militarized actions to suggest the continuity of Canada's involvement in nation-forming military missions throughout history. The Conservatives under Harper used the past to naturalize and provide the continuity of conservative values in the Canadian present, which then bolstered Harper's vision of Canada as a strong, unquestioned military presence on the global stage (Coyne 2014).

While major history, heritage, and cultural institutions such as Library and Archives Canada, Parks Canada, and the National Archival Developmental Program received drastic budgetary cuts, there was also an influx of cash for *more* history and heritage commemoration, albeit for particular events. Between 2012 and 2017, the federal government marked three distinct moments for commemoration that received an influx of federal funds: the bicentennial of the War of 1812, the centennial of World War I, and the sesquicentennial of Confederation. These moments – as opposed to the thirtieth anniversary of the Canadian Charter of Rights and Freedoms in 2012 or the 250th anniversary of the Royal Proclamation in 2013 – shifted the discussion of the Canadian past to feature military involvement and paternal know-how as hallmarks of the Canadian story (Cotler 2012; Dann 2009; Kheraj 2013; Peace 2013; C.Z. Thomas 2015). During the ramp-up for the sesquicentennial of Confederation, for example, Harper (2014) set the tone for how he imagined these celebrations, by stating at the 150th anniversary of the Charlottetown Accord that Canada had become the "confident partner, ... courageous warrior, ... compassionate neighbour" that the Fathers of Confederation had envisioned in 1864.

While the Liberals under Justin Trudeau quickly reversed many of these actions, their long-term effects on Canadian identity lingered. For example, given that the majority of Canadians consider museums and historic sites to be the most trustworthy of all public history sources (Conrad et al. 2013), the cuts and changes to parks and heritage sites altered, and could continue to alter, the interactions Canadians will have with these institutions. These shifts have silently rendered the Winnipeg General Strike less important than the Battle of Lundy's Lane (A. Cole 2015; Rabson 2015) and the personal archival records left in dusty attics less important than the "enhanced, modern access" of digital preservation (Caron 2012). With their majority governments between 2011 and 2015, the Conservatives under Stephen Harper had full rein to make these changes, with the Opposition and lobby groups having only marginal, if any, impact on their actions.[3]

Short term, however, these efforts to construct a Canadian identity based on a traditional vision of unilateral militarism and paternal encouragement seemed to have had little effect on the day-to-day enactment of Canadian identity. While a quarter of Canadians do not see Canada as having a unique identity (Daro 2015), celebrations of Canadian openness, diversity, and a peaceful standard of living continue to mark what is popularly celebrated about Canada ("Canada Day" 2015). In a 2013 poll, Canadians indicated that they were more interested in commemorating social equity than moments of monarchical or militaristic might (CBC News 2013). In focus groups related to the biennial of the War of 1812, Canadians indicated that they would prefer to honour the sacrifices of individuals rather than celebrations of battles (The Canadian Press 2012). These polls demonstrate how Canadians pick and choose aspects of national significance that they feel align most strongly with their vision of Canada. This "blank slate" aspect of Canadian identity leads some to argue that Canada's "invisibility" is its greatest gift to the global stage and to Canada's multicultural population (Todd 2015; Westwood 2013).

On-the-ground Canadian identity has a hard time looking to the past to make sense of itself in the present. Many still draw a hard line between capital-H History and the investigation of contemporary life in all its past, present, and future facets (Martin 2015). Although some have said that "today's Canada is the product of its capacity for mutual accommodation and a belief in an underlying shared order" (W. MacDonald 2015), that has not been our past, which made the lack of public response to Harper's heritage changes sad (Carlson 2012) but not surprising. While a hyphenated Canadian identity has become a familiar and comfortable way for people to identify themselves as Canadians (Andrew-Gee 2015), it does not necessarily indicate an identity that can be reflected in the past and future of Canada. A hyphen "effectively produces spaces of distance ... in which ethnicity is positioned outside Canadianness – as an addition to it, but also as an exclusion from it" (Mahtani 2002, 78). The hyphen can be used to locate a present, and perhaps a future, in Canada, but the preceding identifier honours a past that is elsewhere. Building a future on the hyphen neutralizes the unknowingness of the Other and creates a sense of familiarity based on difference. As a chain, a bridge, or a floating magic carpet, the hyphen is a skeleton of self, as envisioned by poet Fred Wah (1996). It invites people to reach forward and back between home and away, past and present, self and nation to locate themselves in a Canadian present without reaching too far into the past.

If nothing else, the most cohesive vision of today's Canadian identity has often come from the promotional campaigns of Canadian-identified brands and sports teams. These campaigns are designed to broaden a consumer base and therefore signal an inclusive and welcoming vision of Canada that suggests what an idealized vision of multicultural Canada might look like. The 1994 Molson "I Am Canadian" campaign, for example, had a 2014 makeover designed to emphasize Canadian diversity. In contrast to the Joe Canadian "rant" from 1994, a 2015 Molson commercial featured people stating they "were Canadian" in multiple languages so that a beer fridge would open and provide Molson products to the crowd. The implication is that, twenty years on, what now makes "us" Canadian is our multilingual and multicultural diversity – and our love of Molson beer (Molson Coors Brewing Company 2015). Tim Hortons marketing campaigns and presence in every small town across Canada has ingrained "double-double from Timmy's" into the Canadian lexicon and Canadian culture (Cormack and Cosgrave 2013). Commercials featuring recent immigrants working at Tim Hortons, or being greeted at the airport with Tim Hortons coffee and a bag of winter clothes, suggests that Tim Hortons is not just a place to become a Canadian by drinking coffee but also a place to enter the waged Canadian economy. Both Canadian-identified brands operate at the "intersection of commerce and culture," which, while misleading (Houpt 2010), provide strong brand and nationalistic identification that official cultural symbols and narratives have just not achieved. As one journalist writes: "Let's face it – it is more fun to celebrate your Canadianness with beer and a doughnut than it is to read history, follow politics or even vote" (Delacourt 2013).

Canadian intellectual John Ralston Saul (2008) argues that Canada and Canadians need to look at their Indigenous roots to reconcile how to live transnational multicultural lives in Canada today. He contends that a Canadian vision of multiculturalism should be grounded in Aboriginal understandings of inclusiveness and cooperation, because the colonial epistemologies of the English and French were never interested in incorporating difference into their nation-building ideologies. Instead,

Euro-Canadian approaches to ethno-cultural difference were marked by exploitation, miscegenation, and erasure, with tolerance being a compromise that often benefited the bottom line. Ralston Saul (2011) contends that this approach to difference is in stark contrast to Aboriginal epistemologies, which emphasize the circle. Using the circle as a metaphor, one can approach differences with acceptance and understanding and attempt to find ways to ensure that all jointly contribute to the whole.

However, embracing Indigenous epistemologies as the foundation for understanding Canadian diversity is not part of most people's experiences of being in Canada. Celebrating food and festivals may occur on an international stage, but many non-Indigenous Canadians are uncomfortable engaging in First Nations, Métis, and Inuit cultures on an individual level.[4] Canadian colonial history is fraught with so much discomfort and silence that Indigenous and non-Indigenous Canadians have no shared understanding for reconciling and speaking through the violence of the past. Many Canadians still see Indigenous peoples as the shadowy Others on the edges of terra nullius, with federal governments modelling discomfort by failing to embrace colonial history in all its messy complexity. When Stephen Harper apologized for (some) colonial actions, he failed to show an interest in confronting the larger colonial structures and discourses that continue to naturalize Canada's violent attempts at cultural erasure.[5] Justin Trudeau ran on a platform of increased nation-to-nation relations between Canada and First Nations peoples, but, as of this writing, conflicts such as the unauthorized Coastal GasLink pipeline across Wet'suwet'en territory have prompted many to say that the efforts made by the Trudeau government toward reconciliation are dead or never truly existed (Ballingall 2020; "Reconciliation Is Dead ..." 2020; Talaga 2020). Federal parties use Aboriginal issues to gain votes, but fail to act on these issues simply out of a moral obligation for respectful enactments of treaty rights (N. MacDonald 2015). Seventy percent of Canadians believe that Canadian colonial practices, such as forced residential schools, were genocidal (Hensley 2015), but major cultural institutions have been more comfortable providing a "balanced" historical narrative that sanitizes contemporary inequities grounded in colonial relations rather than facing them head on (Logan 2014; Welch 2015).

The 2015 Truth and Reconciliation Commission and the aligned Calls to Action have (re)started the national conversation about the need to include First Nations, Métis, and Inuit epistemologies and histories in mainstream education. The TRC unearthed histories that many Canadians, Indigenous and settler alike, either did not know or failed to acknowledge. While many people knew about the residential schools in the abstract, the testimony of survivors revealed a shameful, racist history that continues to haunt the nation in ways we have yet to reconcile. These practices and policies have resonance today, with self-hate and violence seeping through First Nations and Inuit communities like a cancer that has yet to be treated. On average, in a four-week period, 16,767 Aboriginal people are violently victimized, 91 commit suicide, 712 youth drop out of school, and 22 infants die before their first birthday (Gilmore 2015). It has been through truth-telling, witnessing, active healing, and continued colonial resistance that these legacies of hate and violence have been working their way out of First Nations communities generation by generation (Kinew 2015).

Many Canadian settler communities, however, have not done the work of understanding and acknowledging what needs to be done to confront their own participation in these ongoing colonial practices. This, too, is a cancer that seeps through generations. The apathy, defensiveness, and disavowal of recognizing the ongoing benefits of colonial practices continue when we fail to hear these stories and demand their inclusion in national conversations. As Scott Gilmore (2015) wrote during the 2015 Canadian federal election, "we are not a people, not a nation, not really. If we were, we would not be able to ignore each other, ignore other Canadians, the way we ignore the Aboriginal community." Violent colonial practices against Indigenous peoples have been formative in shaping Canada today, but Canadians have been able to go their whole school career without ever having to learn about, confront, and reconcile the colonial beliefs and actions that are ingrained in Canadian identity and history (Tremonti 2015). It was such a rupture of the ordinary that when British Colombia added mandatory content about residential schools into its history curriculum it made national headlines (Meissner 2015).[6]

In his concluding statements for the Truth and Reconciliation Commission, Justice Murray Sinclair said that there were no shortcuts when it came to reconciliation between Aboriginal and non-Aboriginal peoples. To shape the circle in which Indigeneity is fundamental to Canadian identity – not just as an acknowledgment but as a key to understanding – will take action, understanding, and a willingness to confront the unequal legacy of colonial policies that exist in Canada today. Indigenous educator and theorist Dwayne Donald (2012, 535) writes: "the task of decolonizing in the Canadian context can only occur when Aboriginal peoples and Canadians face each other across historic divides, deconstruct their shared past, and engage critically with the realization that their present and future are similarly tied together." This will involve not only bravery and trust but also Truth, Humility, Honesty, Wisdom, Respect, Courage, and Love, or the Seven Sacred Teachings fundamental to Indigenous epistemologies (Sinclair, Wilson, and Littlechild 2015).

Colonialism is a lived reality in Canada, but the more mainstream concerns of commemorating wars or creating multicultural promotional campaigns have shifted the discussions away from the accountability of respectful and honest understandings of the past, present, and future. While there is an indication that this may be changing – the lacklustre celebration of Canada150 on the heels of the TRC report indicates that Canadians are attempting to reconcile how to value #Canada150 with #Resistance150 – these conversations need to be more explicit about how we move toward the future. Canada has made "dreadful" progress on the TRC's Calls to Action; at our current rate, for example, it will not be until 2057 when all the calls will be answered (Jewell and Mosby 2019). Classrooms are important places to have the conversations about how to create a more inclusive, just, and reconciliatory Canadian identity. As the most consistent and formative site of teaching Canadian history, history classrooms can be places where students are invited to explore these three, at times competing, components of Canadian identity: narrow conservative commemoration, transnational celebration, and inclusive (post/neo)-colonial reconciliation. It is through exploring and triangulating these aspects of Canadian identity that students may be able to find themselves, and a world they want, in the past, present, and future of Canada. These explorations can then act as the foundation for greater, transformative action in the service of justice.

Curriculum Shifts

The current context of Canadian identity influences the lives of young people growing up in Canada today, but it is not necessarily part of the formal history, social studies, and civics curricula. The Canadian history curriculum is often understood as reverence for a list of names, dates, and themes, but when looking closely at the curriculum in Canada, a canonical list of Canadian heroes and events is not what students are intended to learn in Canadian classrooms. These curriculum documents make room for inquiry, for contextualization, for critical thinking, and for the exploration of the Canadian past for the Canadian present. Appreciating the space there is in the curriculum for engaging in transformative work is an important first step for thinking of how our Canadian history classrooms can be ones that facilitate meaningful learning for students.

Given that education is a provincial responsibility, Canada has thirteen different history and social studies curricula that, for the most part, have developed separately within Canada's different provinces, territories, and regions. While these curricula are distinct, there are some prominent themes that suggest a congruence of national values and desires for education that play out across Canada.[7]

History, for example, is most often paired with geography and blended with other social sciences to represent social studies. While many subjects are organized under this "social studies" umbrella, the courses themselves are often not interdisciplinary. Key social studies themes include *diversity, pluralism, active democratic citizenship, the environment,* and *Canada within a global context.* Detailed curricular introductions describe the role of social studies as supporting students' active democratic citizenship. Curriculum documents often use circles to highlight the interconnectedness of how subject knowledge should interact with students' development and self-knowledge. Aligned with this, a range of teaching and learning approaches, as well as "authentic assessment" and evaluation, are emphasized as key elements for how social studies should be taught. This includes an emphasis on inquiry and student thinking, where students set goals, learn through discovery, and reflect on their learning. Taken together, Canadian social studies courses have been designed to support students' growth and development as Canadian citizens who have the means and knowledge to be active, participating members of the Canadian democracy.

As a key component of social studies, Canadian history courses are also envisioned to be experiential, active, and collaborative, with students' full selves welcomed and reflected in teaching and learning practices. Across Canada, Canadian history is taught at both the elementary and secondary levels. Content coverage is organized chronologically, with pre-contact through the late nineteenth century often covered in Grades 3 to 8 and the twentieth century most often covered in secondary school.[8] Along with their mandatory courses, many provinces also offer a more comprehensive Canadian history course in secondary school as an elective. Learning outcomes for Canadian history courses often use active verbs such as *investigate, examine, compare, assess, reflect,* and *determine*. Outcomes are frequently expressed as "big ideas" and/or content-based questions, as a way to blend active learning with specific content knowledge. Like other social studies courses, the history curriculum emphasizes that teachers should use a range of sources, including primary sources, to support learning and that technology should also be effectively integrated into teaching, learning, and assessment. This focus is particularly important for history courses because it indicates that sources such as textbooks need not be the only resource that teachers use. Cumulatively, Canadian history curricula across Canada indicate that we want our students to ask questions, research answers, use multiple sources, and think about big themes as a way to understand the Canadian past. Rarely did history curricula indicate history courses presented as imparting facts for facts' sake; rather, there was a nationwide intent to have students think with and through history as a means of knowing their country and becoming active Canadian citizens.

What was most striking about these documents was the predominance of historical thinking as an organizing concept for any history/social studies revision after 2010. Historical thinking appeared as a pedagogical approach in the 1990s and stressed that rather than teaching names and dates, history education should focus on progressively developing disciplinary skills. The argument was that just as students in a science class learn how to conduct scientific experiments, students in a history class should learn how to construct historical accounts. Although for many this perspective seemed like a breath of fresh air, Osborne (2006) has shown that everything old becomes new again and that a skills focus for history education has been advocated for since the late 1800s. Nevertheless, just because it has been done in the past, this does not make the existing emphasis in history education any less relevant for the present, and a disciplinary skills-focus is the current focus for students learning history, according to the Canadian history curriculum.

While the historical thinking approach has resulted in a greater focus on inquiry and primary source evidence in Canadian history curricula and its adoption in Canada has been relatively "smooth" (P. Clark 2018, 2), it is not above critique. As with any pedagogical approach, it is important to understand the epistemological foundations for historical thinking, and I have argued (Cutrara 2009, 2018b) that if we look closer at the use of disciplinary knowledge as the basis for our history education, we can see how it fails to leave room for the important affective and political encounters with the past that young people need in order for their history education to be meaningful and transformative to their lives in Canada.

Disciplinary Turn in History Education

In the late 1980s, educational theorists in the United Kingdom conducted a multi-year research project aimed at uncovering how young people progressed in their historical understanding. This project was funded by the British government in an effort to revamp the national curriculum and align it to emerging cognitive research in education. By having students reconcile conflicting accounts of historical events, the Concepts of History and Teaching Approaches, 7–14 Project, or CHATA, developed a taxonomy for understanding how students came to learn historical accounts.[9] With the findings from the study, researchers Peter Lee, Rosalyn Ashby, and Alaric Dickinson argued that history education should move away from testing students' knowledge of the *substantive* concepts of history – the "who, what, when, and where" of the past – and toward teaching the *metahistorical* concepts of history – the "skills in a historian's tool box." Lee, Ashby, and Dickinson argued that a focus on the substantive concepts of history did not provide any impetus for students to progress in their historical understanding: they did not need to know about Egyptian civilization in order to understand the Industrial Revolution, for example.

However, by focusing on the *metahistorical* concepts of history, by teaching students the *skills* that go into constructing historical accounts, history education could move students through a progressive understanding of the historical method and give them the tools to navigate the multiple versions of the past they will encounter outside school (for more on this study and argument, see Lee [2004]). The CHATA project became a call for a curricular design that stressed the progressive development of students' historical understanding in history education.

Inspired by this work, educational theorists in other countries started looking at their own curricula to see if these reforms would make sense for them. Peter Seixas, based at the University of British Columbia, quickly became a forerunner in these conversations in Canada, publishing as early as 1993 about how young people understand historical representation in movies. In his early studies, Seixas identified the three elements that made up students' historical thinking: the ability to identify events as historically significant; the ability to refine, revise, and add to their historical thinking; and the ability to recognize and utilize notions of agency, empathy, and moral judgment in the past. Seixas emphasized that the first element, historical significance, was heavily contingent on what the student brought into the classroom because students tend to place themselves at the centre of significance. Seixas used these findings to advocate for a curriculum that moved students away from thinking of themselves as the centre of significance and toward a more reflective and methodological approach to the study of history. In advancing students' *historical thinking*, Seixas argued, students' *historical consciousness* could also be developed (Seixas 1999, 2002a, 2002b).

With international interest in this work, and bolstered by Canada's own explorations of identity at the turn of the century, Seixas quickly became a leader in advocating for a twenty-first-century skills-based history education that could methodically advance young peoples' historical consciousness. Seixas argued that with so many different people and perspectives in today's Canada, and with a history rife with (post/neo)colonial and Eurocentric tensions, teaching and learning a common national narrative was counter-productive to bringing people together. What brought people together instead were questions of *historical consciousness* – questions about where people came from, where they were going, and what would make their future better.[10] Because historians have developed a methodological framework for addressing these questions, Seixas (2000, 25) argued that "rather than promoting identity fissures in a multicultural, multinational, and multiple gendered world," learning the skills in a historian's tool box "offers the promise of deliberative distance" needed to move Canada into a productive and democratic future (see also Seixas 2004, 2006b, 2009; Seixas and Peck 2004). From this work, Seixas developed the "Benchmarks of Historical Thinking" as a framework for curricular design that emphasized six historical thinking concepts: historical significance, evidence, continuity and change, cause and consequence, historical perspectives, and ethical dimensions. These "big six" are foundational for the development of young peoples' historical consciousness as envisioned in Canadian history curricula.

This work on historical consciousness and historical thinking skills struck the history education community in Canada at the right time. The study of Canadian historical consciousness rapidly spread across academic and professional communities and, as a Canada Research Chair, Seixas launched the Centre for the Study of Historical Consciousness in the University of British Columbia's Faculty of Education in 2001. The centre started the Historical Thinking Project, which developed resources and hosted yearly summer institutes that assisted teachers in bringing the Benchmarks of Historical Thinking into their classrooms. Canadian theorists have led academic discussions on historical consciousness nationally (Sandwell 2006) and internationally (e.g., Seixas 2004; Stearns, Seixas, and Wineburg 2000), with multiple projects funded to promote and develop stronger connections between historians, public educators, and formal schooling (THEN/HiER 2015). Academically, there has been research on the intersections between historical thinking and students' identities (Létourneau 2000; Peck 2010), historical thinking and museums (Gosselin and Livingstone 2016), historical thinking and citizenship education (Sears 2011), historical thinking and technology (Kee 2014; Kee and Darbyson 2011), and historical thinking and pre-service teacher education (Sandwell and Von Heyking 2014).

This work has been able to develop, grow, and come together in part thanks to the Social Sciences and Humanities Research Council of Canada-funded THEN/HiER, or The History Education Network, another offshoot of the Centre for the Study of Historical Consciousness, led by Penney Clark and Seixas. This multi-year, pan-Canadian organization, funded between 2005 and 2015, worked hard to bring together researchers, educators, and historians interested in teaching and learning Canadian history, by hosting conferences, publishing books, sponsoring graduate student exchanges, and providing pan-national funding for collaborative public history projects that could "promote historical consciousness, heighten understanding of collective heritage, and improve communication between teachers and historians" (THEN/HiER 2011).

The disciplinary turn in history education has been able to bring together and revitalize the academic and popular discussions of history curriculum in Canada throughout the first years of the twenty-first century, and, as mentioned, any province that revised its social studies curricula after 2010 emphasized Seixas's historical thinking as a key element of its revision. Seixas himself is often acknowledged as a curriculum adviser or influencer for these provincial revisions.

While this community has been able to infuse curricula with greater research and disciplinary focus, older versions of the curricula, and anecdotal stories from veteran teachers, indicate that having students ask questions, conduct research, and use evidence to draw conclusions while thinking of perspective and bias are not new activities in the history classroom. Curricular revisions from the late 1990s and mid-2000s indicate the strong presence of critical thinking skills and inquiry as foundational components of social studies. Discursively, these things read like historical thinking skills but without the explicit connection to Seixas's work.

For example, the 1999 document *Foundation for the Atlantic Canada Social Studies Curriculum* provides a curricular starting point from which New Brunswick, Newfoundland and Labrador, Nova Scotia, and Prince Edward Island can develop their local social studies courses. In this 1999 document, "inquiry" is one of the three "processes" that should be developed in social studies, the other two being "communication" and "participation." The curricular outcomes that supported this process emphasize the use of "critical inquiries," where students are encouraged to actively gather information and draw conclusions about events from the past. Nowhere in this document are historical thinking skills mentioned or emphasized, despite the emphasis on active thinking with and through historical content. However, between 2005 and 2013, New Brunswick revised its local curriculum based on this foundational document and, in any revision made after 2010, the foundational "inquiry process" includes all six of the historical thinking concepts in its definition. In this revision *inquiry* changed from being understood as a *process* to being understood as one of the ways to develop historical thinking skills. Similarly, in Alberta there was a heavy emphasis on "critical thinking" in the curriculum created and used during the 1990s; but, again, in any revisions made between 2006 and 2009, historical thinking and inquiry begin to either augment or replace the critical thinking language.[11]

Discursively, the 1990s idea of critical thinking and the 2000s idea of inquiry are very similar. They both stress that social studies and history need not be subjects in which students learn unquestionable facts but, rather, can be subjects in which students can question and think about multiple perspectives from the past. The shift in language, however, indicates the influence of historical thinking on these later revisions. In 2013, Alberta launched an *Inspiring Education* consultation and report in which the government announced that it would again be revising the Alberta curriculum to have a greater focus on twenty-first-century competencies, skills-acquisition, and inquiry or discovery-based learning. This same language was used to explain New Brunswick's revisions, which resulted in a greater focus on historical thinking skills. What do we gain when historical thinking is used as a way to organize critical thinking and inquiry in history and social studies education? What do we lose?

The Power Written into the Discipline

While it is perhaps exciting that there are similarities in how provinces across Canada have approached history curriculum, I argue that, as theoretically imagined, historical thinking places far too great an emphasis on the discipline of history and far too little on personal explorations of historical narratives. For history to be meaningful, students need to choose to connect their prior knowledge to meaningful material in ways that make them think, feel, and act with the content and each other (Novak 2002, 2010). For students to understand themselves within the stories and absences of Canadian history, space needs to be available for the emotive and thoughtful examination of what these stories and the absences mean, rather than just understanding the methods used to construct the stories themselves.

A skills focus is attractive to provincial governments because the methodological examination of primary source evidence has the dual effect of removing politics from history and helping students develop the transferable skills that will help them contribute to the economy (B. Davis 1995). With a discipline focus, neoliberalism becomes coded into the curricula as skills and an ethno-cultural attitude that prepares students for the dynamism, change, and innovation of a world in which individualism and profits are prioritized (Cutrara 2009). This focus implicitly makes social justice a secondary issue, a compromise after the fact, rather than the main goal of history education (J. Cole 2016, 50).

The skills-based disciplinary focus was designed as an approach to history education that circumvented the messy politics written into history. An early advocate for the disciplines approach to history education, British theorist Peter Lee (1991), said that politics have no place in the history classroom. Over twenty years later, Canadian educational theorists Marc-André Éthier and David Lefrançois (2013) demonstrated how little has changed in the argument for this approach:

> history classes require scientific rigor, which in turn requires that teachers avoid imposing on their students their sociopolitical views, but instead that they help them develop a more profound interest towards the world, so they can transform the common-knowledge representations they have (about the nation, for example) into concepts (e.g. nationalism) that are rational and can be validated within the discipline. (53)

This emphasis on scientific rigour, rationality, and validity through the discipline, and the fear inherent in the potential of teachers "imposing" their "sociopolitical views," are an appeal for history education that is without the messy complexities that come from a political and affective approach to reading, writing, learning, and living history. Removing politics from history leaves an uneven commitment to the nation because it ignores the affective legacy of power and privilege (Cutrara 2010). History education is political, even when (especially when) it is posed as not being so. Primary sources used to teach and learn history are political, even if (especially when) we think of them as objective records in archives and museums (Cutrara 2019; Duff and Harris 2002; Trouillot 1995). The attempt to avoid the politics and the politicization of history is an attempt to temper the tempers of history; but these tempers are where the passions, the emotions, the anger, and the need for justice lie. They cannot be negated in the study of the past; both the knowledge *and* beliefs of the past need to be attended to in the classroom (Wertsch 2000).

Learning the skills of a historian was meant to be a neutral way of learning history, where the discipline, in all its objective glory, could be prioritized over competing claims and subjective encounters. However, theories such as postmodernism and poststructuralism have shown that the discipline of history is not neutral. The discipline of history, like other formalized Western disciplines, is based on androcentric and colonialist traditions that have written women, labourers, people of colour, and Indigenous peoples out of academic disciplines because their artifacts of experience were not viewed as objective, relevant, or correctly crafted enough to contribute to the subject writ large (Carroll 1976; A.D. Smith 1999). This critique of Western disciplines originally came from Indigenous peoples who recognized their displacement from, and in, Western epistemologies (Battiste 2004; Tuhiwai Smith 2008). A focus on the discipline fails to account for or invite the silences of the Others to be attended to or acknowledged because these silences have often been the result of the discipline itself.

Thus, a focus on developing disciplinary skills in the history classroom is not neutral. It is only with a secure sense of privilege that one can advocate for ignoring the emotional, visceral, and redemptive aspects of the past in favour of a sanitized, seemingly objective approach to examining evidence. A skills-based approach to learning history leaves no room for emotion, for oral tradition, for memory, for story – for the things that make history personal and meaningful to one's life. These things do not comfortably fit into a model for assessing significance, testing the validity of evidence, establishing continuity and change, demonstrating cause and consequence, or exploring the ethical dimensions of stories. By focusing on the discipline, an educator teaches students how to build a house of cards that relies on particular structural rules to bolster the appearance of its stability while obfuscating absence. A focus on skills mirrors what

Morgan Anderson (2015, 83) refers to as Dewey's "quest for certainty," whereas through scientific rigour, rationality, and disciplinary validity students can develop a more "profound interest towards the world" free from the imposition of socio-political views (Éthier and Lefrançois 2013, 53). But in learning about the past – a "foreign country" we have never been to (Lowenthal 2015) – certainty and rationality are impossibilities; we can never know the ways we and the Other come to stories, and we have to hold room for the ways we may travel separately and together in exploring these foreign lands.

Emphasizing the pastness of the past through the examination of evidence negates a discussion of the legacy of oppression and its long-term effects on students inside and outside the classroom. This is not adequate for building a history curriculum that can address the many ways of being a Canadian in the twenty-first century. Peter Seixas (2002b, 2006a) has twice used the example of a speech John A. Macdonald gave to Parliament in 1885 as a way to demonstrate a historical thinking approach to learning Canadian history. In arguing that people in Canada with Chinese ancestry should not be given the vote, Macdonald rationalized that "while [the Chinese man] gives us his labor and is paid for it, and is valuable, [it is] the same as a threshing machine or any other agricultural implement which we may borrow from the United States on hire and return ... to the owner." With the historical thinking approach, Seixas uses this quote to demonstrate that we have to take historical perspective and ethics into account so that we do not judge Macdonald too harshly. He is a product of his time; we cannot use modern measures of morality to assess him or other people in the past, Seixas argues. For Seixas (2002b, n.p.), the "richness of this document as a text for historical study is made clear by the questions of historical consciousness" – questions such as, In what ways has there been change between 1885 and now? Does the change represent progress in racial attitudes? How should we judge Macdonald?

Seixas reads this account and sees an opportunity to rationally and categorically discuss the historicity of the text and its content. He sees it as a way to compare past and present, to explore cause and effect, to look at perspective and significance, to recognize the ethics of history. But all these ways direct the study of history to become a form of productive knowledge (Giroux 1984) or knowledge that is measurable and quantifiable rather than emancipatory (Habermas 2015). Macdonald's quote is not then used to help us "understand how social relationships are distorted and manipulated by relations of power and privilege" (McLaren 2003, 73). When I read this quote, I feel gross. I feel sad. I feel shame. I feel anger. Where do these emotions go when we are asked to focus on the questions of, "In what ways has there been change between 1885 and now? How should we judge Macdonald?" There is no room for these emotions – nor any other emotions – because that is not where the focus is when we are using history as a means to understand the discipline.

Macdonald's statement in Parliament is not just a historical perspective we can explore in contrast to others. Macdonald was making this statement in 1885 in order to influence the discussion about the enfranchisement of Chinese workers which would directly influence how people of Chinese ancestry would be treated and understood within Canada. A discussion about the different perspectives and beliefs of historical actors does not address the fact that John A. Macdonald's perspectives and beliefs informed and became policies that have lingering effects on Canada today, with people of colour, including Canadians of Chinese ancestry, continuously constructed as outside Canada (Zhang and Guo 2015). And if we are asked not to judge the past from the perspectives of the present, how far back do we go in giving amnesty? John A. Macdonald was speaking in 1885. How about the 1919 Immigration Act amendment that allowed Canada to bar immigrants based on the perception that they would not adapt to the "climatic, industrial, social and educational, labour or other conditions or requirements of Canada" because of their "peculiar customs, habits, modes of life and methods of holding property and because of their probable inability to become readily assimilated" (quoted from "Immigration Act Amendment 1919" n.d.)? Or in 1955, when it was stated that Black British citizens would not be a "tangible" immigration asset to Canada because "they do not assimilate readily and pretty much vegetate to a low standard of living" (quoted in Carty 1994, 217)?

Macdonald's statement, and the law and political memo quoted above, *are* rich texts for learning. They can be used to dismantle the taken-for-granted operations of power and privilege in Canada. They can also be used to show students how to deconstruct why the "perspectives and beliefs" of people like John A. Macdonald were and continue to be privileged over those of people whose (exploited) labour built the Canada we live in today. These pieces of historical evidence can invite a discussion about the ramifications of racist and sexist policies that were, and are, central to the building of the Canadian nation-state. This account can be a vehicle for students to engage in thinking through the realities that we live in and to recognize that they are historically-based and ever-present in the public space of the classroom. But they cannot be engaged with in any ways that are not political. Desmond Tutu is often credited for the quote, "If you are neutral in situations of injustice, you have chosen the side of the oppressor." It is not an imposition of politics to acknowledge and explore politics in history because politics *is* history. The stories that we have been allowed to hear are political, they are politics (Burton 1992). They are a "fantasy echo" of the past that has come before (Scott 2001). They are the stories told because of a desire for truth and a will for power (Chambers 1997).

Lévesque (2003, 119) found that students feel no connection to past Canadian "heroes" in that these people have no impact on their collective identities and thus are not perceived as necessary for the understanding of the past, present, and future. They are not significant to young people because young people define significance in terms of how close something is to themselves – the very finding that helped rationalize why a disciplinary focus in history education was needed (Seixas 1993, 1994). But I question how students can have a connection to someone or something that they have been taught to methodologically buffer. How can students find significance in someone or something when the elements of the past that connect to them, the emotions and beliefs that come from learning about the past, are not invited in to learning? Marginalized students cannot connect to a narrative that sanitizes and shrugs off as "perspective" the racist policies that continue to haunt us, nor can students with privilege recognize how they are implicated in structural inequity unless we name white, patriarchal, capitalist supremacy for what it is. Addressing and confronting these issues in the classroom will allow history education to do what it should do: transform. Teaching skills over content removes personal ties to history, which makes history education a perfect training ground for employment but not for life (B. Davis 1995). As veteran history educator Bob Davis (1995, 77–78) wrote: "to find your place in the universe is profoundly different from having a bundle of techniques in your pocket."

What would history education look like if we used it to promote a "we" the would enable people to have free and equal access to legal and social justice, political participation (in whatever form that might take), and material resources, and that would enable people to acknowledge, and be committed to challenging, unequal structures of power (Sears and Hughes 1996, 127–28)? Instead of saying that we will become bonded as citizens because we have similar questions that bring us together, we need to "shift our conceptual frameworks for citizenship education in ways that engage questions of identity and inequality, and that educate youth for social change" (Abu El-Haj 2007, 309). This is what history education can do if we acknowledge and develop its transformative power in how we teach the Canadian past in our classrooms today.

While the historical thinking approach to history education has been integrated into the history and social studies curriculum of many provinces, it is important to note that curriculum writers and editors have not used historical thinking without revision. Writers have expanded, edited, and merged the historical thinking concepts into earlier curriculum to emphasize a focus on *inquiry,* rather than *skills,* as an overarching concept. The Ontario 2013 revision, for example, only emphasizes four historical thinking concepts in its secondary-level history course: historical significance, cause and consequence, continuity and change, and historical perspective. In Prince Edward Island, there is an emphasis on project-based learning at the elementary level, which includes historical thinking subsumed under a broader focus on inquiry.

Thus, with a general focus on inquiry and critical exploration found in Canadian history curriculum, there are ample opportunities for teachers to bring student-centric, deconstructive practices into their classrooms in ways that could lead to more transformative and meaningful learning in Canadian history. In fact, provincial curricula are set up well to respond to deconstructing history because "skills in interpreting and using primary sources will have to include skills in deconstructing earlier interpretations and detecting remnants of colonial thought systems" (Nordgren and Johansson 2015, 15). Thus, while skills are part of today's history curriculum, the broader concept of *inquiry* can do more than historical thinking alone.

A curricular focus that has moved away from direct instruction and toward active learning has created a teaching and learning context where students' futures can become part of the fabric of the Canadian past and present. If Canadian history curriculum is interested in students being able to ask questions and explore answers about the past, we, as educators, can apply Freire's (2006) problem-posing approach to our study of the past. This approach can invite a classroom to dialogue with and for each other so that educators and students can learn from and with the narratives that structure their lives. This focus, this personal, affective focus, this focus on relationships and politics in learning history, is a radical focus that "returns our attention to power and hierarchy, as well as to emotions and human agency" central for transformative, meaningful learning (Gardner 2012, 892). Thus, while I argue that, when left on its own, a focus on disciplinary skills can sterilize history as much as the memorization of fact, the curriculum documents across Canada indicate that there is room to do transformative, student-centric inquiries that hold space for the margins and centres of transnational and (post/neo)colonial identity, citizenship, and belonging.

If Canada is a young country, then we can use this youth as strength rather than weakness and craft a vision for education that includes the active exploration and deconstruction of the processes and power in the Canadian nation that get obfuscated in the face of political processes and marketing campaigns. A history classroom can be that place to explore Canada's past, present, and future by having students inquire – ask questions, find and use a variety of resources, challenge perceptions of the world, explore answers they discover – into how Canada has become what it is today and how a greater knowledge of the past can inform what Canada can be. These goals are important, in line with provincial curricula, and can do more critical work than expected – but are they what students want? In the next chapter, I focus on students' needs and wants in their Canadian history education, by using their voices to articulate what meaningful learning would look like in Canadian history for them.

3

Students Speak
A Desire for Connected, Complex Canadian History

Beyond the discussions about this moment in Canadian and curricular history, this chapter brings us back to what should matter most in our conversations about Canadian history education: the student. Like many adults, I came to my research assuming that students would have to be convinced of the value of history. In fact, my first interview question asked students if they thought it was fair to assume that young people disliked history. Over and over, students told me that, while it was a fair assumption, *they* in fact liked history and wanted to learn more.

In the previous chapter I explored the current landscape of Canadian identity by looking at public and curricular conversations; but it is important to note that the voices of youth are rarely included in these discussions. Today's youth will be inheriting the nation we are debating, and yet conversations about Canadian identity rarely include young people's thoughts about the Canada they see and want for the future. For the youth with whom I have worked, large-scale commemoration practices or the debate between historical skills or content have done little to shift the master Canadian history narrative away from a white, European story of founding, settlement, and expansion. They have heard this story before and know that it does not reflect their lives today. Instead, this generation of youth is navigating a transnational and (post/neo)colonial Canada that they are defining while exploring.

Across the three schools that I conducted research in, in written surveys, in formal interviews, and in informal discussions in and out of class, students from multiple neighbourhoods, ethno-cultural backgrounds, and experiences with school all said that they wanted to learn Canadian history, and they wanted to learn Canadian history *meaningfully*, but instead were taught history as if it had nothing to do with them or their place in the world. I define meaningful learning in history education as learning history that has significance to students' lives now and in the future, both inside and outside the classroom, framed with interpretations of the past that align with students' sense of familial or community history in and for the wider world. In this definition I draw on Joseph Novak's (2010, 18) concept of meaningful learning, which he describes as the "constructive integration of thinking, feeling, and acting leading to empowerment for commitment and responsibility." For this to happen, Novak stresses, three elements must be in play: the content must be meaningful, there needs to be connection to prior knowledge, and there needs to be a positive emotional climate where the learner assents to learn. Interestingly, when asked, students' articulation of how they wanted to learn Canadian history was very similar to this conception of meaningful learning. Students wanted to learn content that connected to who they were and demonstrated the complexity of the world around them, taught by a teacher who cared about the complex connections students could and wanted to make in their history class.

However, students still have a hatred toward their Canadian history class. Students who participated in my research often said "hate" to talk about Canadian history. They saw it as boring and irrelevant to their lives. Students who did not directly participate in the research said it was because they did not see the point given how demoralizing their past experiences with learning Canadian history had been. When faced with such apathy and resentment, we, as adults and educators, tend to develop a moral panic about the decline of reverence for the past and blame students – their youth, their backgrounds, their interests – for not accepting what we are offering. In reality, we, as adults and educators, are not doing a good enough job responding to and reflecting upon what students need from the historical narratives that frame their lives.

When I think of these things, I am reminded of one focus group I held at a mainstream, urban, multicultural high school. When I asked students taking their mandatory grade 10 Canadian history course about whether Canadian history should be taught in schools, students said that learning

Canadian history was important, but they were not sure if what they were taught demonstrated this importance. One student said that the Canadian history they learned in school was "like generations before we ever came here, for Canadians that were here for a long time, like their parents, their grandparents and the parents before them. It's their history, it's not our history." Another student quickly and forcefully disagreed, stressing: "No, it *is* our history because we're Canadian, so therefore what we're learning – there is a purpose. But we're not learning our ethnic background history." The original student, faced with this logic, backed down from his original point and said: "Yeah, that's what I was trying to say."

To quell the original disagreement, a third student ventured that, along with learning Canadian history, they should be taught *another* class that focused on race-based Canadian narratives. A frustrated fourth student contributed that they should be taught Canadian history, and that it "should still be called Canadian history," but

> *instead of learning about the white men that came ... [we should learn about] what makes Canada what it is now. Like the different backgrounds and all the multiculturalism. So, how did the Chinese people get here? How did the West Indian people get here? And stuff. Instead of just, "Oh, all the white people from back then."*

While students seem to be disagreeing with each other in this exchange, they are only disagreeing on a solution to the problem they all shared: How can you be Canadian but not present in Canadian history? This exchange between the students, and the confusion about how ethno-cultural diversity intersects with the Canadian nation in practice but not in teaching Canadian history, demonstrates the gap that exists between the desires students have for connecting to the complex narratives of belonging in Canada and the singular story of the Canadian past they most often encounter in their classes.

In this focus group of six students, for example, I had one young woman whose grandmother had immigrated to Canada from Grenada in the 1970s; another young woman who had an Asian Caribbean background and identified herself as Canadian; another young woman who had emigrated from the Caribbean a few years earlier and who spoke with a heavier accent the more comfortable she became; one young woman who described herself as "African American" although she had not lived in the United States; a young man who identified himself as white and stated he did not connect with Canadian history; and, finally, a young man who had Irish ancestry but whose family had lived in Canada for generations.

Students in this focus group came from two different Canadian history classes where students had family links all over the world, including the Philippines, Turkey, France, and Vietnam, as well as different Caribbean countries, including Barbados, Grenada, Jamaica, and St. Lucia. I knew about these connections because talking about their ethnic and cultural backgrounds was a central way that students expressed themselves to their peers and teachers – differentiating themselves from the norm, while also establishing belonging somewhere else. In this sense, their ethno-cultural identities demonstrated a kind of a "two-directional process: in the process of claiming who one is, one is also announcing who one is not" (Yon 2000, 102) – I am in Canada but my connections are also elsewhere.

In today's transnational world, young people are looking for ways to connect and historically understand their complex identities, to learn what it is like to be both home and away, in whatever ways that means to them (Abu El-Haj 2007; Grever, Pelzer, and Haydn 2011; Warikoo 2011). While much of the literature on youth's transnational identities focuses on immigrants or first- or second-generation populations with fluid or flexible identities, or identities that straddle or inhabit two worlds, transnationalism is not just a feature in the lives of immigrant or first-generation youth, nor are transnational experiences binary (Brisson 2018; Malenfant 2018; Ostashewski, Frey, and Johnson 2018).

This country with many ties, stories, and connections across and around the world is the Canada that students are familiar with. These complex connections that are part of their transnational Canadian identities echo through the questions students ask and the opinions they hold regarding Canadian history. Transnationalism is enmeshed in how youth come to understand themselves as Canadian. The pride they have in this multicultural Canadian identity (Grant 2016; Tastsoglou and Petrinioti 2011; Wenshya Lee and Hébert 2006) guides their "visions of Canada" (Ahmad Ali 2008, 99). Students want to learn history that reflects this vision of

Canada and so, Canadian history taught with this transnational vision in mind is history that will be meaningful for students because it will demonstrate a Canada that includes them.

In this chapter, I use the voices of students to narrate the Canadian history education they want to see in their classrooms. Drawing on their words, experiences, and my own observations from having been an educator in traditional and non-traditional sites of education for over fifteen years, I have come to understand students' strong desires to learn history, especially Canadian history, as connected, complex, and taught with care. I argue that the combination of connection and complexity taught in a care-full way can be the start of a purposeful conversation regarding what a new "we" would look like in Canadian history education. This emphasis on connection, complexity, and care shifts our focus in the history classroom to a place where students can be in conversation with a past that includes them, rather than receivers of a narrative or set of tools that are able to exist without them. When we listen to what students want and need from their history education, what they *desire* from it, we come to see their needs as learners to be more present in the classroom than they have been. When we privilege connection, complexity, and care in our history teaching, we begin to teach in ways that strengthen the bonds between self and other and can engender a greater sense of belonging and recognition for our students and the histories they share. This focus allows us to redefine Canada and Canadian history premised on a "we" rather than on an "us and them" that often excludes the very students who have a desire to understand their histories in this place.

I make this argument by drawing on the words and experiences of students who can be easily ignored or overlooked because they may act in ways that seem to indicate that they are not interested in learning. Most of the students you will read about in this chapter are not the typical "good students" who were academically successful and well-liked by teachers. Many of them were failing, some had already failed, and some had failed out of two or three different schools before enrolling in an alternative school. The majority of students quoted in this chapter are students who can be easily dismissed as just not willing to learn because they enter the classroom with such opposition to being there; but these students, these resistant students, are the ones we should listen to: the students who have been active in their rejection of an education that has yet to provide them with what they need or want for the future.

Connection

Stripped of connection to everyday life, national history taught in schools has been shown to be devoid of context with little relevance for students' lives (Almarza 2001; A. Clark 2008; Harris and Haydn 2006). With a pedagogical and curricular emphasis on rote memorization of names and dates, students have no impetus in their formal history education to create meanings between the past, present, and future of the nation. Educational theorists interested in the emancipatory possibilities of education believe that the goal of education should be to empower learners to take charge of their own meaning making and gain the confidence and knowledge needed to make change in the world (Freire 2006; Novak 2010). Yet, when history is relegated to "school knowledge," or "an artificial set of facts and generalizations whose credibility lies no longer in its authenticity as a cultural selection but in its instrumental value in meeting the obligations teachers and students have within the institution of schooling" (McNeil 1988, 191), then history fails to empower students and invite them to create meaning of their worlds in different, and more empowered, ways.

One of the most common ways students in my research talked about their Canadian history education was by saying how much they wanted to learn "interesting" history over "boring, dry" history. While the idea of "interesting" and "boring" may seem simplistic and one-dimensional, I found that when unpacking what these concepts meant for students, "interesting" and "boring" were discursive markers flagging students' desires to learn Canadian history in ways that connected to them and that demonstrated the complexity of the world around them. While these two elements – connection and complexity – often overlapped in students' conception of what "interesting" history education meant for them, in this section, I focus first on connection.

I define *connection* as historical content that links to students' prior knowledge and provides depth to their interests, identities, backgrounds, worldviews, and/or futures in ways that meet students where they are, not dumbed down for their digestion nor self-righteously enforced as relevant.

Connection in history education means that students are given opportunities to actively develop connections – to *negotiate meaning,* in the words of Novak (2010) – between their lives and historical content through verbal, written, affective, and/or artistic instruction, assessment, and/or evaluation. In my interviews, I found that what made something "interesting" or "boring" meant different things to different students, but a student's conception of "interesting" came down to this: Could they connect new information to their prior knowledge and were they actively invited to explore these connections as an integral part of their learning?

For some students, "interesting" history was history that linked to their interests outside of school; for others, "interesting" meant that the content was tied to current events; still others thought content was "interesting" when it connected to their racial or gendered identities. Some students expressed an interest in learning about topics such as Greek or Egyptian history for no other reason than that "it would be interesting just to know, to sit and talk about it." Others wanted to know more about themes they read about in popular books, like *Guns, Germs, and Steel* by Jared Diamond (1997). In the interviews students often posed rhetorical, content-based questions such as, "Were there such things as pirates?" or "What was a woman's mentality like back in the 1950s?" Although seemingly off topic, these questions were driven by curiosity and a desire to better understand things they thought about. In the same vein, other students asked questions to fill in the gaps of what they already knew because, as one student said when reflecting on the focus of Napoleon in one of her courses, "he's come up in my life and been, like, 'Napoleon, Napoleon, Napoleon,' but I have no idea what he does or anything."

While this conception of "interesting" may seem scattered, overwhelming, or irrelevant for teaching Canadian history – why would you learn about pirates in a twentieth-century Canadian history course?[1] – what is clear is that students' understanding of what constituted "interesting" history was history that provided context and depth to who they were and what they wanted to know. Content that was "interesting" answered questions, provided background, and developed new understandings of things that shaped their world. It was not content just for the sake of content. It was content that could help narrate who they were and who they were becoming. While this is an integral part of young people's psycho-social development (Brighton 2007), this notion of connection also links to young people's desire for belonging, especially for racialized youth (Booker 2006).

For many students there was a distinct emotional dimension to wanting these connections. For students who wanted content to connect with their interests outside of school, learning interesting content was a way to quell boredom and energize them in class. For students who looked to content to validate their personal identity, "interesting" was a flag waved in anger, sadness, or confusion for a desire for content that recognized them as insiders, rather than outsiders, to the narrative. In response to the survey question, "What do you think is the purpose for studying history?" one student at a mainstream ethnically diverse school wrote: "I don't really see the point, considering the fact that I don't get to learn about my own history." Another student at the same school wrote that she hated history, especially Canadian history, because "if it's not about my background history then I won't get involved with it." In another class at the same school, another student wrote that in class "they only talk about white folks and black people don't play a role in the history we learn at school." All the statements, anonymously written on paper, reflected a defensive anger about the way they were learning histories disconnected from their lives. On many of the surveys, students wrote large, underlined, or capped words, inscribing their anger onto the page that the history they learned in school had nothing to do with them. These comments confirm the findings that students ascribe historical significance to histories that closely align with their own ethnic identities (T. Epstein 1998, 2009; L.M. Harris, Halvorsen, and Aponte-Martínez 2016; Marker 2011; Peck 2009, 2010; Terzian and Yeager 2007) and when their ethnic identities are disavowed, it creates a sense of anger and apathy about their education (Almarza 2001; Dei 1997; R. Harris and Reynolds 2014; Wane 2007).

Thus, connection is not just about learning interesting material, but about being seen in class as worthy of attention, worthy of consideration, worthy of what is being taught, worthy of representing a past and future of this country and land. Connection in history education means teaching history with a pedagogy of belonging, a pedagogy of connectedness (Beck and Malley 1998; Doherty 2018) that places students and their questions about the world at the centre of why and how we teach about the past.

When students are looking for "interesting" content in their history classes, they are looking for the attachment, the attention, the *connection* that who they are is as important as what is being taught. When history connects, is relevant, and answers the questions students have about the world, students find it interesting and want to know more; but when students encounter histories that lack meaningful connection to the present, when students have no clue where the information or story is heading, it contributes to a sense of demoralization about learning history (Misco and Patterson 2009, 74).

Students talked in binary terms about learning history – yes to interesting, no to boring – because their experiences with history education often creates this dichotomy between history they see as interesting and related to their lives (history at home) and history that they see as boring and disconnected from their lives (history at school). Their mandatory Canadian history class was the class most often associated with "boring" and disconnected history because students saw it as "biased and based on one group" or what "the government wants you to learn." While they recognized that a Canadian history course could be relevant to their lives, students found "It's not always geared to look that way." As one of them said, "some of the stuff that [the teacher] says, sometimes I think it relates to me, because, like, you know, this is Canadian history, so obviously I relate to it, as a Canadian. But, like, I don't know, sometimes I don't."

These students' reflections about their Canadian history classes demonstrate the gap that exists between students' needs and desires for an interesting history education and what they have found in their Canadian history class. These comments beg the question as to what the split is that we, as educators, are exacerbating when students' connections are not prioritized when teaching Canadian history. It bridges to broader national questions of who belongs and how they know this, how to belong and how to show this (Subedi 2019, 119). Are students, for example, forced to choose between dichotomous ways of being in Canada – the colonizers or the colonized (Khan and Cottrell 2017) – or can we help them legitimize a third space where they can relate, where they can recognize themselves, and where they can see how to map a road to greater justice?

My research as well as that done by others indicates that it is content that has a connection to students' prior knowledge and cultural experiences that students find interesting, engaging, and trustworthy for learning history (L.M. Harris, Halvorsen, and Aponte-Martínez 2016; R. Harris and Reynolds 2014). As one student said, "the history I've learned [at school] ... has been from a white supremacist, patriarchal, and capitalist point of view, in contrast from the community history I am usually learning in the rest of my life." Other students articulated the secrecy they expected from formal learning, with one student saying that "school has guidelines for what the teacher may or may not speak or teach about whereas outside everything is out in the open." While formal school curriculum is one-directional, students saw the history outside the classroom as "open," "passed down and told by mouth" and "shared by your grandfather or mother." It is these connections, the emotional and personal relationships students have with the topic, that determine students' level of trust with historical sources and their willingness to learn from them (Jacobsen et al. 2018). Thus, while students are interested in learning history, they draw a contrast between these two types of history – the kind they learn in school and the kind they learn at home – because they see "interesting," personal content outside the mandate for school learning and beyond what is considered essential for their education. The result is that students have to bridge the gap themselves between the history they have learned at home and the history they have learned at school in ways they will not find subtractive to their sense of self (Valenzuela 1999).

Without personal connections inside the history classroom, students have to wrestle, alone, with why they sometimes relate to the Canadian history legitimized in the classroom but sometimes not. However, the question of personal connection and belonging should be at the nexus of what national history education is about: How does Canadian history reflect, relate, and contextualize my experiences in the Canadian present? What can my formal Canadian history education tell me about the world outside the classroom? How can history education be both a mirror and a window to the Canadian future I will inherit (Style 1996)? When there are no invitations to explore these tensions, these questions, both historically and in the present, students resist, rebel, disengage, and "hate" Canadian history; but it is not really Canadian history they hate. It is the way the Canadian history they learn in class fails to connect to the Canada they live in outside of class that is the source of their hate.

Historical content, when taught with students' connections in mind, can link students' pasts and presents, giving them the contextual knowledge to understand the world around them. This shift to a *student-centric* approach to history education is one in which students' learning, rather than teachers' teaching, becomes the focus and basis for the development of students' understandings of Canada and their place within it. Connection in history supports a pedagogy of belonging (Beck and Malley 1998), a humanizing pedagogy (Freire 2006), a pedagogy based in a belief in democracy (hooks 2010) because it is these pedagogies that see students as people who need answers to their questions about the world. Seeing "interesting" content in their history class helps strengthen the bonds between the students' present and "mirror and window" experiences of the past: histories that can reflect who they are and that broaden the view of the world they can imagine (Style 1996). Interesting content, content not to entertain but to inspire and grow, is content that connects to students' prior knowledges and reaffirms their legitimacy in this place.

However, while content that connects is important, connection is not just about content; in fact, "we need to move beyond the assumption that teaching is just about content but also focus on pedagogy and practices that support students' need for relatedness" (Fredricks et al. 2019, 519). Connection can be engendered through instructional methods that prioritize students' meaning making between self and others.

Discussion, for example, is a valuable instructional tool that can support students in making connections with one another and with who they are outside of the classroom. With discussion, learning becomes interesting because it becomes more than a one-directional flow of content; students can play give-and-take with the content, with each other, and with their opinions, building a contextualized and connected understanding of history within a community. While Hess (2010, 207–8) warns that teachers can often limit connections in discussions by asking inauthentic questions or dominating the conversation with their own opinion, students in my research talked very little about these problems and instead identified that discussion was an important way for them to think through what Hess describes as "the complicated discussions of a complicated world."

One student said that he "really [liked] discussions when it comes to history" because discussion with his classmates helped him understand broader perspectives on the topics they were covering. Another student identified:

> *You get interested when people talk from their perspectives cuz it's the whole class, so then you get interested in it, and if every class is like that then even students that don't like history, as myself, they'll probably find it more interesting.*

This student's classmate agreed that being involved and connected to your classmates made class worthwhile and interesting and rejoined by saying: "We have more questions because we learn from each other."

Teaching history through discussion involves students, but also models a citizenry that acknowledges and values difference. Research has shown that low-income and racialized youth are exposed to the least amount of civic education and current event discussions than any other group (Kahne and Middaugh 2008). Discussion holds an important place for demonstrating to marginalized students how important their experiences and ideas are to understanding a full and inclusive Canada. One student from a marginalized, "at-risk" population said that having discussion in class would provide opportunities for students to voice their perspectives and that this would allow them to "realize that they can have an opinion towards things as well." Another student identified that learning about the connections between history, race, and their experiences – topics that teachers often shy away from (Almarza 2001; T. Epstein 1998; Levstik 2000) – can result from discussion, saying:

> *I'm an African American girl sitting in the class and the girl next to me she's white or whatever. And me and her have two different histories, and maybe we can learn from each other. She could go home and ask her grandparents, her mom or somebody, about their history, and I could go home and ask people in my family about my history. And we could come back and exchange information. And then we'll be more knowledgeable.*

This student identified that discussion, through the "exchange" of information, would make students "more knowledgeable." This is not surprising given Patricia Halagao's (2004) finding that it is not just learning information about your ethnic group that is valuable for ethnic minority youth, but being able to *teach* that history too. Thus, the connection the student made about making each other "more knowledgeable" by sharing in school the histories they learned at home, demonstrates how discussion can be a valuable instructional tool for students to be both learner and teacher in ways that support greater learning of the many histories present in the classroom.

By sharing their perspectives and stories in classroom-based discussion, students are able to demonstrate, to themselves and others, the differing ways to be in and connect to Canada. This is not to keep students' perspectives the same but rather for them to (re)develop their own positions, invest more in the lessons, and ask more questions, as the students gestured to above. Discussion is a form of storytelling that "honours the historicity of the other by allowing students to share truths that are historically situated, embedded within culture, and which do not reflect the worldview of those in power" (Griffith 2014, 107). In this way, discussion can be an important instructional tool that implicitly prompts youth to "reimagine the meaning of citizenship and allows them to exercise radical forms of citizenships that [reflect] their community experiences" (Subedi 2019, 120). Through discussion, students can explore their identity and develop a sense of autonomy necessary for pushing beyond limiting stereotypes imposed by others (Fredricks et al. 2019). Teaching with an ethos of bringing students' experiences and prior knowledge into the classroom through discussion can transform the history classroom into a generative space for developing a national "we" that includes and is strengthened by sharing and listening to difference.

Novak (2010) identifies that for meaningful learning to occur, students need to be able to think, feel, and act with meaningful content. While discussion can elicit both thinking and feeling, students I worked with indicated that history can be enhanced through affective learning strategies that can help them do all three: think, feel, and act. Affect and emotion are important yet overlooked parts of history learning (Jacobsen et al. 2018); tapping into the emotionality of the past may be a way for students to process complex ideas in the safe place of make-believe. Through activities such as writing-in-role, watching movies, and even role play (which older students said would be awkward but "kinda funny too"), students can develop *historical empathy* with the past in ways that can be important for their learning.

O.L. Davis Jr. (2001) defines historical empathy as the "enriched understanding within context" that "arises or develops from the active engagement in thinking about particular people, events, and situations in their context, and from wonderment about reasonable and possible meanings within, in a time that no one can really know ... It is robust, tough, and insightful even as it is imaginative, and it is always based upon available evidence" (3). This active engagement of learning and thinking through historical content can activate a deep and critical encounter with elements of the past students may not have considered. This is not about teaching false or fictionalized histories, but rather connecting with the creative possibilities of interpretation that can come from fiction and creative non-fiction – the *wonderment* of meaning, as Davis articulated.

Students gestured to the ways historical empathy connects them to their emotions and imaginations when they talked about the use of fiction or creative non-fiction in their classes. One student said that he enjoyed being able to write in-role because he could "let [his] mind really wander." He explained that "I'm really into war movies, seeing war movies and then being able to put it down on paper what I think someone's experience was. I just really enjoyed being able to, like, let my mind wander and really get into it."

Other students also said that their learning was enhanced when the wonderment of history was present. Watching a Hollywood movie, for example, "grabs you and you want to, like, pay attention," one student said. Documentaries are fine, another student said, but movies are *movies*, she emphasized. Although watching movies in class is often associated with a day off from teaching, historical movies can provoke a certain type of learning grounded in historical empathy that students identified would be important for processing information. As one student said: "Even in Careers [class] and stuff when people who don't normally come to class or don't normally participate or don't really care about that class, when there's a movie being put on, everyone leaves the back of the room, comes to the front of the room and they're, like, really, that's what's going on?"

Although her friend challenged her by saying that students like movies because they do not have to do work, the student emphasized that "when the teacher comes back and asks questions of certain people that don't really participate, you'll have a little bit more hands saying 'this is what happened in the movie. I understand this.'" Another student said that after watching a movie "you, like, develop feelings and then you would be more passionate with your answers. You would be like, 'I saw this da-da-da because' and then we'd have, like, discussions and debates about it."

For these students, movies do not act as a distraction from learning, but as an important and affective hook into thinking about and discussing a historical moment. Because affect invites new and deeper ways to create meaning, inviting students' imaginations to class can activate their learning as connected to emotion. As another student emphasized, these imaginative and affective connections are important for learning history because "sometimes that's what you have to do in education: understand how the people think and have empathy." Students identified that affective approaches to learning history can *enrich* discussion and invite critical explorations of the presentation and interpretation of the past, especially when the viewing is structured for critical learning.

In sum, students found history interesting when it was taught in ways that connected them to others in the past and the present. This connection to others was not just important for class, but for the future. As one student said:

> *It seems like people who know more about history like people in general. They seem to be more attached to the world. Like, people who don't know anything about* [history] *and they just know the way it is now, they're very detached people. They don't connect with the world as easily. They look down on people more and they're more judgmental towards things. And they don't have an empathetic hand to lend, kind of thing.*

As this student articulated, a background in history gives students those connections, those attachments, that can help them help others and also themselves. Often evoking the Santayana adage that those who do not know the past are doomed to repeat it, students talked about how history connects the past to the future, because "if you don't know what happened, you're never going to know what to change about it." Students identified that these connections – connections between self and others, their past and their future – were based in knowledge of history because when you "start making connections in everyday life, seeing where stuff comes from, you get a greater understanding of why things work the way they do." These connections, these *interesting* connections, are the fodder for an interesting history class, a class that informs students of the world they live in, a class where they are included and can work through the world they know to imagine a version of the world they want.

Connected Learning

While this theme of connection may seem obvious to educators, it is important to understand that connections must be grounded in a holistic understanding of who the student is and the types of connections they may want to make with history. It is this respectful consideration of the depth and breadth of students' lives that can contribute to a more student-centric approach to history education – an approach that can court a sense of "we" among the people in the room.

I have defined *connection* as historical content that provides depth and scaffolding to students' interests, identities, backgrounds, worldviews, and/or futures in ways that meet students where they are, not dumbed down for their digestion nor self-righteously enforced as relevant. The second part of this definition – "dumbed down for their digestion nor self-righteously enforced as relevant" – is of particular importance for thinking about the connections students could and want to make with Canadian history.

As I discuss further in the next section, it is not just connection that students want in their history education but also *complexity* of the Canadian stories they are learning. Teachers can make the determination of how and with what students should be connecting and thus fail to notice the connections that have a greater alignment with students' sense of self and needs for the future – in other words, the stories that demonstrate the complexity of who they are as people and as Canadians. With an expectation of predetermined connections, teachers can sever an authentic connection between the student and history and instead enforce the acceptance of stories and histories that actively deny the complexity of who a student is and the questions they have about the past.

In the most striking example of this, I observed a Canadian history lesson where the teacher attempted to connect students to their "grassroots" (her word) by starting a lesson on World War II by featuring the geographic community where the school was located. To begin, she showed a panoramic photo of soldiers lined up on the school's football field and asked students about the young men in the photo. While the current demographic of the community was ethnically and culturally diverse, at the time the photo was taken, the community was not, and so the changes in demographics over the preceding sixty years meant that in focusing on this place, the stories she wanted to feature with this photo were indistinguishable from the mainstream history students had read about in their textbooks. Students were initially intrigued by the familiar setting, but quickly disengaged when the teacher asked them to look at the photo and determine who could not go to war. "Black people," one student shouted. "We couldn't do anything," her friend responded.

By highlighting the lack of ethnic or cultural diversity in the photo – diversity that would have been there but was not apparent because the soldiers seemed homogeneously white – the teacher immediately created a learning environment that precluded the connections her ethnically and culturally diverse students could make with this history. By focusing on the absence of racialized diversity, the teacher highlighted a vision of the local past that was inaccessible and alienating to her racialized students. Students could only connect with the past if they imagined themselves as absent, discriminated against, or divorced from their racial and cultural heritage. These connections could have engendered a sense of victimhood and potential feelings of shame for the Black students, a common reaction for African-Caribbean students who are only taught histories of discrimination and injustice within the Black diaspora (R. Harris and Reynolds 2014). Thus, as Halagao (2004) found: "Although it may be one's first inclination to rush into teaching content about ethnic peoples, spending time understanding students' prior knowledge and sense of ethnic identity is crucial to setting up a learning environment that is open, honest, and reflective" (474). Connections, therefore, are not just what a teacher deems them to be.

Despite not seeing faces that resembled their own, students could have found connections in this photo. The soldiers lined up on the school's football field were not much older than the fifteen-year-olds in the class – the teacher could have asked, How might it have felt to have your friends and family members enlist in a war? As transnational students with links and connections across borders, the students could have connected with the idea of being separated from family – what if your communications with family were not instantaneous but took weeks? Students even tried making connections between their lives and World War II by linking the idea of living with war to the idea of living with gang violence, of which they had first-hand experience – how might the feeling of war be different if the fighting took place overseas and not around the corner?

Although students were not invited to connect with the lesson as the teacher envisioned, at one point a student interrupted the lecture and asked the teacher how "Toronto" got its name. Happy they were engaging on any level, the teacher stopped the lesson and talked about the origins of the names "Toronto" and "Canada." Never before or after had I heard the class so quiet. It was as if, all of a sudden, they were hearing information that provided context and connection to their lives in Canada: What is Toronto? How did it come to be? How was it named? With this student's question, and the rapt responses to the answer, the class demonstrated that they wanted to understand the past of this place they currently called home, and that interrupting the lesson was the only way their connections could be met.

The teacher developed her lesson as if connection to the local community was enough to make the students care about the same content they saw and disregarded in the textbook: the story of white soldiers in a white country fighting a far-off war. In doing so, the teacher precluded her students from making their own connections to the history by using this photograph as a prompt to complicate students' understanding of local development, waves of migration, or how not everyone in Toronto who looked white had the same rights and privileges as others. In other words, her decisions about connections precluded her students from seeing and speaking to the local and transnational connections they might have seen in the photograph – connections that have been shown to be important for racial minority youth (R. Harris and Reynolds 2014; Martell and Stevens 2019). But the question the student asked about the name of Toronto, off-topic as it was, demonstrated the desire students have to make active connections to the city they call home. Their quietness at the answer also demonstrated the respect students were prepared to show for content that prioritized these connections.

When the teacher moved back to the lesson, the students' behaviour returned to normal: talking, texting, and listening to music. Moving back to the prescribed content meant that students rightly assessed that the official story would be prioritized over their need to actively discuss and connect with the history that framed their lives. Thus, they actively, if rudely, resisted this approach to Canadian history by ignoring the remainder of the lesson.

If students are looking for history that frames their worlds, then superficially adding content that the teacher feels will resonate with students – without fully providing the space to see and court the connections that students need, and want, to make with history – will not ultimately satisfy students' desires to learn history meaningfully. Students want history and their history class to be interesting. This is not about entertaining students, but about creating a classroom environment where students connect to the material being taught. Teachers have to take the lead in creating these interesting and meaningful connections, because as adults with a greater knowledge of the world, students are relying on them, on us, to provide perspectives on the world around them. Students already see a "we" in Canada – a "we" that includes them. Their desire in history education is for their time in the classroom to provide them connections with the stories of how that "we" came to be.

Complexity

Closely tied with the concept of connection in history is the concept of complexity. Students are drawn to history because of complexity, not because of national allegiance (A. Clark 2009; Levstik 2000); yet, as "school knowledge" (McNeil 1988), history often loses this complexity and becomes a one-dimensional story of progress and national triumph. Students look at the Canada they see before them and see a country negotiating its place and space as a transnational, (post/neo)colonial nation in a world fraught with populist politics, corruption, war, environmental devastation, as well as compassion, resistance, and resilience. They then encounter a historical narrative that offers a flattened perspective on the country's past, with no precedent for the world they see around them. Alternatively, with a skills-based focus in history education, students may also encounter their history class as a site to methodically and unemotionally examine and assess evidence. Neither approach to history education draws students into thinking about who they are in Canada – the "we" of the Canadian past, present, and future – and neither approach is designed to invite students to think about how they too can engage in the resistance and resilience needed to create a more just world.

As the past section demonstrates, students are looking for history to connect with who they are. However, one-dimensional, superficial connections with history will not ultimately satisfy students' desires to understand and explore Canadian history. They recognize the complexities of being Canadian and have an expectation that history education should reflect these same *Canadian* complexities. Thus, along with connection, *complexity* is the second component of Canadian history education that can centre students' meaningful learning in the Canadian history classroom.

I define *complexity* as content that reflects the multiplicity of experiences in the past and present, taught with instruction that requires students to think about how the world is open to interpretation, not a superficial story with a definitive beginning and end. In this definition I draw on the concept of "counterstories" advocated by critical race theorists. Counterstories are *complex* stories, or stories taught in *complex* ways, that inspire and uncover narratives of action and hope because they better reflect and connect with the complex world we live in (L.A. Bell 2003, 24). As part of one's teaching practice, counterstories can provide us with the "necessary contextual contours to the seeming 'objectivity' of positivist perspectives" (Ladson-Billings 1998, 11) and, in doing so, can "shatter complacency and challenge the status quo" (Delgado 1989, 2414). Teaching with counterstories can demonstrate the complexity and richness of history, and can highlight the "métissage" of history with lives and texts understood as "relational and braided rather than isolated and independent" (Donald 2012, 537).

Students come into the classroom with a desire to learn about the complex world around them and yet in many classrooms, students find a singular story taught in an uncomplicated way that strips that complexity from the past and present. Learning history then provides no space, nor impetus, to participate in the telling and learning of history, to challenge assumptions, to jar complacency, to lift spirits, or to lower defences (Delgado 1989, 2440). While students I worked with did not necessarily use the word "complex" to talk about the history they wanted to learn, they often referred to the textbook when talking about the history they did not want to be taught. Although I did not see the textbook used heavily in any of the classrooms I was in, the repetition of students talking about the textbook indicates how it operates as a kind of spectre of an uncomplicated history education that students both expected and detested in the classroom. Students said the textbook was "evil" and that it made history "boring and dead" to the point that they were "not into it." When asked what they wanted from history education, students readily shouted out "less bookwork" or "no textbook." One student said she did not like her experience learning Canadian history because the class was "very textbook-y." In the interviews, students often lowered their voices and bodies when speaking about the textbook – as perhaps a subconscious indication of the way the textbook dragged down the class. This response suggests that perhaps it is not the book itself, but the *way* the textbook is used as a replacement for exploring a complicated past that is the real root of animosity toward history education more generally.

Students willingly shared that when the textbook predominated as a teaching method, they actively resisted by tuning out of class. Disengagement may seem to indicate students' disinterest in the subject, but actually demonstrates resistance to instruction. Misco and Patterson (2009, 76) found that teaching history from a textbook contributes to isolated and meaningless learning experiences for students in history education, because teachers treat textbooks as the fountainhead of curriculum, as the ends rather than the means. Students referenced how teaching from a textbook presented a linear, unimaginative, and stagnant view of Canadian history that provided neither the complexity nor the connection they were looking for. One student found that teachers use the textbook "like [it's] an accurate description of what really happened, without any analysis of where the perspective is coming from." Another student explained that, in her previous Canadian history class, she had an

> issue with textbook work that assumes that ... "this is the text and this is what happened, memorize the dates and this is how it went down," and there's no real discussion about, like, "Okay, what was the other side of that?" Or like, "Who wrote this textbook?"

Another student I talked to, a student who failed his first attempt at Canadian history, said he had a real problem with his "dry" Canadian history class:

> It was basically, "Read this passage out of the textbook, here are the questions for it." And there was no, like, in-depth conversation; there was no, "Can I ask you questions about it?" It was kind of just like you're fending for yourself. And it's like, how do you learn that way?

Like many students learning "dry" history from a textbook, this student expressed frustration that learning was supposed to take place when students were just looking for simplified answers about history in a textbook. The student may have resisted such instruction by refusing to do work or even showing up for class. These behaviours could have been interpreted by a teacher as that student "hating" history, but the student's desire to ask and be asked questions about the content indicates an interest in the subject but an aversion to the instruction. The student followed this comment by saying: "when I had a conversation about something I can get more out of it."

By denying students the opportunity to participate in their learning by focusing on a one-dimensional story found in a textbook, we simplify the experience of learning Canadian history to the lowest common denominator, leaving students isolated and alone, fending for themselves, and memorizing dry, decontextualized facts that have little to do with the world around them. When we use textbooks as the only way to enter into the study of history, they become the centre, a bounded centre, from which an understanding of the nation resides. There can be no counterstories, for example, or stories told in complex ways, when the textbook is used to bind a narrative in place.

This is not to say that the textbook should be thrown out, however. Students are not opposed to the textbook as a resource; they are opposed to the textbook being used as a stand-in for teaching. When used on their own, textbooks leave no room for history to be presented and discussed as a connected collection of complex counterstories that can expand and challenge how students view the world and their experiences. When there is space for greater complexity in the history classroom, then there is space for the textbook to be one resource among many for thinking about the past. As one student said, a history teacher should have "balance, don't just do notes and discussions ... every now and so often do like a video, and then every now and then ... teach the textbook, and so on, and so on." Another student said that the highlight of her history class was the different resources her teacher brought in, saying that "there was every different kind of media and we thought about it in different ways. And that's something that I'd love to see more of in every class."

As I found in my earlier research with Grade 10 and 11 students (Cutrara 2007), different teaching and learning resources can provide perspectives on history that make students think about the past and present in broader and more complex ways. The textbook, as a readily available and recognizable resource, can still be a part of that. In this research, I asked pairs of students to compare an interview published in an Inuit newsletter about the 1953 Grise Fiord relocation with how this relocation was featured in the textbook. Larry Audlaluk's (2005) interview in *Naniiliqpita,* a Nunavut Tunngavik publication, described the forced relocation of the Inuit community by the Canadian government as well as the lasting ramifications this relocation had on him and his family. In comparison to the textbook, students found Audlaluk's "individualized" account, using one student's word, clearer for understanding what happened during the relocation. By providing "vague" information and not discussing "how much [relocation] ruined their lives," the students found the textbook "biased" toward the government. However, when placed together, students could use both sources to discuss a broader, more historicized perspective on the Canadian government's treatment of Indigenous people as well as the lasting ramifications these types of policies have had on Indigenous nations. Although some students showed ignorance of Indigenous issues that still needed to be worked through – we cannot forgo teaching just because we are focused on learning – Audlaluk's interview and the opportunity to compare it with the textbook provided students with a greater sense of complexity about the past, its presence in the present, and students' own relationships with the ways these stories are taught and understood.

While the history of the Grise Fiord relocation was in the textbook, students were introduced to the *complexity* of this history through a primary source written by and for Inuit people *and* through the invitation to compare the primary source with the textbook. As a static text designed to respond to the curriculum in a broad enough way that can support large-scale sales across districts, the history textbook has never been, and never will be, a resource that can respond and reflect the complexities of the past. Instead, it is inviting the complexity of history into the classroom through complicating and questioning resources and perspectives available to us that provides the kind of complexity students are looking for in their history education.

This has been one of the benefits of having contemporary history curricula foreground primary source inquiry as a way into history. With the inclusion of inquiry and primary source investigation in the Canadian history curriculum, there is now a greater curricular emphasis on, and thus more access to, diverse teaching resources from which to teach and learn Canadian history. When used in ways that foreground complexity, multiple resources in learning history provide the counterstories that narrate a sense of "we" in Canadian history – a "we" that complicates and challenges our understanding of history and provides difficult, and perhaps even controversial, knowledge into conceptions of how and what we know. A "we" not bound to one text or one interpretation, but that can reverberate with the multiple voices heard from the margins and centre of the past and the present.

When the textbook is used as the main entryway into learning history, students' frustrations about history education often come out as hatred for a class resource that could be used as one resource, among many, to teach and learn history. Instead, when used on its own, the textbook acts as an anchor that keeps the story bound to one place. This is what students hate. Their comments about the textbook are simply a shorthand, an effigy, to denounce an uncomplex, disconnected, content-focused teaching and learning experience in their Canadian history class – a focus that discounts them and their own messiness and complexity from being in the world.

While the need for connection and complexity is important for all students, the presence of both as a way to develop a greater sense of "we" in the Canadian nation is especially important for students who, by virtue of their racialization, are often constructed as outside of Canadian history. It is this particular dynamic to which I will now turn.

Complex Learning

As mentioned earlier in this chapter, the lack of connection in history was most personally and emotively felt by students of colour who were angry that history education did not reflect their prior knowledge and cultural connections. Similarly, the heightened need for history to demonstrate the complexity of being a Canadian was most viscerally expressed by these same students. In the Canadian history classes I conducted research in, most of the students were students of colour who articulated aspects of their identity opposed to Canadian norms. They embodied what Ong (1996) called a "flexible citizenship," where students may have felt that they were "born here, but [that their] home is not here" (Abu El-Haj 2007). While many of these students were referred to as immigrants by their teachers, the majority of the students, many of whom were Black and aligned with Caribbean and/or African American culture and music,[2] were born in Canada or had lived in Canada longer than they had in their country of origin. Complexity, for many of these students, defined their identity in Canada.

Because of their transnational Canadian identities, students I worked with struggled with how to articulate the kind of Canadian history they needed and wanted in their history class, given that their experience with history education was that it neglected to reflect the Canada they saw around them. As one student said:

Okay, yeah, I live in Canada, I guess I'm a Canadian but ...
– I'm not a white man. [Her classmate interrupted] –
... Yeah, I'm not a white man.

As discussed, in many of their history classes, students encounter a simplistic narrative of Canadian history that defines white, male experiences as the benchmark for what and who is Canadian. This benchmark excludes the majority of Canadian students from being able to see themselves as part of Canadian history and, by extension, as a valid part of the Canadian present.

Like other racialized youth, the youth I worked with identified that the curriculum repeats the same story of white legitimacy over and over again rather than complicating the nuances of power and privilege across time (R. Harris and Reynolds 2014). One student expressed her frustration with this version of history when she said: "We learnt about the migration, like when the Europeans came to Canada, so you re-teach that again and that gets boring, we don't want to know what we already know." This fatigue in hearing the same stories does not mean that they have learned things well, but merely that they have heard the same stories again and again. Students "already know" the Anglo-European perspectives on Canadian history because these stories, ideas, and values create the dominant Canadian culture that surrounds them. With an uncomplicated, white-dominated focus in their Canadian history class, a focus often articulated as the "textbook" version of history, students who were not white and/or enacted their Canadianness differently than mainstream culture expressed a frustration that through this focus they become implicitly defined as embodying knowledge that is not valued, not national, and not part of the main Canadian story. With a focus on "white men" over the complexities of students who were not "white men" (which includes all students, even the white boys), students can become constructed as "Other" in need of a remedial understanding of Canada and the Canadian past. I discovered that when teachers found it hard, if not impossible, to visualize Canadian history that connected with the complexities of students' pasts, presents, and futures, then students found it hard, if not impossible, to show respect for a Canadian history class that failed to reflect the complexities of their pasts, presents, and futures as Canadians.

As I discuss in the next chapter, teachers struggle with the question "Whose history do you teach?" when they encounter students who do not fit their understanding of Canadianness in their classrooms. At one school I worked in, because a large percentage of the students were Black students with African/Caribbean backgrounds, teachers often answered that question by claiming that more Black history in the curriculum would connect students to Canadian history and result in greater engagement of these students in school. In interviews and in class, students too, would often call for Black history as a remedy for an uninspiring Canadian history class. However, it is bordering on cliché to just add more Black history to the curriculum and stir. This "drag and drop" method, while providing connections for some of the students, does not provide the meaningful *complexity* with counterstories that can substantiate students' desires for a Canadian history that reflects who they are in Canada – a narrative that many feel excludes them (Cutrara 2016b).

Earlier, I defined complexity as content that reflects the multiplicity of experiences present in the past and that students witness in the present. Students live a complicated and complex embodiment of Canadian identity that no single narrative will ever adequately address, thus, if students are looking for history that frames their complex worlds, then superficially adding Black history to the curriculum will not ultimately satisfy their desires to learn a Canadian history that acknowledges the cultural complexities around them. In one interview, a student recollected how her teacher "just gave us a sheet about Black men in the war, and that was it; she didn't discuss anything about it. It was just like that's the sheet and then that's it." Another student said that, while she had learned about the No. 2 Construction Battalion (an all-Black battalion that participated in World War I) in her history class, the teacher "said that it was hard for them to come in, but then after that, once they were in, that's all they said. They didn't go on about actual accomplishments." These students said that when Black Canadian history was part of their history class, there was not a "whole lesson on it, that we could sit down and talk about it and talk how we feel. It's just, 'Okay, today we're doing Black history but tomorrow we're going back to Holocaust.'" These students, who identified as Black Canadians, recognized that simply adding stories about Black people to the curriculum was not enough to make them feel more seen and more legitimate in the nation. As Carla Peck (2011, 317) found, students bring "complex identity-related frameworks to their study of history," not just a one-dimensional understanding of race and identity, and they want history education to reflect this too.

It is understandably easy for these students, and their teachers, to draw on the concept of "Black history" as a way of creating a more engaging Canadian history class. The popularity of Black History Month, the proliferation of excellent popular and academic texts on the contributions of Black peoples to Canadian history, and debates about Afrocentric schools in large urban centres all seem to suggest that adding Black history to the curriculum fills the quota for celebrating diversity. While these resources can, and do, provide counterstories that can force new ways of seeing and being in the world, most often the difficult and complicated parts of these histories are ignored, flattening Black identities, cultures, and histories into a familiar script that fails to have lasting meaning in students' lives. As Doharty (2019, 124) argues, Black History Month can play a "functionalist" role in schools in a way that mainstream, white history does not. Tokenistic Black history content can "counterbalance whiteness" rather than challenge the liberal democratic tradition that manages diversity from a white centre. This means that Black history can be rote for students, because it is not being taught as a way to deconstruct whiteness. In explaining why they do not teach more Black history at school, one teacher said that, while it was "sad" that they did not teach more of it, "it's like once you've already heard it once, have you heard it?"

However, it is not that we should not attempt to bring in Black histories, or bring in histories that connect with students' ethnicities or local communities, to our history classes. Quite the contrary; as the previous section demonstrated, students want history to connect with them and often this means connecting to their ethnic and/or cultural backgrounds. What I suggest, however, is that to make these histories meaningful, these histories cannot just be added to a standard curriculum because they connect to students. The *complexities* of these histories, the counter-ness of these stories, the way they *challenge* dominant history and shine a new light on the past, have to be included in the class as well. To learn history that represents the Canada that includes the students in the room – the new "we" of Canada – students need to learn the connection *and* the complexity of the Canadian past and explore the struggles, successes, heartbreaks, and hopes of many people who have called Canada home, often in the face of prejudice, discrimination, and forced (violent) assimilation.

To return to the example of the teacher who wanted to connect to her students' "grassroots," the teacher held up the photo of white soldiers going to war and asked students who was not able to fight. As I shared previously, two Black students in the class answered "Black people," with another student commenting that "we couldn't do anything." The teacher, a white woman who had strong connections to Canada and military history, and whom I discuss in greater depth in the next chapter, did not respond to either of these comments nor explain why she had asked that particular question. Instead, she asked the class what the backgrounds of the people in the photograph were. One of the students said, "white people," with her friend responding, "That one was easy!" There was no direct response from the teacher, who then took the students down to the front of the school to look at the photographs of alumni veterans. She asked them to look at the last names of the soldiers and guess what their backgrounds were. While students would have had to know and understand the ethnicities of surnames for them to correctly answer her question, all the teacher really wanted students to do was take note that the majority of the soldiers were white. She then pointed to one Black World War II soldier on the wall and emphasized how he was the *only* Black soldier among the dozens of white soldiers. Rather than acknowledging the details of his service, his accomplishments following his service, or details about his life in the community, the teacher highlighted how he was *"the only one"* there, making his presence the embodiment of absence.

While this was supposed to be a moment of connection for students, by highlighting the absences of people who shared ethnic or cultural similarities with them, this moment lacked the complexity to be meaningful. Students knew about the absences already. It "was easy" to say they were not there or were only there on the margins. Students wanted to know the stories that were less easy, the counterstories that told them who they were in this place.

Complexity, like connection, could have been explored in this same lesson. The teacher could have discussed how some of the soldiers were immigrants themselves, or that whiteness is construction and that not all the soldiers who look white would have experienced whiteness equally, or that masculinity was, and is, constructed with principles of militarism and therefore we do not know nor honour the men who were conscientious objectors during the war. The teacher could have done some research on the Black community in the 1940s and had students imagine the experience of that Black veteran before, during, or after the war. She could have held onto students' questions and comments about gang violence and interracial relationships as a way to frame a discussion about the war and the xenophobia and anti-Semitism around it. There were ways to focus on a complex story, or a complex reading of the standard story, but because complexity was not the focus in the class, the teacher tried but did not know how to respond to students' questions in a way she felt was valuable to her main objective. She was anxious to get back to the main lesson and nervously laughed about how frequently her students go "off the rails."

However, when students look around at their peers, their neighbourhoods, their workplaces, their churches, mosques, and temples, they do not see the Canadian history that teachers are telling them makes Canada. These questions are not "off the rails," these questions beg for connection *and* complexity in learning Canadian history, neither of which students are getting in their classrooms. While histories that narrate their ethnic and cultural backgrounds are part of students' desires, they want more: they want integrated, sustained explorations of the history that informs their identities as racialized people in a transnational and (post/neo)colonial world. Yes, students want Black history, but they want these histories to have meaning and depth. They want history to reflect the cultures and cultural practices that they are creating in their interactions and relations with their peers (Yon 2000, 44). They want answers and historical complexity to the Canadian identities they embody daily. They recognize that the history they are learning ratifies a Canadian identity that they cannot identify with and that sees their very presence as challenging. They want Canadian history that allows, nay, that *invites,* these complexities into the classroom for discussion and exploration.

This sense of complexity in teaching and learning Canadian history is not an easy task, but it is not as insurmountable as it might seem. The main requirement for a complex and connected learning environment is one that is facilitated by an educator who is comfortable opening up the Canadian history classroom so that a one-dimensional story of both the students and the Canadian past is left behind. The educator has to be able to prioritize instructional approaches that connect to students' prior knowledge by thinking, feeling, and acting with meaningful content and has to be okay with the messiness that arises when students explore complicated ways of being Canadian in our transnational and (post/neo)colonial world. A connected, complex, and meaningful Canadian history classroom seems like a difficult task, but creating history classrooms where students can learn meaningfully only requires one thing: a teacher who will invite a sense of "we" into the classroom through their comportment, affect, and pedagogy. As Shiho Main (2012, 82) writes, formal curriculum is only half of education, "the other half, which cannot be taught directly, is effected through the personality of the teacher."

Care

A key element for developing meaningful learning opportunities in the Canadian history classroom is the willingness and affective demeanour of a teacher in inviting connection and complexity. Students identified content and instruction that made history interesting, but they also talked about how important it was to learn history in a positive environment shaped by a teacher who listened to and cared for them as people. Students want the promise of education to be fulfilled and are understandably angry and frustrated when they do not encounter this in class. Students astutely identified that it is often the teacher who breaks the promise of an engaged and interesting learning environment because they do not "act like proper teachers," in the words of one student. Thus, the third element of student-focused learning that can lead to a new "we" is care.

According to students, "proper teachers" were teachers who communicated their enthusiasm for the subject, were knowledgeable about the content, and had a genuine interest in what students thought. One student said that learning was enhanced when "the teacher [was] acting like a teacher" and interacting with his or her students. Another student said that class was better when the teacher was "being active about it and excited about it and talking to you with their hands and looking at everyone in the class." Enthusiasm and content knowledge, however, are not always what students encounter in their history class. As one student said, "Some teachers, they don't know how to teach, they just give you work and work and expect you to know everything. They don't expand on it, they don't tell you and they don't explain properly."

Across all three schools I conducted research in in 2011, students readily shared examples of teachers who they felt did not care about them or their learning. One student, in thinking back to her Canadian history class, said she wished her "teacher [had] said to me, when I was falling asleep in history class: 'Pay attention!' I don't know, involved me more and made things more fun." In this statement, the student did not identify any particular content that she wanted to learn; rather, an acknowledgment that she was in class, had something to offer, and wanted to be engaged in learning. Another student said that the raison d'être of schooling was to provide students with the knowledge they needed to go forth in the world, saying: "This is all for us, we go to school to actually learn the material for ourselves. All this is for us really. Like, yes, we do marks and all that, but the primary reason we even take these courses is because we want to learn it." In the interviews, one student at an alternative school talked about teachers who "don't know how to teach" when he recalled:

> When teachers are giving you homework and be like, "Read this overnight and then do it," half the time I'd read it and not understand it, and I'd be so frustrated that I didn't understand it that I wouldn't be able to do the work. And then I'd get into trouble the next day and lose marks. And it's like, why do that? You're there to help, so do it in class.

While a frequent comment in teachers' staff rooms is that students do not complete their work because they are lazy or uninterested, this comment indicates the opposite: the student had an expectation that his teacher would guide him through his learning and knew he would be penalized for not finishing the work that he needed support for in order to complete successfully. By pushing back and bringing in incomplete work, the student was signalling to his teacher that he wanted *more* support, not less.

Students also had an expectation that teachers would know the history they were teaching and teach in ways that supported students' questions about the world. During one focus group, a student said that a history teacher needs to be "specific and exact and know what she's talking about." Another student related that, when her teacher was teaching about genocide one of her Black classmates pointed out that the slave trade was an example of genocide because "they took us out of Africa, then [they] killed off our heritage." The student identified that the teacher never followed up on this comment nor provided more information and context for the class. As the student recalled, her teacher "didn't really know that, so she couldn't teach us. If the teachers don't know then you can't learn."

When I asked students what they thought about teachers not wanting to cover certain material because of the controversy that might ensue, one of the students interrupted and emphasized: "But then those aren't proper teachers, because if they don't know how to teach a concept like that then you can't be a history teacher cuz you're not supposed to hide those things." This student's classmate was equally frustrated:

I don't think that's a logical statement because people can feel offended when you talk about the Holocaust. Jewish people will go, "Oh well, that's not exactly true from what my grandparents said," and they can get offended like that. There's German people who can get offended ... some Germans still deny that happened; Germans can get offended.

Aboriginals can get offended when you talk about their past because they think that [the] white man switched it up to put in their textbooks.

So just by saying that one group of people will get offended, that's wrong, because every group and any group can get offended once you talk about them. But teachers still talk about them, so it's not fair to us.

Research indicates that students want to learn the controversial content that teachers often avoid (Dion 2009; T. Epstein, Mayorga, and Nelson 2011; James 2008; Levstik 2000; van Hover and Yeager 2007), but in this interview, the students make a very logical argument for the ways this material is falsely constructed as controversial. Students are interested in learning about difficult histories even if teachers are not up for the challenge (Dion 2009; Lazare 2005; Levstik 2000). Rather than leaving students angry or despondent, a commitment to dealing with issues of power in history education has been shown to encourage them to learn more about the period outside of school and to have a positive effect on their identity and peer relationships (M.H. Schultz, Barr, and Selman 2001; Terzian and Yeager 2007).

When I asked students about teachers who may want to shy away from histories in the Canadian past that they do not know, students emphasized that teachers can open up the classroom for input rather than just ignoring the content. One student said, "The teachers should open up discussion so anybody that knows anything could help." This student's classmate laughed and said: "Yes, it's funny how sometimes kids actually know more than the teachers themselves." In my own experience with the class, I found that saying "I don't know" and following it up with the promised research prompted the same level of respect as actually knowing the information. In our last interview, one student said: "Remember with me, the [Dionne] Quintuplets? Like, I asked you and you brought it in. And then [one student], he asked something and you brought it in. So where people are asking and then they get the information out." Echoing this student's comment, other students wrote in their final surveys that people felt "more comfortable to ask questions now" because of the acknowledgment of these questions as having a place in class. It is not having a bottomless fountain of knowledge that students look up to, but the *promised follow-up* that validates students' desire to know and be part of their learning of the Canadian past. It is this action that demonstrates to students. the importance (and ease) of research to follow up on new information, but also maintains the teacher's place as the facilitator of community learning.

Students were also aware that teachers had the power to control the tone and tenor of the classroom and that they could elevate their status as teachers at the expense of students. When I asked students if they felt that they could express their opinions in class, a student who was barely passing most of her classes answered:

> *When you put up your hand and you have something to say, to defend what they taught [most teachers are] going to overpower it and bring it back down to what they thought, cuz they like to know they're the teacher, they're standing at the top of the room, and they've got the university degree, so they know their stuff ... They want to feel they're right so they probably would avoid [discussion] and they would just teach the content instead of ... debating.*

This was an "unsuccessful" student and teachers could (and did) ignore her opinions in class; but this student was acutely aware of the ways in which teachers secured their place in the classroom by limiting the boundaries of what was discussed and how. She was aware of how these moves were prohibitive of a healthy and supportive learning environment for her and her classmates. The student's status as "unsuccessful" contrasted with her articulate understanding of power in the classroom and provides evidence that students are using active resistance strategies to push back on the dominant power in the room and set the terms for their own learning (Almarza 2001; Giroux 2001).

Students articulated that teachers listening to them, *really* listening, empowered them to be active in their learning and to feel acknowledged in the classroom. I asked students to provide two pieces of advice for a new history teacher and one student said simply, "Ask the kids how they feel about what's being taught." Another student talked about how listening to students can make them feel acknowledged because: "If you make the students feel like they're important, then they might want to learn more or feel better about learning and be encouraged more." Another student said that she enjoyed being part of the research because "[my] voice is heard and I get a say in what's going on," but she ended this comment with an acknowledgment that having a forum in which to speak is only half of the issue; the other is being listened to and acting on what is heard. She said she liked being part of the research because "we get to change it up a little, if the school actually listens."

On my last day in the mainstream school in which I conducted research in two Canadian history classes, I bumped into one of the students who, when I first arrived, had been particularly vocal about hating Canadian history and demanding more Black history. During the first few weeks, she was rude, dismissive, and insolent regarding both the research and Canadian history. But, as the weeks moved on, and especially during the lessons on the West Indian Domestic Scheme and Africville, she began to be a leader among her peers, calling out answers, asking for clarification, and telling her classmates to be quiet. Throughout my time in the school, I hoped that I was able to convey an unconditional invitation to learn so that if the students made the choice to learn from me, they could do so without fear of reprimand or self-righteous gloating regarding their previous behaviour (Kohl 1994; Kohn 2005; Purkey and Novak 1984). We had covered histories in her class that we hoped would connect to her and students like her and had taught them in ways that demonstrated the complexity of the past and present so that students were able to think, feel, and act with historical content.

When I asked her on the last day what she thought about Canadian history after the work we had done in class, the student smiled, looked me in the eye, and said, "Good, I like everything now." This response was a turnaround from the reception she gave me during the first few weeks, and I was sad that we could not build off these positive feelings in a longer research period. I felt that I had gained her trust as an educator and that she was more open to taking the unconditional invitations for learning I tried to provide with the connected and complex histories we brought to class. While we did not have a chance to talk more, this interaction reminded me of an answer in one of the exit surveys where a student wrote that their opinion of history changed after the research intervention because "I have a more positive approach to learning about new units, cuz I realized it's not boring if you can see how it relates to you."

Despite the belief that students do not care about Canadian history, the students I worked with were clear that history education could and should connect them and provide historical depth to the complexities of their present. However, students also talked about how they would wilfully demonstrate resistance, rejection, and anger toward a class that failed to take seriously their desires to connect with a complex understanding of self and the past. This is why students articulate such an exacerbated split between "interesting" history and "boring, textbook" history; this split is how they have experienced Canadian history education. Thus, to lessen the gap students see between interesting and boring history, history education needs to be organized with a belief in connection, complexity, and care that serves students and their meaningful learning in class. Believing that history "relates to you" is an important factor in learning Canadian history, and caring enough to bring these complex connections out is the primary job of every educator.

4

Teaching the Others in the Room
Limiting Connection, Removing Complexity

With students' desires strong and clear, the possibilities of classroom practice are endless. Essentially, a history teacher has a class full of students interested in learning, thinking, and discussing the narratives that frame their lives, but we all know that this is not happening. Why not?

Despite all the innovations in teaching Canadian history, Canadian history education is disengaging for young people because it is often not designed to be about them. To teach for and with an ethos of connection, complexity, and care that could invite the opportunities for meaningful learning into the Canadian history classroom requires that teachers let go of what they think they know about their students, their ethnicities, and their histories, while also acknowledging and committing to these as valid elements of pedagogy and practice. Teaching in ways that are transformative to students' experiences learning Canadian history requires that teachers foreground students' connections and complexities as the centres, not the margins, of teaching and learning history, allowing those complexities – for example, a student saying: "I am a Canadian, but I am not a white man" – to be acknowledged and given weight in the classroom. As the last chapter demonstrated, students want to learn in the very classes teachers want to teach in: a place where content is interesting, instruction is differentiated, and respect is demonstrated by and for all. Thus, while students' transnational and (post/neo)colonial identities may seem outside the scope of a Canadian history course – as educator Schaun Wheeler (2007) found when he realized that he spent the majority of his time in his national history classes teaching about things *other* than national history – teaching so that students are able to meaningfully connect with the past will mean teachers will have to re-evaluate the methods, modes, and structural beliefs that underlie their approach to what national history may mean in the context of today's world.

In both my research and my practice I have found that a teacher's desire or need for familiarity, combined with their unchecked assumptions about their students, have resulted in many Canadian history classrooms being structured with an emphasis on *teaching* Canadian history rather than *learning* Canadian history. In these classes, the importance of students' learning is secondary to the teacher's teaching, where the retention of the "right" story becomes the mark of success rather than the mutual and meaningful exploration of the many stories that frame our lives in Canada. To be clear, this is both an individual issue and an institutional one. Schooling is not set up to privilege learning over teaching. So while individual teachers enact elements of meaningful learning in their classrooms, the institutional context in which they work does not support a holistic approach to teaching and learning that places students, and their learning, at the centre of an exploratory classroom space either. (This will be discussed at length in the next chapter.) However, to get to a place where one teaches Canadian history in ways that hold space for the connected and complex lives of Canada's transnational and (post/neo)colonial youth, teachers need to start from a place of care, a belief in connection, and a vision that together they form a beautiful and complex "we" who can address, explore, and develop Canadian history together.

To explore this theme more closely, I now feature a case study of one Canadian history teacher who, despite the best of intentions, undermined the possibilities of meaningful learning in her Canadian history class in subtle but consistent ways. While she had an interest in teaching to her students, her expectations of what they were capable of, combined with the comfort she took from teaching a traditional narrative, meant that student learning, especially students' meaningful learning, was not a priority. The priority instead was the acceptance of a historical narrative that reflected her own perception of good teaching. In this teacher's class, students were not invited to engage in history learning in connected and complex ways. They were meant to know what the teacher identified was important for them to know, so she rationalized away moments of connection and complexity as outside the purview of the course. The result was a self-fulfilling cycle of resistance and disengagement from the students and frustration and pedagogical limiting from the teacher.

By zeroing in on one teacher's practice, a successful award-winning teacher's practice, this case study is meant to demonstrate the patterns of practice that circumvent the possibilities of meaningful learning in the Canadian history classroom – how teachers, without meaning to at all, can deny their students the meaningful learning of Canadian history by limiting connection and removing complexity, the very things inspired by a diverse and inclusive vision of a Canadian "we."

Erin: A Teacher Primed for Meaningful Teaching

Erin was a white, mid-career history and language teacher who had worked at one mainstream urban, multicultural secondary school for the whole of her formal teaching career. She was recognized and rewarded for her "out there" approaches to teaching Canadian history, and she used innovative teaching and learning strategies to engage her students in the study of the past. For Erin, "history was object" and involved "solving mysteries" about the "fragments left behind." She had a background in Canadian history and the school administration supported her in providing mentorship in her department. She was critical of other teachers' lack of care toward students and said that, sometimes, "no one [would] give a damn" but her.

Erin was exactly the right teacher with whom to explore issues of engagement and inclusivity in a research project intended to create meaningful learning possibilities in a Canadian history class: she knew Canadian history, she wanted to engage her students, and she was open to innovative teaching and learning methods. Erin wanted to participate in this research to share what she knew and to discover more instructional strategies that she could use in class. She was excited that this project could address, or at least help her explore, issues of relevancy and engagement that she faced in her ethnically diverse class.

However, it was Erin's practice – the practice that was most rewarded in comparison to the other teachers I had worked with – that was most contradictory to her intent and philosophy of teaching Canadian history.

If on paper she was the ideal teacher to embark on this research with and we had content and instruction that appealed to the students' learning styles and backgrounds, then why were there so few opportunities for students to learn meaningfully from the Canadian past?

While Erin wanted to teach history in ways that invited her multicultural students to meaningfully engage with the Canadian past, what this work would involve – the connection, complexity, and care of students who had experiences and histories different from hers – ultimately unsettled her practice and what she knew, and wanted to know, about the Canadian nation. These challenging stories, and her students' possible interaction with them, decentred her authority as teacher of Canadian history. In centring students' learning, Erin would no longer take on the role of Expert Canadian History Teacher; instead, she would only be a facilitator of students' connected and complex narratives, narratives she could neither predict nor control. In this way, Erin would no longer be the *manager* of a larger Canada-first nation-building project, a project that included diverse stories but was not constituted by them (Mackey 2005). Instead she would be another person in the classroom, a person open to learning from and with them in a spirit of collaborative Canadian exploration, a person who would be an ethnic and cultural minority in the room – and this being unfamiliar to her made her uncomfortable. Thus, to offset this discomfort and gain back control of the classroom, Erin reverted to teaching a personal and linear narrative of Canadian history, leaving students and the opportunities for their meaningful learning behind.

For the remainder of this chapter I will highlight the ways in which Erin's underlying beliefs about her students and Canadian history created a history classroom that prioritized her comfort with teaching a mainstream historical narrative over creating opportunities for students' connections and complexities in learning about the Canadian past. In particular, I will focus on how viewing students as Other can create barriers to seeing their potential to actively and meaningfully connect with history. For Erin, this meant going back to a narrative that centred her and her experiences as the barometer for what connection in Canadian history would look like. I will also explore how seeing current ethno-cultural diversity as at odds with Canadian history is limiting for exploring the complexity of the Canadian past. For Erin, this meant teaching a mainstream chronology at the expense of histories that could challenge this chronology. With both of these beliefs in play, the result was a classroom environment that privileged Erin's "personal curriculum" (Gudmundsdottir 1990) over a curricular approach that could invite connection and complexity into students' study of the past.

Limiting Connections: Students as Other

Students want to learn history in ways that connect with who they are and what they know inside and outside of class, and these connections can be engendered by both content and instruction. However, a key element of connection is that if we want students to make meaningful connections with the past, then we have to believe in the multitude of ways in which students can, and want to, connect.

The relationship between teachers and students is a fundamentally important relationship that affects everything from in-class behaviour to school retention (Bosworth 1995; Cornelius-White 2007; Gholami 2011; B.D. Schultz 2011; Vogt 2002). bell hooks (2010) writes that while a teaching relationship is a hierarchy, that hierarchy does not necessarily have to result in damaging power relations. An appreciation of *mutuality* between teacher and student can produce a partnership with "affection and friendship at the same time [as] deserved respect for the role of the teacher" (114). In this way, teachers can be facilitators of learning and can guide students toward their own understanding of the content in ways that are respectful and open to what these understandings may be. When teachers think of themselves as *in-relation* with the students, or when teachers present themselves as being one with the students and able to learn *from* them and *with* them "in the ethos of mutual presence, trust, responsibility and appreciation" (Harjunen 2012, 148), then students become more than empty vessels in need of filling. Teachers have to take the lead in these relationships because "the teacher's way of being opens understandings for the student that are beyond what is officially prescribed" (Giles 2011, 63). Moving away from perceptions of teaching, learning, and interactions in class allows the classroom to be one in which students' connections are invited, and kept safe, as a key part of their learning.

The problem in Erin's Canadian history class was that Erin did not see her students as people with an interest in and desire to learn about the

Canadian past. While she had taught at this school for her whole professional career she admitted that she was thrown off by these students because she had not expected such overt rejection of Canadian history, nor the (perceived) behavioural, academic, and cultural challenges they brought to the classroom. Students in this class were chatty, not overly academically inclined, and demonstrated resentment, and thus resistance, toward education in general and history in particular. The students could often be flippant, dismissive, and rebellious, but when listening and watching them closely, they also seemed bored, needy, and astute.

As a rewarded and successful teacher in other circumstances, Erin was confused and frustrated that these students were not connecting to the Canadian history she was teaching. Predictably, she began to do what many people do when they feel rejected: she pushed students away even more, painting them as Other and unknowable from self. These controlling and counter-aggressive behaviours are commonly used by teachers who try to save face and maintain a hierarchical position in classrooms they see as uncontrollable. They have the opposite effect, however, and result in greater conflict with students rather than greater control of the classroom (Beck and Malley 1998). For Erin, these behaviours manifested in her articulation and enactment of the belief that her students had learning styles, were part of a certain generation, and had home lives that prevented them from being able, or willing, to learn. She talked about her students as different from her, so different that there was no common ground for teaching or learning Canadian history. The result was that Erin kept reverting back to a narrative of herself, a narrative she was comfortable with, a narrative that was disconnected from students, to set the parameters for what meaningful connection might look like in Canadian history.

Erin's previous teaching experience had been with International Baccalaureate (IB) students, pre-IB students, or students in upper-level French – students who were arguably more comfortable playing the role of "good student" in mainstream schooling. While Erin was proud that she was assigned this "difficult" class because of her success and enthusiasm with other classes, she struggled because her so-called "crazy class" had "mixed abilities and mixed interest and mixed liking of school" that were outside her previous teaching experiences. She struggled because she found that she was "the most motivated person in the room" and did not know what more she could do to engage her students. "It's school. It's not a circus," she once lamented.

As racialized minority students, most of the students in this class had been identified by the school board and principal as being "at-risk urban youth." Many of them had a long history of disregard, benevolent pandering, or falling through the cracks of an education system seemingly not designed to support them. Through the implicit and explicit messages they encountered throughout their school career, many of the students believed that academic success was not in the cards for them, especially in a class like history that was divorced from who they were and what they wanted to know. This meant that students entered their history class believing that it was not going to be a place where they would feel an unconditional and unsubtractive invitation to bring their full selves to class (Kohn 2005; Valenzuela 1999). Students were in their own world of texting and music, parties and clothes, and all that changed during the day was the room where these conversations took place. But in small ways, through their resistance, the students demonstrated that they were keen to learn, they wanted to connect, but were skeptical that they could consistently get teaching that was meaningful to them. And they were right.

To make sense of students' rejection of her instruction, Erin distanced herself from her students by viewing them as Others, unwilling and unable to learn. As an expert teacher, Erin was quick to use educational rhetoric to diagnose her students as non-thinkers. This perception framed the parameters for how the teacher/student relationship could manifest itself in class. As educational theorist Jerome Bruner (1997) emphasized, a teacher's conception of a learner shapes the instruction he or she employs, so if the teacher sees his or her students as unwilling or unable to learn, his or her instruction will be rote, with few opportunities for students to make deep connections in class. By not seeing her students for who they were, for what they were bringing to class, and for how these perspectives could enhance learning Canadian history, Erin limited the opportunities for them to connect with Canadian history in meaningful ways.

One way Erin counterbalanced her students' resistance to the content and instruction was to draw on something she knew – educational discourse – to define who (she thought) her students were. Of the four teachers I worked with, she was the most tightly bound to her status as teacher and frequently used these institutional(izing) discourse(s) to make sense of students and their potential to learn. While I worked with teachers who overtly rejected the "edu-speak"[1] of formal learning, Erin found comfort and familiarity in it, in that it could provide her with a mastery over the concepts it represented. In using this language, she was able to articulate students' rejection as pathology. Through the lenses of perceived learning styles and multiple intelligences, she could diagnose the problems in her class as originating with her students and their learning styles, and not with her practice. In relying on this discourse to understand her students, Erin negated the students as individuals and limited their possibilities for connections in learning Canadian history.

Throughout the research period, Erin would assess the feasibility of new content or instruction based on how it would speak to the "more chronological learner" or the "conceptual learner" or the "visual learner." She understood good teaching practice as that performed by one who could "appropriately select resources that reflect the various learning styles of students – visual, auditory, kinesthetic learners." She identified that creating a "safe space" in a history classroom meant a place that met "the various learning needs of students." Erin used edu-speak to predict her students' reactions and responses to proposed content and instruction and we had very few conversations where she did not draw upon these discourses to reaffirm the importance of students' learning styles as a consideration in creating lesson plans. However, even as she talked about her students using these labels, they were often separate from students' own understanding of themselves, even by her own admission. When explaining the possible failure of one activity to me, Erin commented that, "I know this sounds kind of weird, some of them don't know what they are good at. Some of them do, some of them don't."

While edu-speak does have a role in institutionalized schooling and differentiating for learning styles and multiple intelligences is an important consideration in planning, the fetishization of these discourses can shape the ways we think about, and enact, educational practice, especially for racial minority students (Bartolomé 1994; A.V. Kelly 2003). These discourses can result in a distancing between learner and teacher where the learner can only be what the teacher diagnoses and the connections students make come only from the opportunities explicitly provided. How educators engage in these practices becomes a hidden curriculum that shapes what and how students have the opportunity to learn (Cherryholmes 1987; McCutcheon 1982; Portelli 1993).

When edu-speak is used as the foremost way of understanding students and their behaviour in the classroom, it maintains mastery over students' needs in ways that can ignore verbal and non-verbal cues students use to communicate their experiences in class. Students in the room cease to be individuals and instead become a set of pathologies that only the teacher can remedy. A teacher can be so intent on aligning with, or making concessions for, these learning styles that little space is left for the students to think about, discuss, explore, or question the content in ways that differ from the predicted response envisioned by these methods. In Erin's class, her reliance on edu-speak meant that she never felt like she had to understand students' behaviour as a call for something more or different than what she was offering. Through her use of edu-speak, students became pathologized learners needing her diagnosis, not individuals wanting more, and different, connections with the content.

However, it became clear that although Erin used this language constantly, it was frustratingly superficial. Words and concepts would be used without any weight or meaning attached to them and would not result in any change or improvement to educational practice. For example, Erin would often describe her class as "verbal." She would repeatedly emphasize that her students were "*very* verbal" to explain how talkative they were in class. While Erin would talk about this as a negative, I heard "verbal" as an opportunity to bring in more instructional activities that relied on students talking through content, such as presentation, role play, and/or debate. Also, as discussed in the previous chapter, in interviews and surveys with me, students indicated that they wanted to learn through "verbal" instructional methods such as discussion and role play because these allowed them to be active thinkers in a community of their peers.

I suggested to Erin that our cumulative lesson on Africville would be a great opportunity to invite students' "verbal-ness" into the classroom. In this activity, we would give students a portfolio of primary sources and ask them to write a statement as to why an individual would advocate for or against Africville being destroyed. Students would then present these statements to the class and, if time allowed, respond to each other's statements in a mock Town Hall. This activity was designed for students to affectively connect with the material, learn both individually and collaboratively, examine primary sources and define a position, and verbally communicate their findings to the class. It was an activity that aligned with what I observed about the students as well as how Erin characterized them as learners.

I found that students' presentations were good, if a little awkward, but I was disappointed there was not a greater community for listening and responding to each other's presentations. As "verbal" students, I expected to see confident presentation skills, especially because this was the second half of term and students presumably had months of practice. I also expected to see students eager to respond and debate with each other as a way of expressing their frustration about the injustice and racism found in Canadian history that they discussed, unrelated to the lessons, in class all the time. While I was happy but not thrilled with the students' work, Erin was floored – speechless even. Erin could not believe what students were able to accomplish in this class and said multiple times that some of the students did their "best work" in that class.

Because there was clearly a disconnect between my experience and Erin's, I asked her how students had done on their previous presentations. I had assumed that these students had previously done presentations because of Erin's repeated insistence on the students' "verbality," her desire to adhere to differentiated learning strategies, and her assertion that students did not like presenting. Instead, Erin said they had never done presentations in the class. In this, *I* was floored: How could they have gotten to May and never done a presentation although the teacher repeatedly said that despite being *very* verbal these students did not like presenting? It then made sense as to why students lacked more polished skills for presenting and listening: there had not been any progressive skill-building throughout the year for students to understand how a presentation would work in a class community.

Thus, although Erin had labelled her students as "*very* verbal," she never used that talkativeness as an entry point for students to connect with Canadian history. Because students talked through class, Erin drew on institutional discourses to diagnose them as "verbal," without actually listening to what students' verbality was saying. In her class, students asked for, even demanded, content and instruction that prioritized more Black history – history that connected to many students' ethno-cultural identities. Sometimes students would ask for this content outright but more often they would communicate their dissatisfaction with the course content by talking over the teacher, yelling out remarks about exclusion and racism, and discussing their social and cultural lives outside of class. Rather than consistently and consciously responding to students' demands for connection, Erin characterized students' talk pejoratively, saying that they were "misfiring all over the room."

Talking out of turn is a problem behaviour that is predictable, preventable, and can be remedied through modifying one's instruction, such as providing greater opportunities for students to respond in class (Landrum, Scott, and Lingo 2011). Instead of listening to her students, Erin diagnosed her chatty class as having a pathology she had to work with and around in order to teach. By labelling them as "verbal," Erin framed students' unfamiliar behaviour within a familiar discourse to take (back) discursive control over a class she could not behaviourally control. In doing so, she limited students' interactions with the content and ensured that their (perceived) out-of-controlness did not interrupt her teaching. This is not a unique instructional tactic. Many teachers stay away from verbal, opinion-based instruction as a way to maintain control of the way the content is received and their performance as a "good teacher" is perceived (Childs and McNicholl 2007; Dion 2009; McNeil 1988; Saye and Brush 2004). Because it is the language of educators, not students, Erin's constant use of edu-speak worked to separate her from her students and to augment her place in the classroom over their rejection of it. Rather than adopt a value-based praxis that would begin with recognizing the strengths and questions students were bringing to class, Erin's use of edu-speak provided an institutionalized evidence-based discourse to frame the possibilities for how and in what ways students could engage (Biesta 2010). In this way, through her reliance on these discourses, Erin did not need to get to know her students well enough to understand how they wanted to learn. She had already determined how they were going to be taught.

Along with learning styles, Erin often invoked students' age or generation as a reason that students were not connecting with Canadian history. In explaining why an activity did not work, she rationalized: "I think ultimately it is that they're fifteen. Right?" While generational labels are not the same as edu-speak, when Erin spoke of her students as different and unknowable because of age or generation, it often achieved the same effect as when she emphasized their learning styles: it created a distancing between herself and her students that, because of students' resistance to the content, pitted an effective teacher against a hopeless group of students. It was their generational differences that made her teaching ineffective, not her approach to these students.

Erin would often go back and forth between learning styles and age to talk about the burden she bore as a Canadian history teacher in the twenty-first century. Commenting that maybe because of their generation, if she taught the course "through social networking and had the kids tweet the entire time, we might have more success." She stated:

> *This is a generation of students that doesn't like to read. Or at least the type of learners that I teach are not students who like to read long things of text. And because they are so used to this kind of computerized high-tech text messaging – high graphic, low text – there's way too many words on the page for the kids to look at.*

Students' use of communication technologies is certainly different than it has been in generations previous, but these new technologies do not make teens unknowable, nor does it make them unable to connect with history. Like many generations of teens before them, today's teens are interested in their friends, pop culture, self-expression, and a future away from school. Just because today's youth use different tools to express these things does not mean that they are different students. They still have a desire to learn and connect with ideas and issues, although perhaps not always academically. Students have to balance the often-dichotomous worlds of youth culture and school culture in their daily lives, but their participation in youth culture does not necessarily mean they are unable or unwilling to participate in school culture (Warikoo 2011). Demonizing students' connections through communication technologies and the use of social media in the classroom reinforces the idea that they are only tools for social interaction, not for academic learning and community building (Emdin 2016). Integrating them, even supporting students' use of them through explicit digital literacy development, can encourage student-centric learning in the connected and complex twenty-first century and even invite greater civic participation in the world around them (Drexler 2010; Kim and Yang 2016; Rheingold 2008).

However, in discussing both generation and learning type, Erin places the emphasis on things neither she nor her students could control to lament and excuse students' disengagement when reading-heavy tasks are in front of them. This idea supports a methodological and mechanical idea that teachers need to find the "right" instruction for serving underachieving students (Bartolomé 1994, 173–74). This view of students meant that we never had to acknowledge the power imbalances in inner-city schools where strong literacy skills may not have been prioritized in younger years, or that many of us in our technologically-connected world prefer image- and video-rich apps over a page of heavy text, or that maybe students were not given things to read that they were interested in (Almarza 2001).

At the end of the post–World War II unit, for example, I designed a lesson where we gave students multiple primary sources from activist groups in the 1960s and '70s. As the lead educator for this lesson, I asked students to go through the documents and summarize their findings by writing a profile of a group to present to class. Although many students were curious about the activist groups I featured – groups involved with the Black Power movement, the Civil Rights movement, feminist liberation, among others – students quickly went off-task and onto their phones. Some students though, students who had been resistant to Canadian history when I arrived in their class, did try to complete the task by leaving the room to read in the hall or by wearing headphones to tune out their off-task classmates, but the lesson generally devolved into social hour with music, texting, and internet surfing, leaving my meticulously researched primary documents behind.

This class was "puzzling" for me (Ballenger 2009) because while it incorporated many elements of content and instruction that I thought students could connect to, students were active in their rejection of the task. In a later group interview, I asked some of the students what happened during that class. Students (respectfully and tactfully) told me that the reading-heavy, primary source investigation I gave them was boring and overwhelming. Students told me that I had provided too many documents and that they did not know where to start or how they could finish. Even though we were covering topics they found interesting and had a connection to, students said the text-heavy task "wasn't as fun because we're reading it." While students wanted to learn the content, I had unintentionally set them up to be disengaged from the activity because I relied solely on reading, and reading a lot, as the way for them to connect with the histories and actions of these activist groups. One student suggested that if they had been given one document to read and the opportunity to engage with that document through role play, they would have found the class more interesting, because they would have been able to affectively connect with the content and actively process the ideas with their peers. It was not that the material was "boring," she said, but "the reading and the overwhelmingness just made it kind of sink the interest."

Their articulation of the tension between their interest in the content but disengagement with the instruction demonstrates the strength of teachers' perceptions in deciphering and directing students' behaviour in class. Erin deciphered students' popular and cultural use of these technologies as prohibitive for being good, engaged students. She then labelled them as being uninterested and unable to read or engage with text and (reticently) expected to provide them with less academic forms of instruction (i.e., her articulation that if we "had the kids tweet the entire time, we might have more success"). By speaking to the students, I came to see that my intentions in developing a lesson could be easily eroded by tasks that were not interesting or connected to their lives, and thus how easily they relied on entertaining distractions to reject content and/or instruction. In the future, I could direct their attention toward a more affective connection to the material, perhaps through role play, as a way to ensure the material could connect with their interests. What is important to note, however, is that students want to make these connections; their phones and other technologies were just distractions from teaching and learning experience that prevented these connections from being possible.

Further, just because students were on their phones using social media does not mean they were not actively and productively connecting to and creating meaning in their world. As Emdin (2016) found in his research with urban youth, whom he refers to as "neoindigenous," communication technologies such as Twitter and Facebook can serve an important function for youth in building community, venting frustrations, and talking back to dominant culture. He writes, "just as hip-hop culture pushed the norms of music production technology and shaped the ways that microphones, speakers, and turntables were designed and used, the neoindigenous have done the same thing with social media" (194). By using invention, delivery, ritual, and audience participation, the same elements of Black culture found in hip-hop, social media like Twitter allow for "rapid discussion between groups of connected users" that serves as an important cultural communication medium for Black people (A. Brock 2012, 545). These real-time, transnational connections across the diaspora can encourage young people to become active civic participants and participate in larger conversations about issues that directly connect to their lives, such as the #BlackLivesMatter movement (Carney 2016). While educators can bring these out-of-class connections into class, for this engagement to have a positive impact on students' formal learning, it must be recognized and developed as an important element of students' productive and critical literacy of the world around them (Rheingold 2008).

However, Erin saw students' use of digital communication technologies as prohibitive of positive communication or connection. She theorized that maybe it's "the 21st-century teacher's challenge" to teach students how to use today's communication technologies because "do the kids know the technology? Yeah, they know some of it. Do they know how to use it? No." She characterized students' use of the technologies as being similar to "being in a cage with your mouth duct taped," where students are "constantly communicating" but "misfiring and cyber-bullying" because of how unaware they are of how to communicate properly.

By linking her expectations of how students *should* communicate to their use and enjoyment of current technologies, Erin saw students as unable to connect to history *because* of these technologies. She explained that "this is not the generation that sits around the dinner table and talks politics anymore. It is not. That was my generation, right? And my parents'. And so on, and so forth." In this statement, Erin references three very different generations as being the norm that this generation of students challenged: her own, her parents', and the generations before them. Erin links these very different generations to invoke a notion of stability that these students and their use of communicative technologies are now upsetting. Erin seems to miss that referencing her family only works to idealize a mythical past that she feels her students do not share, rather than to accurately describe normal generational and technological change.

Talking about generational differences was not the only way that Erin pathologized students. She also referred to students' home lives as key to why they were resistant to learning history. Because the students were not showing an interest in national history, Erin rationalized that it was because their home lives were not places that bred an interest in or appreciation for learning about the past in the way she felt her own upbringing did. In the working-class, urban multicultural neighbourhood in which the school was located, Erin saw her students coming from poor, immigrant households where they had little opportunity or interest in connecting with history. Erin contrasted the education level of the parents in this class with the parents of students she had in the IB program, saying that the parents of the students in this class were blue-collar workers who "faced the brunt of economic disparity" and who were not planning for post-secondary education for their children.

Erin saw it as her role to remedy the apathy bred in these households, where parents, because of socio-economic factors that were out of their control, were not taking an active interest in their child's education, especially related to history. She said that part of her role as a history teacher was to "be a bridge" where she could connect the past

> to an understanding of [students'] own identity, because many of my students who are immigrants do not have these conversations around the dinner table like I did when I was growing up. The students are definitely from a different generation where, because of the trials and past of their parents, they may or may not have any dialogue whatsoever about any of that.

Erin's deficit-based perception of her students' home lives and parents was not only wrong and stereotypical, but misguided and ill-conceived. Erin may be indicating care for her students here, but her performance of care replicates a patronizing deficit discourse, where a teacher, especially a white teacher, feels sorry for and mothers her students of colour (S.E. Epstein and Schieble 2019; James 2012; Valenzuela 1999). She speaks about her role in the classroom as the "helpful hero" (Hyland 2005) or the "white knight" (McIntyre 1997) – mythical tropes white teachers have been found to use when talking about how to effectively teach Black students. While the perception that racialized or low-income parents do not care about their children's education is pervasive, this belief does not acknowledge the many ways parents demonstrate the value of education (and history) to their children. Similar to the white teachers McIntyre (1997, 668) worked with in her research, Erin's talk was "embedded in a caring and sharing storyline, [that] propels [teachers] further into the maintenance of myths" of deficient home lives of racialized students.

When Erin saw her students, she saw them as Other to her understanding of a "typical" Canadian household and surmised that it was their home lives that prohibited connection with history. She explained that her students "aren't the kids that go home and say, 'Hey Mom and Dad, we had this conversation about so-and-so in class.' They don't do that." However, students said in their interviews with me that they *wanted* to learn content that they could go home and talk about with their parents and that this was missing in their Canadian history education.

In one focus group interview, one of Erin's students, a student who was the least academically successful of all the students I interviewed, said that she wanted to learn things in her history class that she and her classmates could connect to their families, because if they did, they would

> *probably go home:* "Mom, this is what I'm learning in school." "Dad, this is what I'm learning in school." *And they'll get opinions and probably have discussions with grandparents and stuff that probably were around in those times and they'll have time to come back and debate in class.*

This student's eager and involved description of how she could, and would, connect her learning to her family, and then bring the connections back to school, indicates how important these connections are to students who seemed to be disengaged and unwilling to learn Canadian history. As Beck and Malley (1998) highlight, "most children fail in school not because they lack the necessary cognitive skills, but because they feel detached, alienated, and isolated from others and from the educational process" (n.p.). While Erin is trying to excuse and forgive the differences she saw between her students and her own upbringing, she missed the opportunity to see her students' desires for connection in Canadian history as the same and equally important as her own.

Whether it had to do with learning styles, generation, or home lives, fundamentally Erin did not see her class as a class full of engaged thinkers who wanted to learn Canadian history. This got in the way of her being able to get to know them and what they needed in order to learn history in meaningful ways. On multiple occasions Erin talked about students as not wanting or not willing to think and be engaged in class. Partially she blamed this on the culture of other teachers, but mostly she talked about students not wanting to think because of students' own mindsets around this, saying at one point:

> *I just want them to be able to think critically about what is going on around them, to understand their roots, where they come from, to understand that history is complicated. And I think that is why most of the kids are resistant to thinking, right? Because it isn't cool to think or to be critical, because it makes you a nerd, right?*

While all adolescents are hesitant to commit too enthusiastically to anything that makes them stand out from their friends, I found that the students in Erin's class desperately wanted to think and be critical about history and the world around them. In fact, many of their outbursts in class were critical challenges to the one-dimensional history they were presented with. If and when her students had the opportunity to ask questions, share what they knew, and be respected about their possible contributions to class, students demonstrated they were able and willing to both connect to history and commit to learning in critical and worldly ways.

If "*who we are* is central to relational connectedness in education" then "*how* a teacher comes to the teacher-student relationship is important" (Giles 2011, 61). Erin came to the teacher-student relationship seeing these students as Others unwilling or unable to connect with Canadian history, and so she limited the connections they could make in her Canadian history class. Her classroom was set up to make her comfortable in an uncomfortable situation where students were active in their resistance to Canadian history. Thinking of students in deficit, hindered by their learning styles, age, and home lives meant Erin was unable to conceptualize learning opportunities where students could, or would want to, connect with the Canadian past, and as a result, she impeded opportunities for doing so. Because Erin thought she knew everything she needed to about her students, she set up her teaching to remedy the deficits she diagnosed, further isolating her students from the content, from her instruction, and from herself.

Privileging Self: Telling My Own Story
Because Erin did not know her students well enough to see who they were in class, her expectation of how, or why, to connect them to Canadian history was flawed from the start. Erin thought of herself as a "bridge" between the past and students' presents and so she wanted students to make personal connections with the past to develop "a sense of understanding and a sort of spirit of empathy about the life experiences of people that came before them." She said that students thought history was boring because "[one,] they don't understand it and two, because they find that they have no relationship." Erin believed that history was about "understanding people, and relationships and interrelationships and how particular events have either brought people together or broke people apart" and felt frustrated that students did not see this "big picture" of learning history. While connection is essential to students' meaningful learning, connection is problematic when teachers and students do not understand each other enough to understand the connections they share. When there is a separation between teacher and student, when there is no sense of a "we" that they share together, the appeal to connection limits the relationship students can make with the Canadian nation. In Erin's class, because she distanced herself from who her students were and what they were bringing to class, she was unable to see how their personal stories could fit in the past, and thus made her own personal experiences the barometer for the connections students could make with Canadian history. The effect was a reaffirmation of mainstream Canadian history as well as a self-fulfilling prophecy of students' Otherness.

As a white woman whose family had been in Canada for generations, Erin often talked about how major events in the twentieth-century aligned with her family's history and at one point explained, "I always tried to find ways of reflecting the kids. And I think part of it is that I was always really comfortable telling my own family story if I didn't have any other way of connecting in." In choosing her own family story as the way to "connect in" and make history personal, Erin tied history so closely to herself that any experiences outside of her own were immediately delegitimized as irrelevant to Canada. She understood these connections as ideal for a Canadian history teacher, because

> *history teachers who were not born in Canada have a different perspective on – or if their parents were immigrants – then their perception of history affects how they teach it, right? Or if you're a first-generation Canadian because your parents immigrated from Vietnam or Poland or whatever displacement that might have been, I think that sort of frames part of it.*

Because Erin "was born here, and [her] parents and grandparents and grandparents and grandparents, so three or four generations," she did not see that her "perception of history" fragmented the nation the way others' may have. Her "frame" of Canadian history was soundly "Canadian."

Her personal connection as a basis for understanding Canadian history was so strong that Erin rationalized that she taught "World War I and II because my family's history is connected to it." This rationale meant that she was not "reflecting the kids" in her attempt at connection in history; she was reflecting herself and the history that she was comfortable with. Because she felt in alignment with mainstream Canadian history, her focus on this history as *personal* history narrowed the frame of connection for the students even more, setting up an implicit dynamic that if students rejected history, Erin felt they were rejecting her.

Erin's attempt at connecting with her students through an emphasis on herself was especially obvious when she discussed an activity she did to introduce history to students. She said that on the first day of class she brought in an "archive box" of objects that represented moments in her life. She explained that she then told students to imagine that "one hundred years from now, the archives has come to them with a whole box of stuff and they have to look at the evidence and identify what information it provides." She said that the purpose of this activity was to show students the connections that they could have with the past and also to demonstrate the ways in which artifacts and records provide historical evidence. Erin was proud of this activity and said that "instead of me introducing myself to them, they introduce me as a historical figure" or that "things that I've done as an individual are historically significant."

This activity is a great way for encouraging students to think about connection and evidence in history, but it can also set up a taxonomy that privileges certain sets of experiences as important and historical, and others less so. Erin said that after showing her students the artifacts of her experience, the next step was to encourage them to bring in objects to fill their own archive box. While she was very excited for the ways this activity was conceptualized, Erin's enthusiasm waned when I asked her what her students brought in. After thinking for a second, Erin answered:[2]

> Umm ... Medals. Like medals that they won, from track-and-field type medals. Photographs ... umm ... I'm trying to remember ... Things that were kind of cool ... I mean, some of the kids just said, "I don't know what to bring in. I don't know." But most of them were photographs ... Some of them I think brought in a book that they liked when they were growing up as kids ... or some certificate or whatever.
>
> And I had crazy stuff in mine like my passport, plane tickets, journal entries, things like that. But they were empowered by that.
>
> And then the next question following that was [laugh], "So, this year are we going to be studying Black History in February?" So the conversation of, "Now that we recognize that, as students, you care about us and you care about what we're doing here, now when are you going to talk about us?"

While she searches to remember things that students brought in, the ones she does remember do not seem to hold the same weight and excitement as her own items, describing the objects that students brought in as "things that were kind of cool," "some certificate or whatever," and "most of them were photographs." Her enthusiasm picks up again when she returns to talking about the "crazy" things in her archive box, things that "empowered" students.

By Erin's own admission, this introductory activity positioned her as a central and important figure whose experiences became the marker of what and who could be considered "historically significant."³ The activity had nothing to do with her students making personal connections to history, understanding their own experiences as historically significant, or introducing themselves to her. As Erin defined it, the activity framed her as the benchmark for personal connections in Canadian history, with her personal artifacts acting as badges of honour for the ways she was historically significant.

Following this statement, Erin paused and referenced a student asking if they were going to learn Black history in February – a moment she talked about often. It is ironic that she could not remember what students brought in and was more excited by the objects she brought in, yet she understood the student's question as an acknowledgement that students saw that she cared for them and found their personal connections important; but, really, this question emphasized the opposite: "When are you going to talk about us?"

Because Erin taught Canadian history as a story so overtly and closely tied to herself, she interpreted any challenge to mainstream Canadian history as a challenge to her own sense of self and history. She took any resistance as a personal rejection, articulating a "self-righteous despair" (Beauboeuf-Lafontant 2002, 83) that categorized students as non-thinking Others who would not, or could not, connect with history. The extent of Erin's connection between a rejection of self and a rejection of the course came out when she talked about regrets she had about the course. She said that the role of the teacher is to learn something about her students every day. When I asked about what she learned from her students, Erin focused on the rejection she felt from them, and answered:

> *I think I have learned from students that you have to be persistent.*
> *And that when they don't do the assignment [it] doesn't mean they don't like me. It may mean that they just don't like the assignment.*
> *And I think I have learned that it's hard, and this is kind of a weird one, but I guess, I think the students need to know your context. Like, I don't think a student would ever criticize my context at all really. But I can understand that they would think, "What is her authority in understanding the history of this place if she isn't like me?"*

In this statement, Erin begins to articulate how her own selfhood became bound to students' rejection or acceptance of the experience she provided in her history class. In this more thoughtful moment of the interview, Erin begins to identify that students may be resisting aspects of their education that are unrelated to her: they may be expecting a low commitment from teachers to encourage them, they may not like the assignment, they may prefer to learn history from someone who shares their background. These are important observations for coming to know what students are bringing into the classroom. Separating rejection of instruction from rejection of self is an important aspect of creating learning opportunities that invite more of the students' whole selves into the classroom.

However, when it came to rejection of content, Erin took it personally. She identified that the cultural differences between her and her students might be part of the reason why they were not embracing Canadian history, but she angrily explained that this position was not a valid one to take, because:

If they actually talked to me, they would know that I lived in Anguilla. And then they know I've lived in Aruba for a little bit, and they know that I've travelled in the Caribbean. And like, I don't understand all of their culture, but I understand some of it. It's like me sitting in a Native Studies class and saying, "Well, you can't possibly understand, you're not Aboriginal." Well, that's garbage. Because I've tried.

By setting up a learning environment that provided her own history as the baseline for connecting to Canadian history, she was only able to respond with the need to validate herself and the ways she had "tried" to understand others. In this statement, Erin referenced an experience she previously shared when, during her undergraduate degree, she felt personally insulted when an Indigenous student in her Native Studies course congratulated a guest speaker for overtly and explicitly calling out white supremacist colonialism. In that story, like the one above, Erin wanted to be congratulated for making an effort to learn about cultures and history that were not her own, and thus prioritized her self-congratulatory stance over and above someone else's lived experiences. By blending certain histories and experiences into her own understanding of Canadian history, Erin felt that she "tried" enough to understand different perspectives so no one should take issue with her sharing and teaching these histories. But you do not get a "good white people's medal" just because you "showed your whiteness" (C. Hayes and Juárez 2009, 740). Erin's self-righteous attitude shut down the space for exploring others' perspectives, which limited how and what she could hear from those she saw as Other.

As a note, I never saw students demonstrate any disrespect to Erin or her history, but I did see students enact a disregard for a class that failed to provide meaningful connections for them. The students asked for Black History *every day* and they communicated their dissatisfaction that they were not learning more of these histories by disrespecting many of the lessons. But students still came to class. They still asked for what they wanted. When given opportunities to venture beyond the grand narrative, they demonstrated enthusiasm and desire for more. By paying attention to what they were paying attention to, I began to see the students' keen desire to learn Canadian history in ways that held meaning for them, but this did not mean celebrating a conventional understanding of the Canadian past – even when it reflected your teacher's family story, even when you liked that teacher.

Because of how the students rejected mainstream Canadian history, Erin pushed them away even more, articulating her hurt in their rejection by thinking that maybe they did not want or were unable to learn, saying: "We're teaching them how to learn, maybe they are not ready to learn yet because maybe we're pushing them along too fast." While Erin saw that students had to understand her context, she never saw the importance of understanding her students' contexts as different than she believed them to be. Her approach to her students and the content aligned with her "personal standards of good teaching practices" (Goldstein and Lake 2000, 869), and because she had been recognized and rewarded for being a good teacher in other contexts, she never felt like she had to question how her beliefs in her practice undermined the actual operation of her practice.

For connected learning in Canadian history to happen, the classroom environment must be directed by a teacher who wants to engender a community of learners where collaboration, dialogue, conversation, and the sharing and telling of stories are able to thrive. Teachers need not only pedagogical content knowledge but also knowledge about their students in order to teach effectively (McCaughtry 2005). In an attempt to foreground students' connections with the Canadian past and the complexities these might have highlighted, I recommended we start the post–World War II unit by giving students an oral history assignment where they would ask a family member what they remembered about the early Cold War period. Erin liked the idea of this activity, but when she handed the assignment out, she announced that it would not be graded and, as a result, it was left to the wayside both by students and herself. For the students who completed the assignment, the experiences they uncovered, or were *not* able to uncover,[4] were astonishing. However, Erin did not know what to do with these connections and never added them to her planning. In our first interview, before we even gave out the assignment, Erin said that students would be unable to complete it because they "are fifteen [and] don't know how to ask the questions."

Some students did know how to ask the questions, however, especially because we provided them with a worksheet of prompts, and about a week after students had submitted their assignments, Erin mentioned how upsetting some of the assignments were. Visibly shaken, she said that one assignment was very "disturbing" and she did not know what to do about it. She told me that in that assignment, the student shared that his grandmother shaved her head and wore men's clothes to avoid being raped during World War II. Erin was shocked and shaken by this disclosure and did not know how or if she should address it with the student. I had never seen Erin so personally and professionally unsettled and she insinuated through her tone that it bothered her that the student brought something to class that she was unable to handle. I, too, was shocked by this story, and suggested that she should indeed say something to the student. She should tell him that the story unsettled her but that she was appreciative that he brought it to class. She should also ask the student how he felt about his grandmother's disclosure and if he wanted to do more research on it outside of class. Erin nodded at these suggestions and went back to preparing for class. I found out later that she never spoke to the student about the assignment, thus failing to provide the *critical care* that racialized students need as learners within marginalized cultural communities (Antrop-González and De Jesús 2006; Garza 2009; Rolón-Dow 2005).

While this was a moment of connection, because it was a connection that featured "difficult knowledge," it confronted Erin with "feelings of helplessness and loss, and the impossibility of undoing what has already happened" (Farley 2009, 542). Erin did not have room for this knowledge, so she pulled back and denied its presence. However, confronting this difficult knowledge, like all difficult knowledge, "may lift the veil on some of the illusions that drive teaching: illusions of self-mastery, or perfect authority, or enlightenment." It can invite the "conflicted and embodied relations that education cannot school away" and privilege those connections that highlight students' complexity (Farley 2009, 550). Erin was not prepared for this, however; she was not prepared for her "illusions of teaching" to be lifted and her knowing be challenged. As James Loewen (1996, 287) writes, a teacher saying "I don't know" "violates a norm," and in losing control of the answer a teacher can be fearful of losing control of their authority. For Erin, this authority was all she had in class that was outside her understanding of teaching and learning; losing this authority meant losing the only ground she felt she had.

By the end of the year, once the rawness and shock of the assignment had worn off, Erin celebrated the opportunity this student had to share this history. As will be discussed in the next section, she did not see her multicultural students as sharing a common narrative, but in her final interview, Erin emphasized they could, if they were "connecting their own personal stories to it," and used this as an example of how students made connections. She said when "that kind of story emerges," it is "amazing what you find out." Amazing, yes, but apparently not important enough to acknowledge to the student. Even as Erin said that the story was "amazing," she also stressed that: "Did it fit into what we were doing? No, not necessarily, but it has to do with reframing one's course to make room for all those voices, right?" In our interviews, Erin often took the role of expert to explain what did or did not make for good history teaching. In this statement, she did the same: she moved from the shock of the story, to gushing over the amazement of it, to acknowledging that these voices needed to be added into the class, but saying that, logistically, there was no room for them.

Erin was completely right. Students do need to share personal stories to make connections with the past, and history teachers do have to make room for these voices to be present, but Erin had to practice this philosophy for it to result in a new and more inclusive way to teach and learn Canadian history. Erin had to be comfortable being uncomfortable with histories she did not know. She had to be comfortable confronting the painful connections students might make when sharing family stories. She had to be comfortable with her students and the fact that they had lives as Canadians that were different, more layered and complex, than she perceived them to be. As educators, we have to be comfortable being uncomfortable with the stories we do not know, so that there is a classroom environment where we can say: "Let's look that up together!" Perhaps there was no space to talk about this student's experience in class, but there was plenty of opportunity to acknowledge this history outside of class and demonstrate the respect for sharing this type of story outside the family. Erin, though, was so unsettled by the student's disclosure that she was unable to attend to this story in ways that were meaningful and respectful, and made his connection the problem rather than the solution. Feeling accepted by one's teacher is important to students' experiences of school (Andersen, Evans, and Harvey 2012, 218) and has direct results to academic achievement and retention (Gehlbach, Brinkworth, and Harris 2011; Giles 2011).

When teaching becomes viewed as "an interactive relationship between student and teacher," where teachers "discover what the students know and what they need to know," and demonstrate a "willingness" to "engage students beyond a surface level," a humanizing, engaged pedagogy can emerge in the classroom (hooks 2010, 19). Regardless of how deep a student's desire is to learn, it is the teacher-driven relationships that have the potential to move both teacher and student, and their interactions in the class, away from a structure that places teaching over learning. Teachers have to take the lead in building these relationships because there are very few institutionally accepted ways that students can communicate their frustrations with the system and their roles within it (T. Brown and Galeas 2011; T. Brown and Rodriguez 2008; Dei 1997; Thompson and Bell 2005). Because of Erin's Othering, this element of respectful community based in love and engagement was missing from the class. As a result, students' full selves were not invited in to learn and they were therefore not able to meaningfully connect to Canadian history.

Removing Complexity: Whose Histories Do You Teach?

Knowing, learning about, and trusting your students well enough so you can invite their connections into the classroom is important for developing a sense of "we" in Canadian history education. With the realization of these beliefs in practice, students become seen as complex individuals able to learn meaningfully about narratives from the past and present. Earlier, I defined students' desire for complexity in the history classroom as a desire for content that reflected the multiplicity of experiences present in the past, taught with instruction that encouraged students to explore how history is more than just a one-dimensional story of national accomplishment and progress. The complexity imparted through content and instruction is what reflects the world students know – a world with complex, transnational, and (post/neo)colonial experiences of being Canadian. I also discussed how important complexity was for students grappling with the intricacies of being people of colour in a country like Canada that celebrates multiculturalism while also privileging a past that has denied, even attempted to assimilate, such diversity. Focusing on complexity in the Canadian history classroom means focusing on histories that are *counter* to a mainstream "textbook" version of Canada that flattens and simplifies the past to one easy narrative. As complex individuals in a complex world, young people are looking to the past to be both a mirror and a window (Style 1996) to the diversity of the nation they see before them.

However, while students want to learn Canadian history that reflects their identities as Canadians, they fail to see this complexity in their history class. This does not mean that teachers are unaware of the complexities of the past (although they may be). It means that complexity is not being invited into the classroom as an integral way of holding space for the complex and historically situated lives of young people today. It means that students' complex identities are not being recognized as the starting place for learning about and developing a sense of "we" in the Canadian past and present. At worst, it can mean that students' complexities may be seen as a hindrance for engaging in history rather than a benefit.

Erin was a teacher who saw complexity in history. She said that Canadian history was "multicultural, multi-faceted, multi-event, multi-contribution," emphasizing that "It's not just one straight narrative. And it can't be." However, when faced with teaching this complexity to "multi-cultural, multi-faceted" students, Erin was unprepared to confront these complexities as pedagogy. The result was a teaching practice that privileged a simplified narrative of the past for a simplified vision of the student.

As the last section showed, Erin continuously talked about how students' learning styles, generation, and home lives posed a problem for her Canadian history teaching. However, she also emphasized that when she walked into class on the first day of school, she realized that she would be teaching to a group of students who were "not Canadian" and that she had to change her approach to teaching Canadian history. Students as learners posed a problem for Erin, but students as "non-Canadians" were the biggest problem of all.

As stated earlier, many of Erin's students were students of colour who expressed complex Canadian identities that aligned with global youth cultures (Yon 2000; see also Warikoo 2011). Many students spoke with an accent or used slang words when talking among themselves, using their cultural capital to resist a situation that undervalued who they were and what they could offer in the classroom (Almarza 2001). Erin looked at her students of colour, noticed their different food and drink choices, heard them talk about international sports teams or music stars, saw their rejection of mainstream Canadian history and compounded these things together to determine that they had no connection to Canada. In particular, she saw her students as immigrants with no legal stability in Canada, attributing citizenship with a clear understanding of one's place, saying "I think citizenship solidifies one's space, right? You are a resident of *this* space, therefore, you hold *a* passport from *this* country." While there is no data on students' legal citizenship or passport status, neither are they indicative of one's understanding of belonging to one's country of residence (Yuval-Davis 2007).

When looking at available data, Erin's characterization of her students as non-Canadians was one-dimensional and racist. According to the available figures from the school board,[5] while many teachers at the school would refer to the students as immigrants, less than fifteen percent of students at that school had been born outside of Canada or had lived in Canada for less than five years. Fifty-five percent of students' primary language was English and it was the language most often spoken at home. The numbers as well as my discussions with students indicate that the majority of the students were first- or second-generation Canadians, but because they were visible minorities and/or because they articulated aspects of their identities as aligning to other cultures, teachers at this school, including Erin, viewed these students as immigrants with no solid Canadian roots. At this school, like the school featured in Dan Yon's (2000, 30) book *Elusive Culture,* students' perceived immigrant status disrupted the "imaginary coherent school identity now fragmenting under the impact of cultural pluralism and competing interests." By using this population of students as a contrast to the imagined simplicity of earlier times, the difficulties of pedagogy and practice could always be discussed as the fault of the newcomers. "Immigrant" is often a label that "sticks for life" (Philip 1994), even when it more accurately describes someone's racialization than their nationality. In thinking of these students as immigrants, teachers and staff at the school could always position them as different from the norm.

In her Canadian history classroom, this perception of students as immigrants supported Erin's view of them as other to, and outside of, Canadian history. While she wanted to connect her students to Canadian history, she saw their diverse backgrounds as prohibitive to doing so. When asked if she thought her students had any shared narrative, Erin first clarified if I meant before this class, and when I said yes, her answer was no, explaining that the Canadian narrative is a "tapestry" where "each one of them holds a string." She said reconciling those strings was one of the "challenges" a twenty-first century teacher had to overcome.

To confront these challenges, Erin often drew on Jack Granatstein's book, *Who Killed Canadian History,*[6] to frame the question: "Whose history should you teach?" Oft repeated in formal and informal conversations throughout the research period, "Whose history should you teach?" was a guiding question for Erin's attempt at reconciling diverse histories for her diverse students. Erin identified that Granatstein presented three options for addressing this question: teach to who was in the room, look to the greater community, or use what resources are available. Erin said the "obvious choice" was to teach to who was in the room. She felt that appealing to students' ethnicity in the study of Canadian history would maintain engagement and fulfill the requirements of being a good teacher who taught culturally relevant material. Teaching to "who was in the room" could provide the connection students said they wanted when learning Canadian history.

While connection is essential in the Canadian history classroom, Erin's articulation of "whose history to teach" sets up a dynamic in which students' ethno-cultural diversity becomes simplified to a pathology that can only be remedied through cultural-specific content: Asian students need Asian history, Black students need Black history, Inuit students need Inuit history. While she is putting forth a pluralistic national identity, it serves the function of a "flexible strategy developed to manage diverse populations" (Mackey 2005, 13). Her concept of race, ethnicity, culture, nationality, identity, and history that she frames as a key "challenge" for her as a twenty-first-century Canadian history teacher draws on larger Western liberal ideologies that separate people into unique categories, hindering a contextual understanding of how experiences and narratives are interconnected and shared (Bannerji 2000). Thinking of some histories over others relies on the simplification, separation, and management of differences, often by a white majority (Bannerji 2000). As Mackey (2005, 17) argues, it is "the *construction* of culture and difference, and not simply its erasure, [that] is an integral part of the flexible Western projects, practices and procedures" (emphasis in original).

The diversity that Erin saw her students embodying represented a vision that they had multiple identities that were "constantly at battle with each other" (Mackey 2005, 11). But this battle is imaginary; or, more accurately, it is the result of a white liberal order that places people of colour in competition with each other so that they fail to see their shared similarities of class oppression (Bannerji 2000). Racialized students want to learn complex histories even if these do not align with their own cultural backgrounds (Martell 2013, 80). But simplifying history by thinking of "whose history to teach" fails to acknowledge that students want to learn the complexities of transnational and (post/neo)colonial Canada that rely on seeing the interconnectedness of these stories. "Whose history should you teach?" fails to see everyone in the class, teacher *and* student, as embodying a "we" that can be explored through Canadian history.

Not only does seeing ethno-cultural difference as a competition between different identities put the burden on the Canadian history teacher to know and be able to teach many different histories, which is impossible – "Where do I find this stuff?" Erin asked – but it also makes it impossible for teachers to teach Canadian history with diverse people in the room. While the majority of students in Erin's class were Black, for example, with family links to the Caribbean, she had students in the class who were white with European backgrounds, students from the Philippines, and students next door who were from Slavic and Arab countries. While she wanted to teach to "who was in the room," she had problems answering this question because she did not see a clear "who" in the room. She surmised that in a culturally homogeneous but still ethnically diverse classroom, this choice of "whose history should you teach" would be somewhat easier to answer than in her current classroom because

> *if we were teaching this [at another school] where the majority of the population were Asian or the majority of the population were a couple of other different cultures, then obviously different spotlights would go on, because obviously the research shows that you want to be representative of the students.*

However, in her classroom, a classroom with more diversity than at another school, the choice of which "spotlights" would go on was not as "obvious." For her, her students from multiple Caribbean, European, and Asian backgrounds represented so many ways of being Canadian, she was not able to pick one to spotlight.[7]

Although Erin's educational background emphasized that the Canadian past was "multicultural, multi-faceted, multi-event, multi-contribution," when deciding what to teach she found that this multi-ness meant there were few opportunities for convergence, rather than a collection of interconnected stories. Erin did not see a way to operationalize a vision for teaching and learning history that would reconcile Canadian history with the multiplicity of ways that students came to be in Canada. It was Canadian history and Other, placed at an impasse, with points of intersection ideally negotiated to respect both. Erin could only see choosing one history over another as an option of integrating "alternative" histories to Canadian history. There was Canadian history, proper, and then alternative histories that were there too. This dichotomous understanding of Canadian history leaves no room for a community of respectful discussion that acknowledges and deconstructs the complexities of identity, nationality, and belonging when learning Canadian history.

While Erin questioned whose histories she should teach, it became evident that choosing a "spotlight" representative of the students in the class was further complicated when the majority of the students in the class were not white. For the research intervention, we chose the histories of Africville and the West Indian Domestic Scheme as complex counter-stories that could *challenge* a traditional textbook version of the postwar period (see more details in Chapter 6). These histories featured Black people, which would connect with the dominant Black student population in the class, but would also demonstrate the complexity of identity and belonging within the larger narrative of economic and familial growth of this period.

Erin was very excited to cover Africville, especially because she was about to travel to Halifax and could do primary research. She said that Africville represented the "*real* history stuff. It's, like, *what's left behind that has not been fully resolved that made me, like, made me read.*" Erin brought back books, pictures, and documents all designed to enhance her teaching of the subject. She said that preparing for teaching about Africville in this way was important for her because she felt like she could now "talk about Africville and its impact because I've been there and I've read and I've had conversation with some people that live in that part of Canada." But even when being so prepared, Erin acknowledged that she was "struggling" with our choice of covering histories that featured narratives of Black people because we were isolating other students in the classroom, especially students who were white. In making this argument, Erin would circle close to the concept of "reverse racism" that she brought up during one of our late-night conversations. She fully discussed her thinking at one of our interviews and said:

> *I guess the part that I kind of struggled with a little bit, and I tried to think, um, if I were Yvan in the class, right? I kind of thought to myself that it is important for students like Yvan, a white French student from France, to*

> have an understanding of what the alternative history is, no question. But the question is: Is his history that appears to be more mainstream than the others dealt with as much consideration?

As Erin tells it, "Yvan," one of the only white students in the class, needed an understanding of "alternative histories," but she struggled with whether we were dealing with his history, his white mainstream history, with as much consideration. However, as a French national who had been in the country for less than a year, Yvan had even *less* connection to Canadian history than his second-generation Black Caribbean Canadian classmates. Of all the students, Yvan was the most "non-Canadian." But, in Erin's mind, Yvan's whiteness tied him to a mainstream Canadian history that she saw as not being considered with the same weight as the "alternative" histories she felt only appealed to a segment of the class.

Erin also explained that focusing on Black history left students like Caribbean Canadian "Estelle" at a disadvantage because, according to Erin, "kids like Estelle and others saying, well, 'I'm Scottish,' 'I'm Jamaican Scottish,' right? Or 'I'm whatever identity.'" The way Erin describes it, students with "whatever identities" were coming to her complaining that we were isolating them from history because we made content choices that only privileged Black history. Although "Estelle" was one of the most vocal students in the class for asking for Black history, Erin's recollection that Estelle identified a partial Scottish background was enough to say we were putting her at a disadvantage because we were not focusing on histories that "appear more mainstream."

Through these sweeping statements, Erin removed complexity from the classroom in how she saw her students and how she interpreted history. Black history was for Black students. We were leaving white students out. We were also leaving Black students out because some of them had mixed heritage. We had to consider "mainstream" – that is, white – students and stories, which we were leaving out in favour of "alternative" history. Our focus on "alternative" histories meant we were not dealing with mainstream history with the same "consideration."

Erin was only able to reconcile our focus on covering histories featuring Black people when she was able to link these histories to white people. She came to explain that

> *I don't think that there's anything wrong with teaching Africville because there's two sides to that story and I think everyone's voices would be heard and they would feel that they were represented, particularly in that scenario. Because I think that the white students in the class have been in scenarios where they also have felt that oppression.*

With this characterization of Africville – that there were two equal sides to the story and that this story needed to appeal to white students, of which there were fewer than five in the class of twenty-five – Africville was conceptualized as an "axis around which African American[/Black] stories turn" (Vaz 1995, 32).

Covering Africville – or any other history that privileged the complex engagement of race, nationality, and belonging – could only be engaged with in simplified ways: there was oppression, there are two sides to the story, and everyone's voice needed to be heard. While teachers know how important it is to ensure multiple viewpoints are presented in the history classroom, approaching this multiplicity by ensuring "both sides" are equally and democratically heard results in "the possibility of simplifying and painting black and white pictures of the past ... thereby inadvertently [promoting] its understandings in caricature-like terms" (Zanazanian and Moisan 2012, 263). With Erin's approach to Africville, we would not have been able to cover Africville as a counterstory that could "bear witness to social relations that the dominant culture tends to deny or minimize" in any way that challenged "the mainstream story or master narrative that constitutes the public script" (L.A. Bell 2003, 8). The "public script" of white, mainstream Canadian history needed to remain intact so that the parity of histories could be sustained. The notion of *complexity* that Africville was supposed to engender as a counterstory that could open up new ways of seeing and being in the world (Delgado 1989) was missing.

Erin's question – "Whose histories should you teach?" – while perhaps a familiar one for historians and teachers, is premised on the fear that focusing on "alternative," Othered histories will fragment and abandon a foundational story of the nation. Saying "Whose history?" and then doubting the presence and validity of histories that may be able to answer that question makes those histories – and the students who connect to those histories – Others, and if you make students Other, there is no room for the mutuality needed for a community of respectful discussion that acknowledges and deconstructs the complexities of identity, nationality, and belonging when learning Canadian history. Even if you ask, "How do you teach a story without making others Other and without interrupting the story?" you are presuming a structure that places the story and Others at an impasse where they need to be reconciled. There has to be *work* to get them to fit together. This work, the belief that an effort has to be made, denies the fundamental complexity of the past because underlying this belief is that there is one true narrative that all others circulate around.

With an emphasis on the importance of complexity in the classroom, I continuously emphasized to Erin that our focus on the histories of Africville and the West Indian Domestic Scheme were *Canadian* histories that allowed us to think about the power and privilege woven into the past, especially related to race, gender, and class. We were not looking for these histories to play a "functionalist" role in "counterbalancing whiteness" (Doharty 2019, 124). Students are neither looking for this superficiality nor do they find it intellectually satisfying. Rather, I strived to communicate to Erin that the histories that we were going to cover explored the complexities of belonging, identity, and legacy that, as a community, we could think about and question together. These histories happened to feature Black Canadians, but we could have featured any histories that invited discussions of how race and racism signify a complex set of relationships in the nation (T. Epstein, Mayorga, and Nelson 2011, 4). However, Erin was only able to see our focus on Black histories in Canada as a flattened history chosen over another – *that's whose history we'll teach*. In doing so, she failed to see that the belief underlying the question, "Whose histories do you teach?" is the very belief that maintains a simplified history that rationalizes a separation between "us" and "them."

While Erin's concerns may be common, the beliefs latent in her concern of "whose history to teach" worked to decentre complexity as having a place in the classroom. As I discussed earlier, students are looking for Canadian history to connect with, explore, and challenge the complex stories that frame the world they live in. They want history to share these complexities, maintain them, hold onto them, unravel them, question them, make them central to their learning about and with the past. However, these complexities cannot exist if teachers believe in the separateness of histories, experiences, and identities in Canada. As Mackey (2005, 90) writes, although in a liberal democracy "'cultures' (defined in a limited way) may be multiple, the project of nation-building is singular." In this way, the separateness, the complexities, of different identities cannot exist in the singular nation. Instead, there is a competition of cultures that prompts the question, "Whose histories should you teach?"

The beliefs underlying "Whose histories should you teach?" are "symptomatic of a semi-paradoxical desire to preserve the national heritage, while simultaneously cultivating a new multicultural narrative of the nation" (Andrews, McGlynn, and Mycock 2009, 367). While she wanted to speak to the multicultural students in her class, Erin also did not want to erode the stability of the mainstream narrative either. In this way, her question of "Whose history do you teach?" worked as a "tool of whiteness" that actively protected the hegemonic stories of white supremacy that she, like many other white teachers, know and are comfortable with (Picower 2009, 205). This question worked to strip complexity from the classroom and shielded her unconscious racism that viewed multi-ethnic students as having histories separate and alternative to the mainstream.

Privileging Chronology: The "Package" of History

Erin's response to the question "Whose history should you teach?" was to avoid focusing on specific "other" histories altogether. She said that she was "conscious of not isolating other: 'Let's talk about Black people in *this* context.' 'Let's talk about women in *this* context.'" Instead, she emphasized, in class "we're going to talk about men, women, children, old, young, and all the different ethno-cultural groups and their involvement as a *package*," sometimes pulling things out, but avoiding relegating them to "a nice little footnote at the bottom of the textbook." However, if one presumes that there is an unequivocal "package" of Canadian history that includes contributions of different groups but is not defined by them, then one inscribes a hegemonic fatality to history that can only be assessed for accuracy and not for exploration. The focus goes on teaching "The Story," not on how the story applies in the present.

Erin's emphasis on learning about everyone as a *package* meant that in her class the *package* could never challenge itself because real, core history cannot be modified or negotiated, it can only be known. While Erin said that she did not want to add-and-stir or pull other out and make it Other, she actually used her definition of Other as the justification for leaving those stories out. "Whose histories should you teach?" she kept asking, but how to not fragment history in doing so?

Erin's fear, discomfort, and unfamiliarity with the complexities of identity and nationality, and their intersections with teaching and learning history, resulted in rote teaching of a linear series of facts that privileged a mainstream narrative of Canadian history rather than an exploration of the complexities of the past. Her metaphor of the Canadian narrative as a tapestry, where each student "holds a string," supported her "enduring understanding" of Canada as "multicultural, multi-faceted, multi-event, multi-contribution," but her fear of narrative fragmenting meant she could not see how these strings could provide anything but disadvantage to the (seemingly stable) Canadian narrative.

Rather than choose one string to pull (answering the problematic question of "whose history do you teach?"), her chosen narrative ("the package" that tied these strings together) was the one she could rely on the most – the traditional Canadian chronology. Through a focus on chronology, Erin was able to rationalize how teaching this simplified narrative avoided the tangles of different "strings." Because of her deficit-based understanding of her students of colour and their perceived distance from Canadian history, she justified that students were both the cause and effect of this focus on a rote, linear understanding of the Canadian past, rationalizing: "You can't just challenge the narrative if you don't know what the narrative is, right?"

However, while Erin felt like she was struggling alone to answer the question of "whose histories should you teach," in her ethnographic study of nation-building discourses during Canada's quasquicentennial in 1992, Eva Mackey (2005, 20) identified an "unmarked, non-ethnic, and usually White, '*Canadian*-Canadian' identity" that many white Canadians use as a marker of national legitimacy and belonging. It is this "*Canadian*-Canadian" identity that prompts people to ask Canadians of colour where they are *really* from, for example (Mahtani 2002; Paragg 2015; Shadd 2001). A key element of the *Canadian*-Canadian identity is a "Canada-first" orientation that privileges this unmarked, non-ethnic, white, *Canadian*-Canadian identity *first,* before difference is allowed in. In her interviews, Mackey (2005, 157) said that many white Canadians discuss multiculturalism "as part of a sequential logic, embedded in a series of statements and assertions in which the conclusion was that 'other' cultures in Canada should be secondary to 'Canadian culture.'" Diversity was fine in Canada, but the *Canadian*-Canadian identity had to come first.

With an appeal to chronology before other histories could be covered, Erin invoked this same "Canada-first" discourse as a way to manage, and sublimate, the complex identities of her students. Her justification was that with so many stories the students could bring into the classroom, it was key to stick to chronology because "there is a lot to be said for some sequencing, right? To understand the cause-and-effect relationship of consequence." Interestingly, this notion of causation is the same rationale that other researchers have found teachers use to revert to a traditional, chronological approach for teaching history, even when the curriculum provides space for thematic, interpretive, or critical approaches to teaching and learning (R. Harris and Reynolds 2018; Husbands, Kitson, and Pendry 2003; Zanazanian and Moisan 2012). Erin echoed these teachers when she rationalized that it was the students themselves who needed a simplified, chronological narrative. As Erin said: "Kids do understand things in a linear way, because they understand that A happens before B, and that B happens before C." While chronology does have a place in learning about the past, privileging a timeline for the sake of linearity leaves no room for the complexity students are looking for. It can provide a national canon to be memorized, but no space for students to imagine how history could be interpreted otherwise.

Mackey (2005, 148) found that a key element of the Canada-first idea is the management of difference by the *Canadian*-Canadians. As the "'real' and 'true' Canadians," they are the ones in the best position to "define the appropriate *limits* of difference" (emphasis in original). Mackey (2005, 151) emphasized that it is not that *Canadian*-Canadians want to do away with difference; rather they want to properly coordinate the "subordinate cultures ... within the totality of a *normative* national culture and the project of nation-building" (emphasis in original). Although Mackey identified this dynamic in 1992, it was still in play in Erin's classroom in the 2010s.

In both interviews and informal discussions, Erin reiterated the story of walking into her classroom on the first day of term and seeing a group of ethno-culturally diverse students she understood as "not Canadian." Because of this, she felt she needed to re-evaluate how she should teach Canadian history. Her plan, she repeatedly recalled, was to "start with themes at the end of the twentieth century," which would "bridge some gaps and some understanding about 'who are you' and 'how do you fit in society' and 'is your culture represented or not.'" Then, she continued "we were able to go back to the First World War and move through it." Erin was very proud of this solution and brought it up on multiple occasions. For her it represented the best of both worlds: connecting to students who were "not Canadian" and retaining a focus on mainstream Canadian history.

While Erin wanted to begin her course by focusing on her students, small instructional changes are not enough to transform the power relations in a class (Depaepe, De Corte, and Verschaffel 2012). Instead, it is the "transformation of the underlying pedagogic and educative objective that transforms the teaching activity" (Perumal 2008, 395). With her solution, and her pride in this solution, to start with contemporary connections and then "move through" the Canadian narrative, Erin demonstrated her interest in managing difference within a larger Canadian narrative, keeping the complexities of difference subordinate to a larger unifying Canadian project (Mackey 2005, 148).

Erin's changes to instruction did not transform the class into one in which her diverse students would continue to explore the complexities of "who [they are] and how do [they] fit in society and is [their] culture represented or not" – as she had claimed. Instead, this brief contemporary connection kept the focus on "moving through" the mainstream Canada-first narrative. This "slightly delayed" the pace of the course, but this was something Erin felt "was worth it" in the end.

In talking about how the class was going to "move through" the content after the students' contemporary connections were covered, Erin betrayed her "knowledge package" (Ma 1999), her *Canada-first* knowledge package, of how her course would be organized. Cunningham (2007, 618) defined knowledge packages as "discrete pieces of knowledge in terms of their related, interconnected roles – not as a sequence, but as the application of several ideas rather than just one – a package, in other words." While knowledge packages can demonstrate a teacher's "expert pedagogical content knowledge" (Shulman 1987), they can also limit the opportunities for students to explore complexity outside the expected response.

While I came to the research with content suggestions for her class, Erin had a clear vision for the content she saw core to teaching the post–World War II period. To her, these histories were the ones that had to be taught before anything else, in order to understand Toronto during this time. These included the development of the Don Mills suburb, the Toronto subway, Hurricane Hazel, Marilyn Bell swimming across Lake Ontario, Toronto's television station, the Allen Expressway, and the development of both Regent Park and Lawrence Heights. Although Erin was critical of teachers who taught from a binder, Erin was similarly *bound* to her "knowledge package" of Canadian history, because for her, there were things that had to be covered first before other content could be taught. This list became a "text" that, while not printed on the page, articulated her "personal curriculum, infused with [her] different values" (Gudmundsdottir 1990, 48).

Erin was open to adding to this text but only if it fit into her larger personal curriculum – a personal curriculum that allowed her to manage histories and cultures within the larger unifying project of the Canadian nation. Erin identified that Regent Park and Lawrence Heights were aspirationally added to her list this year as a response to her current students. She said that she thought that covering Regent Park and Lawrence Heights would be "very interesting in terms of what's going on in terms of the whole discussion about displacement and relocation and, in fact, I read that Regent Park is the first of its kind in Canada in terms of that settlement housing."

Both Regent Park and Lawrence Heights are Toronto community housing projects that were either going through or scheduled to go through massive redevelopment and revitalization in the 2010s. Many racialized and immigrant Canadians live in these community housing developments; however, these people were not Erin's students. The students in Erin's classroom did not live in or around either of these neighbourhoods and the housing around the school was not community housing nor undergoing displacement or relocation. But the students were racialized, and Erin did see them as immigrants. Erin's interest in bringing these histories into her classroom served the function of being able to continue to manage and define the parameters of how diversity would be addressed, but not of giving students more opportunities to connect their own stories to history. These articulations of inclusions only served to maintain her personal curriculum as the one that could "define the appropriate *limits* of difference" as opposed to allowing differences to thrive in the classroom (Mackey 2005, 148; emphasis in original).

For a sense of "we" to be engendered in the Canadian history classroom, the teacher and the student must see each other as complementary pieces within the larger puzzle that is Canada. A sense of ownership over the definition of what and who can be Canadian cannot be a dominating feature in how the content or instruction is approached. However, even two months into the research, after greater connection and complexity had been discussed and modelled, Erin continued to ask, "Whose story do you teach?" She articulated that "if we're looking at engagement and if we're looking at the Canadian mosaic, then I would argue that you can teach to tell the stories of the students that you're with." However, Erin went back to this set content of a chronological, Canada-first narrative of Canadian history and said:

> *I think that using chronology you can provide some sense of that which is linear, but that you can look at opportunities for comparing and contrasting experiences coast-to-coast, north-to-south, urban-rural, poor-rich, and everything in between.*

Thus, even with a research intervention designed for greater complexity, and her own knowledge and appeal to educational research, Erin was able to conclude that a chronology needed to be the overarching framework for approaching Canadian history because it could ultimately provide something "linear," something a "mosaic" could not provide. According to this approach, it is with the solidity of chronology that one could then engage in the complexity of comparing solid history to other, alternative histories. With this distinction, differences become democratized, where ethnicity and culture can be synonymous with geography and economics in terms of comparative potential. The complexities of identity and history become simplified and sublimated under a rubric of predetermined connections. Students' identities become "everything in between," covered when there is time and place to do so. A chronology of mainstream Canadian history always comes first. And by coming first, it is never changed or challenged by the histories that may come second.

Like many approaches to canonical subjects, an appeal to foundational dates and/or people makes a subjective approach to the material seem objective. Learning the main events and people in a time period seems to provide a foundation to build from, but in fact it creates columns and beams of power and privilege that cannot be challenged unless purposefully deconstructed. Privileging the "main story" just to get it out of the way prioritizes and reaffirms these events and people as the core elements of the past, rather than subjective selections of what and who is important. This is a Canada-first knowledge package designed to prevent greater complexity from entering the grand narrative, and thus results in less meaningful learning opportunities about Canadian history for today's diverse students.

Erin was a well-meaning teacher who wanted to be a good instructor to her multicultural students. But she was too tied to her own self-image as a good teacher to understand that her practice was undermining the opportunities for her students to learn in connected and complex ways. Whether it was because of students' learning styles, generation, home lives, ethno-cultural diversity, or supposed proximity to the Canadian nation, Erin always had a reason for why they were not taking what she was offering and it was never because of her. Even with a pedagogical belief and instructional approach that was meant to provide connection and complexity for her students' understanding of the Canadian past, Erin could not leave behind her core beliefs that prioritized her teaching over their learning. As a result she framed her Canadian history course to be about what made her comfortable: a focus on herself as a teacher and as a *Canadian-*Canadian who taught Canada-first (Mackey 2005).

Everyone knows, has been taught by, or is an educator a little bit like Erin: eager, frustrated, knowledgeable, self-confident, overworked, and keen. As an award-winning teacher who was generally well liked and respected by students and professional colleagues alike, Erin was in a teaching situation that unsettled her, and this, combined with a research intervention that provided space for pedagogical and narrative exploration, meant that her practice can now be used as a case study for understanding the slippages between philosophy and practice that can limit the opportunities for today's transnational and (post/neo)colonial students to learn meaningfully in the Canadian history classroom.

In another class, with another group of students, Erin's practice may have been different, but this case study demonstrates why conversations about history education need to shift from teaching through content and instruction to learning through an ethos of connection and complexity. If teachers start thinking about learning, then they start thinking about how to position their work, their difficult and fearful work, to create more opportunities for understanding their students well enough to make connections in their complex worlds. This is what was missing in Erin's class. Erin had all the content and instruction that, on paper, should have engaged her students, but she was so fearful of these students and how, through their resistance to her work, they challenged what she knew about herself as a good teacher, that she used her expert teaching knowledge, her knowledge of "good teaching," as a barrier between herself and her students.

To teach with an ethos of "we" in the Canadian history classroom starts with a belief that the class community already features a "we" – a "we" of smart, capable, connected, and complex students. Ensuring that this belief works in practice means understanding one's work as a teacher to be a learner *with* students as well as *of* students, and to not be so tied to what can work that one fails to see what would work, for these students, now.

5

Meaningful Sites of Teaching
The Need for Time, Space, and Place

To transform the Canadian history classroom into one where connection, complexity, and care for students is the starting point for historical engagement, a teacher must model, support, and believe in a Canadian "we" that includes the diversities of the past, present, and future of Canada. However, just as meaningful learning can be obfuscated by teachers' one-dimensional understanding of Canada, meaningful teaching can equally be obfuscated by an institutionalized understanding of education that fails to acknowledge and provide space for the emotional and affective experiences needed to teach and learn meaningfully.

Thus, it is important to emphasize that for a classroom to be a place where students can creatively and meaningfully explore the ways historical narratives intersect with their identities as Canadians in the present, schools have to be places where teachers are able to creatively and meaningfully develop those intersections with their students. If one is to teach and learn in ways that are open, receptive, and inviting for meaningful learning, then one needs the time, space, and place to reflect on and engage in this work.

In this chapter, I will explore the systemic barriers that may prevent teachers from teaching with an ethos of meaningful learning in the Canadian history classroom. In making this argument, I will broaden my analysis to draw on my experiences as a researcher-educator and participant-observer in both mainstream and alternative schools. It is the contrast between these two types of schools that puts into focus the ways in which the teaching environment shapes the possibilities for learning.

What was most interesting about conducting research in both alternative and mainstream schools was the marked contrast in their environments with regard to supporting students and their learning. It was not only the students who were different – at the alternative schools students were, and felt, older than students at mainstream schools – but the organization of the schools themselves. The teachers who taught at alternative schools generated new possibilities for teaching and learning that seemed unavailable in the mainstream school. On a site-based level – walking in the halls, using the public spaces, sitting in the classrooms – I found that the alternative schools offered greater invitations to learn meaningfully than did the mainstream school.

Teachers at the alternative schools were often more politically aware and invested in the politicized emotional well-being of their students. The mainstream teachers, while interested in their students and issues of social justice, were often too busy in the hectic pace of the day to fully explore these complexities in their practice. While all the teachers struggled with the difficulties of teaching conditions that failed to give them the time, space, or place to develop the connection, complexity, and care required for meaningful learning, the alternative teachers were more able to see and talk through these constraints than were the mainstream teachers. Drawing on the experiences of teachers in these two types of learning environments gives greater context to institutionalized education more generally, and thus will help provide direction as to how meaningful teaching can be better engendered by individual teachers and departments.

Time to Research: Connection to Content

For teachers to develop their history classes into places where students are able to connect with the complexity of the past, teachers need the time to find, synthesize, and develop meaningful content and instruction that invite this type of learning. Without the professional scaffolding needed for discovery, teachers can become comfortable in the stability of set lessons and adopt a view of their work as simply providing information to uninformed students. This approach leaves no room for different or unique explorations of the past with students viewed as complex people who have rich prior knowledges. The result is a classroom environment more concerned with meeting predetermined objectives than with developing the connections needed for the meaningful learning.

In my research it became clear that teachers needed, and wanted, time to find and turn historical information into meaningful material for their students; however, this time was simply not available to them in the daily course of their work. The frantic pace of the year, with few spares and loads of marking, meant that there were no sustained opportunities for teachers to research and develop new, perhaps more meaningful, content for their classes. Even with curriculum focused more on inquiry, teachers often prioritize familiar content because of the suitability of this content for assessment, the rationale that this content covers both the breadth and depth needed for understanding national history, and the perception that this is content that students find interesting (Ormond 2017). Without challenging and innovative content, the class narrative becomes set and relationships between teachers and students become rote, so that teachers, even those with complex ideas about history, begin to see the work of challenging the master narratives as falling outside the boundaries of what they can teach (McNeil 1988, 535).

All the teachers with whom I worked commented on how important it was to stay current with one's historical research, but they also said that they had difficulties finding the time to look for and develop appropriate content for classroom use; a common complaint among history teachers (Cunningham 2007, 609). Early on in the research, one teacher mentioned her difficulty in finding "age-appropriate" resources to support her teaching. She said that it was a "reality" that the search for resources could take the whole summer and that she could see why, "fifteen years into it," teachers might stop looking for new resources. However, she backtracked and stressed how important it was for history teachers, no matter what stage of their career, to continually bring new elements to class because "there's always new resources and new documentaries and revision in history. Whether it's good or bad, it's still a perspective." While this teacher suggested that it could be the more experienced teachers who may feel they no longer need to do research, a first-year teacher with whom I worked estimated that it would take about five years for her to get to a place where she could even start bringing her own perspective and research into the classroom. She said that she had an interest in, and saw the need for, developing "local curriculums" for her history class but that, at this early stage of her career, there was no time for her to do so.

The perspectives of these teachers suggest that mid-career teachers would be in the best position to enrich their practice through research and development. Research says otherwise, however. Studies have found that it is early- and late-career educators who engage in the most professional development (Louws et al. 2017). In my study, a mid-career teacher such as Erin, a teacher keen on history and historical investigation, still encountered barriers to engaging in historical discovery to support her teaching. For her, it was important to bring a variety of different perspectives into the class, yet, she remarked, "it's one thing to make reference to it, [and] it's another thing to have resources to back it up." Teaching with diverse perspectives was of particular interest to her because she wanted to bring culturally relevant material to her students, but she said it was difficult because, it was "a resource question ultimately." "Where do I find this stuff?" Erin asked rhetorically.

Teachers are most interested in engaging in professional development and self-learning related to their subject matter (Louws et al. 2017), but when attempting to engage in such learning, they can be faced with a crisis in self-efficacy that makes it difficult for them to bring this desire into practice. Even while being committed and interested in research, Erin admitted that when attempting to

> tap into, like, the [provincial] archives and the city archives – I've only been in there once, right? Partly because I think it's some kind of ivory tower that has too many passwords and too many ... I walked in[to] the [education library at the university] really briefly as I was coming over here and I thought, "My God, there are some old books in here." There doesn't appear to be a lot of new stuff, which to me says they're either digitizing things or all the good stuff is out of the library.

While Erin identifies that she felt intimidated to enter the archives to find the raw materials that she could use to build new lessons, she was also critical of the ready-made resources she might find at a library.

This echoes a problem I have seen in other work I have done with history teachers: while teachers want material to grow their practice, they want this material to be digestible enough so they do not have to spend time making it ready for classroom use, but not *too* digestible, so that they can still determine how the material would be used. This element of *supportive agency* is an integral part of working with teachers. Teachers want the *agency* to develop their lessons according to their own purpose, rhythm, comfort, and knowledge, but they also want the resources from others to *support* them in developing this purpose, rhythm, comfort, and knowledge. This concept of supportive agency, which Vangrieken et al. (2017) identify as the paradox between autonomy and collaboration, is an orientation to professional development that views teachers as active participants rather than passive receivers of pedagogical and practical support. As Louws et al. (2017, 172) summarize, "Teachers show a high level of ownership over their own learning: they themselves decide what they learn from the learning opportunities the workplace offers them." While teachers most often want professional development to support their subject expertise (Louws et al. 2017), without the right balance of support and agency or autonomy and collaboration in the support they receive (Vangrieken et al. 2017), often what gets taught in class is the same thing that has been taught before.

Finding time to research was less of an issue for the teachers in my study because I came to their classrooms with content and resources developed for each class. However, the lack of opportunities for teachers to think about and reflect on this new material influenced how much of it actually altered what was taught. The new content often complemented teachers' "knowledge packages" but did not substantially modify them in ways that shifted the overall narrative of their teaching (Cunningham 2007; Ma 1999). The stories I introduced could be included, but they did not act as *counterstories* to a larger historical narrative. Again, this mode of adding, but not really *integrating*, content is not rare for teachers.

Research shows that primary sources meant to complicate the understanding of a singular narrative are often used as a prop to support the narrative already in place because teachers are not equipped to teach history outside a bound narrative (VanSledright 2008, 118). Teachers can bring in new, challenging stories to their history class but the professional structure of schooling does not encourage their deep learning of these stories – meaning they could teach the content without "really knowing – or being required to know – what [the stories were] about" (Dion 2009, 150). Similarly, without time to reflect on how to teach the new material I had brought into the classroom, the teachers I worked with did not have the opportunity to explore how these stories could expand or challenge their frameworks of knowing. And without this time to reflect on the new content, there were few opportunities to engender different, and perhaps greater, invitations for connection and complexity from this content in the classroom. The new material might be included as a story within their personal narrative, but not act as a specific counter to these narratives, which is needed to teach more complex engagements with the past.

While teachers may stay within the professional structure of good teaching as a way to feel safe in the courageous and unpredictable arena of teaching (Palmer 1998), even teachers who want to challenge historical narratives in their teaching may face the obstacle of time to do this reflexive work (Dion 2009; Palmer 1998; Popkewitz 1998). During my final interview with one teacher at an alternative school, for example, the teacher apologized that she had not done any extra research on the topics I suggested as challenges to the mainstream narrative. She said that the lessons could have been richer if she had done outside research on these topics and folded her findings into the overall themes for the course. While I did not feel that these lessons suffered, she did, and reflected that, "I just felt like I ran out of time to not only research, but, I don't know, embrace." This concept of "embracing" the content, to make it one's own, to bring it into one's framework for understanding, is key for integrating content into lessons that can invite greater connections and complexity into the Canadian history classroom.

At the mainstream school, Erin said she was excited when I suggested Africville as content challenge in her Canadian history class because the suggestion gave her incentive to do more research:

> *As soon as you said Africville I was pumped ... because it's the real history stuff. It's like what's left behind that has not been fully resolved that made me, like, made me read. Like, who has time to read when you're a teacher unless you're reading for teaching, right?*

Erin already knew about this history and was interested in thinking about the effects this history had on the present. However, before my suggestion and support of research materials, she had not found the time to bring this topic into her teaching because, she insinuates, reading without a specific direction was not something teachers have time for. She knew the history but not to such an extent that she could embrace it as part of her teaching.

Thus, we have to be aware that embracing content takes work. Embracing content takes time. Teachers do not have this time in their schedules, and the multiple responsibilities they have throughout the day use up the little time they do have on administrative, not pedagogical, tasks. This places an added stress on teachers to do the reflexive work needed for engaging in critically informed pedagogies that can support meaningful learning outside the normal workday (Warren 2011). As Erin recollected:

> *Someone was walking down the hall and was like, "What's wrong with you? You're kind of down today." I was like, "Look, I was planning some stuff for another class," and I'm one of those people that won't stop until it's done. And that's exhausting. You want to be able to shut the brain off but you can't go to bed because you're in the middle of trying to construct something that you think is going to work, and it might, but it just takes a long time to explain it.*

Erin indicates that the act of construction, of piecing together a class and a story to tell and share with students, is an ongoing process that takes time, time that is not available in the normal course of her day. That time is found in the hallways between classes or at home in bed, but it is outside the set times for teaching and learning. Research has shown that teachers spend an average of 17.5 hours preparing for class outside of school time, with full-time female classroom teachers in their first six years of teaching engaging in the most work out of school time (Higton et al. 2017).

However, the issue of time is not about teachers finding more minutes in the day – although teachers certainly articulate how they need a greater work-life balance to engage in effective teaching (Manuel, Carter, and Dutton 2018). Rather, the issue of time highlights how the structure of schooling can commodify time in ways that preclude the reflective work needed for inclusive teaching and learning practices to be more than technical endeavours to be completed (M.K.E. Thomas and Whitburn 2019). As Loewen (1996, 288) writes, "most teachers are far too busy teaching, grading, policing, handing out announcements, advising, comforting, hall monitoring, cafeteria quieting, and then running their own households to go off and research topics they do not even know how to question." Schools and schooling are directed by time in ways that direct "choice, control and organization within systems" so that "teachers and students always need to be somewhere at some time." With this approach to time, there is no reflective time to do the ontological work of embracing the content, so that even with more time, "inclusiveness remains illusory, and socially just practices become so in name only" (M.K.E. Thomas and Whitburn 2019, 167).

Thus, while teachers may want to learn more to develop their teaching practice, it is difficult for them to do so when they work within an institutional climate that is not built with the time for them to reflect on and develop their teaching practice (Kutsyuruba et al. 2018). A professional context is needed to support deep, meaningful reflection about content, pedagogy, and practice that is indispensable for engaging in critically informed, inclusive pedagogies, like those that support meaningful learning (Septor 2019; M.K.E. Thomas and Whitburn 2019; Warren 2011). Thus, time is not just about minutes, but about the temporal space for reading, for researching, for *embracing* new content and new knowledge – slow time that helps grow one's own practice as an educator. As Berg and Seeber (2016, x) argue in embracing this notion of "slowness" in higher education, educators "need time to think, and so do our students. Time for reflection and open-ended inquiry is not a luxury but is crucial to what we do." Slow, deliberate, *deliberative* time is needed if the work of education is to consist of something more than just depositing knowledge into students' heads. It is this humanizing time, and the professional confidence that develops from it, that create an emotional climate in which both teacher and student are invited to mutually explore the complex connections within the Canadian present and past.

All the teachers with whom I worked were open to having someone collaborate with them and suggest content and accompanying resources, but they also needed time to embrace the content in ways that could more fully support their practice long-term. One could argue that this type of time is not built into daily practice because "teaching was never meant to be a transgressive or subversive activity," especially for female teachers (Beauboeuf-Lafontant 2005, 436), but if we are interested in supporting teachers' practice, then more time needs to be made available to support teaching as an academic and research-filled endeavour that is not extra, but integral, to one's daily practice.

Space to Reflect: Complexity of Individuals
Another component of creating a professional climate in which teachers feel supported in creating more meaningful learning opportunities in their Canadian history classroom is having the space for them to reflect on their students and their work. Teachers, including the ones in this study, put "a great deal of effort and emotion into teaching" and, at the end of the day, often leave school drained (Aultman, Williams-Johnson, and Schutz 2009, 641). Teachers need space to reflect on the experiences of teaching to refuel their pedagogical and empathetic coffers. This reflection on their work and their students can help them think about, and address, these things in more complex and nuanced ways.

However, in my study, I found that teachers had few spaces where they could engage in this reflective work, and the spaces that *were* available often supported deficit-based thinking about their students, leaving teachers feeling powerless and isolated in their efforts to make change (Kutsyuruba et al. 2018, 61). While reflection is for the most part individual, "attention to context is as important as attention to personal and professional development" (L.F. Hayes and Ross 1989, 349). In other words, the spaces available for reflection shape the possible in how teachers can reflect. In my research, I saw three ways of approaching reflection: "bitching"/ complaining, venting, and meditative deliberation. All three were directly influenced by the spaces they were in and the professional climate created by their peers.

In our final interview, a junior teacher at the mainstream school told me that she was happy to be part of the research because it provided her with much needed space and time to reflect:

> These [interview] sessions are really great because I think it's so important to be reflective in your practice and what you're doing. And, like, as bad as it sounds, we don't really do that that often, as teachers ... At least I would expect to do it more, or I would like to do it more.

As a first-year teacher, she was overwhelmed and exhausted by her work in the classroom, and she complained about the absence of a reflective space within which to think through the multiple dimensions of teaching and learning in ways that would strengthen her practice. In the next breath, though, she stopped herself and said: "What am I talking about? I bitch to people all the time. Isn't that reflecting? Talking about it?" The switch from a call for thoughtful reflection to the acceptance that "bitching all the time" fulfills this need suggests an adherence to the cultural or social expectation among her fellow teachers that "bitching" was an acceptable form of professional reflection. "Bitching," as a misogynistic colloquialism, suggests a continuous stream of unproductive complaint not intended to engage the heart (Valli 1997) or clarify issues of practice (Burchard 2001). "Bitching" suggests a professional toxicity (Keller 2000; Nourie 2011) that contributes to the alienation of both teacher and student in the learning environment. "Bitching" is not reflecting, and yet she was suggesting that they could be one and the same.

As a new teacher, she was keen to explore multiple ways to teach and learn. She also frequently talked about the dominant professional culture that discouraged her enthusiasm for trying new things or speaking positively about the students. She said that she made the same "mistake" that other first-year teachers make at the beginning of the year by spending too much time in the staff room, something Nourie (2011) identified as one of the top ten mistakes new teachers can make. Part of the "toxicity" of staff room talk (Nourie 2011) is that it can "allow constructions like 'students who (don't) want to learn' to go unproblematized" (Toshalis 2012, 15). These beliefs can then become normalized for young teachers, such as the one I worked with, who can begin to believe that "there's so many limitations, you know? Like, you could have all these great ideas and then ..." At this point in the interview the teacher stopped herself and said:

> *I'm not trying to be negative and that's what happens, right? That's exactly the stream. It's negativity. That's what it is. It's everyone else's negative attitudes coming in on you saying, like, "Oh, well, don't try that because this is what's going to happen." And, "If you try this, you're just going to get that." It's like, "Can you just let me make my mistakes!?" Like, I don't want to have this attitude, it's just like ...*

She trailed off and shook her head. She could hear herself echoing an unproblematized construction of limitations in her explanation of why her "great ideas" were not getting realized. But she could not get away from these voices, they surrounded her. Because these voices were in the spaces where she could decompress at the end of the day, they echoed through her expectations of what her practice could be and limited what she felt she could do.

To understand the distinction between the reflection she longed for and the reflection made possible in the staff room, I asked her if what we were doing in the interviews was "bitching." To this she replied with a definitive "no." She said that while the interview had some similarities to her conversations in the staff room, what she does in the staff room involves "a bit more bitching."

In our interviews, I asked this teacher questions about community, teaching goals, and the evaluation of success in her class to clarify her ideological position and to understand if or how these ideologies actually were fulfilled in practice. I shared my own observations about classroom dynamics and curricular goals, and together we discussed possible strategies for addressing these in class.

While we would complain about certain aspects of the class, in the interviews we had the space to productively think through them and, with the accountability of future interviews, we also had the incentive to test our learning in class. This teacher's distinction between "bitching" and having time to reflect highlighted the few opportunities she saw for having these types of conversations outside our interviews. This teacher identified that "everyone's negative attitudes" – including those of other teachers, students, and administrators – made it hard to work and thrive in an environment where one's "open-mindedness" and enthusiasm were continuously met with negativity.

A teacher at one of the alternative schools also discussed the "stream of negativity" she encountered while teaching in a mainstream school early in her career. In her experience, she found that in the staff room or at professional meetings, "you hear a lot of complaining about the students." Having realized that we had just left her office where she and her colleagues had talked about their frustrations with their students, she caught herself and said that I had "just heard complaining about the students" but that teaching "can be frustrating" and "it's okay to vent." Like the first-year teacher at the mainstream school, this alternative-school teacher made a distinction between two forms of reflection: complaining and venting. Her conception of complaining was similar to the other teacher's conception of "bitching" in that both referred to a discourse among teachers that was unproductive for practice. This teacher said that "venting" with her colleagues was different from "complaining" and that, as opposed to complaining, venting was both healthy and important for teaching.

Burchard (2001) differentiates between venting and complaining in the workplace by arguing that the concept of venting is more complex and multidimensional than are the negativity-tinged concepts of "exploding" and "bitching." Because people are not "necessarily seeking advice or a solution to a problem" when they vent, venting can be primarily understood as "a process of externalizing, through talk, problems and concerns in our lives" (24). Burchard finds that venting serves multiple purposes in the workplace, including helping people understand or feel better about a situation as well as helping build community among colleagues. While he makes a distinction between venting and problem solving – "once the topic moves to discussing solutions, participants are no longer venting" (10) – he fails to acknowledge what would tip the scale to turn venting into "complaining."

As a participant-observer in the staff rooms of the three schools I researched, I recognized both venting and complaining among the teachers and I found that the distinction between them was contingent upon space and audience. In congregational spaces such as the staff room, teachers' cultural patterns are formed (Mawhinney 2008, 196) and set the tone for what is acceptable in speaking about students and work. Because, as Ritchie (2012) has found, it is important for teachers engaged in critical pedagogies to connect with each other, avoiding other teachers is not the answer. But space is a container of school culture (McGregor 2003), so while some have found teachers' lounges important for building professional networks (lisahunter et al. 2011; Mawhinney 2008, 2010, 2012), others identify that they are incubators for toxicity. What version a teacher encounters depends on the larger culture and context of the school (Nourie 2011; Rankin 2016), as well as who they are and what they need from their peers (Mawhinney 2012).

At one point midway through the research period at the mainstream school, I was in the staff room between classes with another teacher. This teacher was frustrated about the extra work she was doing for students who were failing her classes. In trying to sympathize with her, I began making small talk about the structural difficulties of supporting failing students. While she had various complaints about the administration and the school board (and it was these upon which my comment was intended to build), she abruptly broke off her speech, looked me in the eye, and said: "We all know what the problem is. *These* students ..." When she looked at me, it was with an insider's eye, as if I would understand what she was talking about. But I did not. Her statement was so definitive, so cut and dry, however, that I was speechless as to how to respond, let alone challenge. I was not expecting such a self-assured statement that the problems she was having lay with a group of students, with whom my experience had been challenging, but still rewarding. With this comment, the teacher set the climate for the remainder of what could happen in this space.

The different forms of reflection that I overheard in spaces such as the staff room suggest how important the school environment is for courting teachers' self-efficacy and, in turn, their emotional investment in developing classrooms where students can learn meaningfully. In my own experience after a bad day of teaching – a day when my lesson failed, the students overtly disrespected me, my necklace broke and the students had used the beads to throw at each other across the room – I walked into the staff room ready and able to disrespect the students as a way of dealing with my fragile and wounded post-lesson self. It would have been easy to pick up the conversation and talk about students' supposed deficiencies regarding their inability to conduct themselves with the decorum befitting respectful learners. Even while I knew this was not true, I also knew from past experiences that the staff room was a safe space to save face by putting the blame of a bad lesson on the students and not on the ways my practice could be improved in the future.

However, because of the unstated yet pervasive belief that haunts the micropolitical context of schools with a predominantly low-income Black student body like the mainstream school I was in, this conversation would also have become racially coded (J.B. Diamond, Randolph, and Spillane 2004). The pervasive beliefs that Black culture is "anti-school (Majors 2001) and a challenge to authority" and that Black youth are "underperformers, problematic and unteachable" (Wright 2010, 317) were implicit in the comments I heard in the staff room about the inherent talkativeness of Caribbean students, or the lack of care or control parents had over their Black children, or how a program designed to help students through courses was "educational welfare." To complain, to bitch, about that class and my students would have played into these underlying beliefs even if I did not reference them myself. Sharing my experience would have been another example of "these students" and their inappropriate and disrespectful behaviour.

Thus, while I would have liked to vent because I needed to analytically talk through what happened, the staff room would have only been a place for me to complain about students in ways that would have been damaging to my beliefs and relationships with them. This was something I could not do. For me, this would have been too damaging to my own understanding of my role and goals as an educator. I found an empty room and cried instead.

The fine line between complaining and venting is based on one's perception of hope and possibility in education. When complaining, the situation cannot be changed, the students are the problem, the teacher cannot do anything; when venting, the situation could possibly be changed, the students may get better, the teacher sees that there is more s/he can do. The professional climate of the school determines "the commonly accepted hidden norms and beliefs of the school" (Keinan 1996, 312), which then have a direct influence on teachers' daily work with their students. Shapiro (2010, 616) found in her own return to full-time teaching that in the staff room, she and her fellow teachers were "interacting on a very limited basis. We had restricted the scope of our conversation to topics that were safe but shallow." This reflection made her question if "this limited interaction might be related somehow to our preconceived notions of how educators *should* interact – what they *should* think and talk about." Had they created a culture that only made it appropriate to complain or vent when they came together?

While there is a distinction between complaining and venting, I argue that there is a third way of reflecting, a way that the first-year teacher with whom I worked first suggested, a way that has even greater potential to positively influence teachers' practice and the possibilities of meaningful learning, and a way that (Shapiro 2010) suggests is unavailable when we do not provide the space to think about teachers' emotions. This third way is *meditative deliberation,* and it is demonstrated more by its absence than by its presence in this research.

When the first-year teacher called the interviews "rewarding" because of the opportunities they provided for reflecting, she was making a distinction between her staff-room talk and our more quiet and deliberative conversation, which reflected on practice in an attempt to achieve positive changes in the classroom. Thinking of this form of reflection as *meditative deliberation* suggests reflection that is internal, quiet, and deliberate. It suggests the opportunity for teachers to consciously stop and think through a situation in order to come to a greater realization of it and their own role in making change happen. Even though reflection "can have spontaneous and intuitive aspects, it is also a conscious and systematic mode of thought" (Valli 1997, 68). Many teachers are aware of their need for reflection and, when asked, identify the use of reflective strategies such as seeking stillness and seeking focus to restore self and their practice (Gulwadi 2006). Many cite Dewey's (1933, 100–1) work in identifying that the function of reflective thought is to "transform a situation in which there is experienced obscurity, doubt, conflict, disturbance of some sort, into a situation that is clear, coherent, settled, harmonious." As Kutsyuruba et al. (2018, 59) found, "when confronted with difficult situations, the opportunity to step back and mentally prepare for the next challenge had helped some novice teachers in our sample to develop and improve."

Similarly, it was during more meditative deliberation that the first-year teacher and I talked about the gaps between philosophy and practice, community building in the classroom, and the disengagement of certain students. These conversations were not about placing blame, but about understanding the context of teaching and the complexity of students in order to better support the students and their meaningful learning with historical narratives. Teachers need a vocabulary to understand their work. Traditional educational discourses do not permit such thoughtful reflection (van Kan, Ponte, and Verloop 2013). The space to explore different levels of reflection can invite different vocabularies and ways of thinking to develop. It is in this space where the inspiration and support for connection, complexity, and care for the student can develop into student-centric teaching.

Place to Come Together: Caring about Each Other
While time and space are important for developing a practice that can support meaningful learning, another component of this is place: places for teachers and students to come together to see each other outside the teaching task. Teachers need places to reflect upon, build, and participate in community with their students. When the classroom is the only place teachers and students interact, it facilitates a mechanical approach to education that sanctions a technical, rather than value-driven, space of interaction between teachers and students (Biesta 2010). As Lahelma and Gordon (1997, 130) argue, the more rigid the physical layout of the school, the greater the emphasis is on how "bodies of students and teachers present themselves and take space, time and voice."

McGregor (2003, 370) writes that "the school is not fixed and static but the site for dynamic and intersecting networks of practices which articulate in different configurations of power relations." Thus, thinking of place within school is not just about the school's physical layout (although this, too, is important) but also about how the dynamic and intersecting networks of power exist in the place we call "the school." In other words, what are the places, literally and figuratively, where students can interact with their teachers outside classroom time and feel that they unconditionally belong? How does this shape what teachers and students think about each other during class time?

Mawhinney (2008) argues that because of the high emotional cost of teaching, it is important for teachers to have adult-only places in which to build community and provide each other with emotional support. While these places are important, having only these places for "downtime" during the school day can increase the divide between teacher and student and, in doing so, may prohibit imagining a sense of "we" between teachers and students. It is in the out-of-class contexts where teachers and students can "renegotiate their relationship" in ways that are beneficial to their in-class relationships, and have resulted in teachers reporting greater positive relationships with their students (Claessens et al. 2017, 489). For a community of learning to be present in the classroom, teachers and students need a chance to see and interact with each other as people. These interactions can take place during class, but it is also important that they occur outside class as well.

The importance of understanding students as connected and complex people *outside* of class in ways that result in greater invitations for connections and complexity *in* the class was a major difference between the alternative schools and the mainstream school I worked in. In the preceding section I talked about the role the staff room played in turning the time for reflection into spaces for complaining. At the mainstream school, the staff room was a teacher-only place where students were only allowed temporary access if they had to ask a question or drop something off, but never invited in or expected to stay. Often a teacher opened the locked door and waited until the student got what he or she needed before closing it again and resuming lunch. As an "adult-only" place, the staff room allowed teachers to work through the emotional work of teaching, but it also made it all the more easy to complain, or "bitch," about students once the door was closed.

At the two alternative schools, however, I heard venting about the students, their punctuality, quality of work, and attendance and I heard complaining about the administration, board policies, or increased workload, but I never heard "bitching" about the students. One reason for this was because the staff rooms at the alternative schools were not private places. Students at the alternative schools had access to the places teachers ate their lunch, prepared for class, and/or held meetings. These spaces had computers and couches, and an open-door policy that invited students in. Having these shared places provided students and teachers with the space to sit and interact with each other in a less hierarchical, and more humanizing, way. In this way, the more informal boundaries in the different places within the alternative schools contributed to a greater sense of collaborative living and learning among teachers and students than in the mainstream school.

At the alternative schools, there were no staff rooms, lunch rooms, or offices, and classrooms themselves were multi-use spaces in which students took instruction, lounged, and participated in extra-curricular activities. In the three to five shared classroom spaces that made up these schools, teachers and students were able to interact with each other outside of lessons and to learn about each other as multifaceted people with lives and interests outside school. This was as important for the teachers as it was for the students because "the positive feedback teachers receive from their daily contact with students is what gives teachers a sense of satisfaction from their work and the appropriate reward for the effort they make" (Shkedi 1997, 66). Classrooms were places where teachers marked, planned, congregated for meetings, and ran extra-curricular activities. The classrooms were a home base for the school community and held symbolic weight for the mutual respect needed for teaching and learning in ways that centred the students' connections and complexities. This is not surprising given Friedman's (1991, 331) finding that "in a less organized school, behavior patterns are more flexible, and initiatives and spontaneity are more tolerated and common." Friedman highlighted that schools with these characteristics have a lower chance of burnout for teachers than schools with clearly defined power structures and uni-functioning environments. It is in these more rigid institutional environments that there are fewer places to do the emotional work that teachers need to support their pedagogy and practice (Angus 2012, 241).

In the alternative schools the lack of rigidity in teacher and student relationships was mirrored in the lack of rigidity of school places; what came first is a moot point. The more places for students and teachers to interact outside the classroom, the more room there is to bring that understanding into an interactive teaching and learning space for both teachers and students to develop and court a sense of "we" in the learning relationship. This was a key element for the teachers and students at the alternative schools. Students want personal attention from their educators (Fusani 1994). They want to be seen as having lives, interests, and challenges that go beyond one class. Without the places to share this knowledge with educators, education can be about an "us" and "them," not a "we" that can build knowledge together. Alternative schools often started from a "we" because they were places that took students' complexities as the starting point for teaching and learning.

However, this approach to teaching and learning is not always prioritized in mainstream schooling. One alternative school teacher took issue with how easily students' complexities were stripped from institutional discourses about teaching and learning. She was angry that the prevalent educational discourse indicated that teachers could "rise above" students' individual lives to grant everyone the same education, every time, in every class. She said that this "artificial" emphasis is frustrating because it circumvents real issues and the understanding of one's students. She says this emphasis is

> *not real, cuz you know what, these are people, and as much as you tell us we have to do diagnostics and see where the students are at, blah, blah, blah, you don't care where the students are at because you think I should be able to meet every single one of them where they're at and that's not possible.*

In the alternative schools, where students were older and their family lives and backgrounds were integrated aspects of their learner profiles, students' complexities were present and explicit in the classroom. But in mainstream schools, with more students and teachers and fewer spaces to ask for help, these students get left behind, fall through the cracks, and are diagnosed as the problem, not an educational system that does not recognize their needs. One teacher who taught at an alternative school said plainly:

> *I think a conscious goal is to make the classroom feel like the safest place possible to learn and to be one's self. Because I think you learn best when you're yourself. You know, feeling like you're fully accepted.*

She said that this applied especially to the students in the alternative environment because they needed to know that,

> unconditionally, nothing changes no matter what sort of mood they're in. Business as usual, everyone's here, we're all supporting each other. And I think we make a conscious effort to do that because we have a vulnerable population. And it's the best forum to draw on strengths.

With this focus, it was the "cultural and interpersonal substance of the formal and informal curricula" that resulted in "authentic caring relationships" and the possibility of student transformation that courted a communal sense of learning (Antrop-González and De Jesús 2006, 413). This belief in an unconditional environment for teaching and learning is premised on there being an actual environment for students to be their complex selves. This safety in place is a key element for both teaching and learning in meaningful ways.

In the same way that teachers have to invite a class environment where both they and their students are able to teach and learn from each other when connecting with the complexities of the past, teachers also have to feel that their work is being conducted in an invitational environment where they are supported in teaching in meaningful ways for complex and multifaceted people. A teacher's working environment plays a factor in how they are able to realize the vision of teaching they hold for themselves (L.F. Hayes and Ross 1989; Yilmaz 2008), so that if the school has no time, space, or place for research, reflection, and community building, then it makes it difficult for the teacher to explore the connection, complexity, and care that engenders a student-centric, meaningful learning environment. In other words, teachers need support and a professional context to teach in ways that can support meaningful learning and if teachers are burnt out, overwhelmed, and uninspired, they will transfer this energy to the classroom, moving back into a "defensive" and rote way of managing their work (McNeil 1988) and decreasing opportunities for meaningful learning in the classroom.

While teachers in my study did not comment on the increasingly neoliberal culture of accountability in education, this cannot go unnoticed here. In the almost ten years since conducting my research, I have become aware that at least two of the four teachers I worked with had temporarily or permanently left the teaching profession. Tye and O'Brien (2002) found that mid-career teachers leave teaching because of the increased accountability and paperwork and the decreases in scope for teachers' agency and creativity. Over the last twenty years this notion of accountability and paperwork has only amplified, and young teachers are now entering the profession with a normalized sense of test-taking as learning that they encountered during their own schooling (Hawley and Whitman 2019). The culture of accountability means that things like imposed curricula, standardized testing, and a job climate that does not value security often contrast with teachers' understanding of themselves as teachers, and the choices they make in leaving teaching are often part of a resistance to this climate of schooling, not (just) a burnout of enthusiasm (Glazer 2018; K. Smith and Ulvik 2017). In this way, it is the teachers who leave who could have been the most transformational for our students' learning. But the culture of schooling is designed to isolate these very teachers.

It is easy to blame teachers and say that they are not doing enough or not doing it right, but the issue is larger than any individual teacher. Teachers work within a "pervasive stream of beliefs, expectations, and practices that flow throughout a school" that "guides teacher expectations and sense of responsibility in a particular direction" (J.B. Diamond, Randolph, and Spillane 2004, 76) and without an instructional context that supports connection, complexity, and care as the foundation for teaching, teachers will not have or find the time, space, and place they need to direct their teaching toward the student and the larger sense of community they can, and should be, developing through their history class.

Thus it is not always the fault of an individual teacher when meaningful learning is not able to thrive – teachers work in an environment that shapes what is possible, and often meaningful learning is not possible in these spaces. It is, however, the individual teacher who can find ways to prioritize connection, complexity, and care – a "we" for learning – in their teaching and in doing so create more meaningful learning invitations for their students. By committing to this pedagogy in practice, by imagining a new vision of what can be achieved in our classrooms, a teacher can shift the focus in their teaching to be about learning and do so in ways that make best use of the limited time, space, and place that is available to them.

6

Historic Space
Meaningful Learning in Canadian History

Today's students are looking to understand their transnational and (post/neo)colonial identities in Canada in ways that are historically grounded and supported by a network of caring adults interested in helping them make connections to a complex past. However, this desire is often obfuscated by teachers' expectations of students and personal narratives of history, and is exacerbated by an institutional context that fails to provide teachers with the time, space, or place needed to reflect upon and develop teaching that invites students to connect with the complexity of Canada's past. While these barriers are great, by keeping the focus on the students, their meaningful learning, and the "we" they want to see reflected in their Canadian history class, teachers can transform the Canadian history classroom into a place of historical discovery by and with others. By maintaining a focus on learning – *meaningful learning* – as the goal of classroom practice, educators can adopt the tools needed to do radical, transformative work that invites young Canadians to deconstruct and reconstruct Canadian history narratives in ways that resonate with their transnational and (post/neo)colonial lives.

I conclude this book by recommending a model for approaching history education in ways that develop connection, complexity, and care in teaching and learning while also keeping a keen eye on the constraints teachers have on their time, space, and place. Rather than a prescriptive and didactic model where teachers will have to develop new skills or dig into the archives or history books to find more or different histories to teach, this model encourages teachers to *lessen* control of the classroom, lessen control over content, and decentre themselves as the all-knower at the front of the class. This model encourages the activation of students' learning – not the teacher's teaching – by using readily available resources, focusing on students' connections, and creating the space to explore the complexity of history and its re-presentation. This model reduces the emphasis on teachers and frees up their time so that more of their work, both inside and outside the classroom, can go toward reflecting on and coming to know their students as complex individuals. This greater sense of awareness of the complexities we all share will help engender a classroom environment premised on a "we" in both learning and teaching.

With an interest in connection and complexity in both content and instruction, this model aligns with the inquiry focus of today's curriculum, but within a context that challenges and questions the discipline rather than simply learning it. It supports students' needs as learners, lessens teachers' influence on content and instruction, and meets the objectives of the curriculum, all while supporting a radical and transformative engagement with history. In this way, Historic Space invites an engagement of history in ways that can be viewed as a "métissage" of relational and braided experiences rather than as a series of isolated, independent, and competing narratives (Donald 2012).

To introduce this model, I return to my theoretical grounding in postmodernist and poststructuralist theory. These theories are often avoided in pedagogy conversations because of the belief that they may be too complicated for and/or result in navel-gazing by students (Barton 2006; Seixas 2000). Yet, poststructuralism is not as lofty as it appears. The idea of uncovering and challenging popular structures of experiences and ideas can also be found in critical race, feminist, and (post/neo)colonial theories. These bodies of theory point to how discourses and systems define, and have defined, what is considered Truth and what is considered Other. Rather than leaving students discouraged or without the maturity to move forward in the world (Morton 2000), bringing these bodies of theory into the classroom can help young people understand how systems of knowledge and power function in their own lives and give them the tools, and permission, to redevelop these systems so that they make better sense for their futures. To give them the space to seize the rules, "invert their meaning, and redirect them against those who had initially imposed them"

(Foucault 1980c, 151). To conclude this book, I take a closer look at this three-step poststructural approach for teaching and learning history and demonstrate how it can attend to the connection, complexity, and care of students in ways that are mindful of teachers' time, space, and place.

Historic Space in Theory

In the early 2000s, I developed a conceptual framework for history called *Historic Space* based on my experience working at a living history museum and my background in transnational feminist theory. In my museum experience, I saw how strongly people held on to their simplistic, one-dimensional view of the past. With my educational background, I saw how important it was to dismantle and deconstruct these views. Historic Space is a conception of history that blends the simplistic and popular understanding of history with the complexity of the past as a way to peel back the misconceptions and stereotypes of grand, historical narratives and build a more contextual and inclusive understanding of the past and present. In other words, Historic Space begins with the simplistic way history is often taught and learned in schools and uses it as the starting point for deconstructing historical narratives. As Jocelyn Létourneau and Sabrina Moisan (2004, 119) found in their research, students have an established framework for thinking about history through a common set of cultural references or "mythistories." Unless these stories are acknowledged and replaced "with another representation – equally as strong, probably just as simplistic, and more likely structured metaphorically," these initial beliefs will continue to provide the simplistic foundation, however unstable, for students' future learning. Historic Space is a framework for learning history that is based on deconstructing and reconstructing students' knowledge foundations in a way that is strong, simplistic, and structured metaphorically.

History education can often privilege a textbook version of history that re-presents the past as a timeline – a static, linear timeline – where significant people and events are hierarchically ordered and less significant people and events are left out completely. Even with a curriculum that encourages greater emphasis on themes and/or inquiry, teachers often revert to this chronological narrative as a way of structuring their lessons.

The problem with a timeline, however, is that it leaves no room for students to understand the past as being more or different from what is on that line. Yes, more people and events may be added and their significance debated, but these additions often serve to reinforce the logic of the structure rather than re-evaluate the structure itself. For example, Nellie McClung and the Persons Case could be added to a timeline of the early twentieth century as a way of acknowledging the feminist actions during this period. But simply adding her to the timeline fails to explore the complexities of McClung's racist beliefs, which resulted in the forced sterilization of many poor, and mostly Indigenous, women in Alberta. It also fails to imagine the relationship between her fight for Personhood and other contested legislation during this time, such as the Chinese Exclusion Act of 1923, which ended the Chinese head tax but barred any further immigration from China. McClung's addition to the timeline helps support a vision of Canada's continued progress, but it does not challenge how this progress served a larger context of white supremacist actions in the beginning of the twentieth century. While McClung and the Chinese Exclusion Act may seem unrelated, these histories share important similarities that can invite a discussion of Canada's complicated and prejudicial nation-building activities during the late nineteenth and early twentieth centuries. How can we get these histories to interact with each other, to *play* with each other (Derrida 1978), in ways that allow students to explore their significance in the past and the present?

Historic Space is a strategy that takes the simplistic ways people, events, and ideas are re-presented on a national timeline, and rearticulates them as concepts in space rather than facts on a line. Conceptualizing history as space provides the *space* for students to "play" with the past and gives them permission to organize historical information, pull it apart, and reorganize it in a search for new ideas – to construct, deconstruct, and reconstruct historical narratives in ways that make sense to them. Space is social relations "spread out" (Massey 1994, 2) and thinking of history as *space* allows students to understand social relations structured through the narrative and (re)create them in ways in which social relations are more equitable. *Space* insinuates an openness and possibility to chart new ways of reading history and reading the world. Historic Space provides an opportunity for national history to be a backdrop for discussing internalized judgments dictated by hegemonic understandings and to give students the *space* to explore how and why these judgments are made.

By re-imagining grand national narratives as *historic spaces,* a different reading of what history is and what it can do can allow students to explore different ways of understanding and being in the world. This strategy implicitly encourages students to think about the connection between what we know and the ways our knowledge is "disciplined" (Foucault 1980a, 1980b, 1980c, 1995) and how insecure a seemingly secure narrative is (Derrida 1978, 1997).[1] This strategy invites students to challenge the fixity of historical narratives privileged in a chronological textbook version of history and ask:

- Why are these particular stories important for understanding the nation? According to whom?
- Who and what are included? Why?
- Who and what are left out? Why?
- What is common among the absent histories?
- What is common among the included histories?

Structuring history education around these questions teaches students the names and dates of the main story but also helps them learn about the power structures that placed them there. It gives students the opportunity to think about the narrative, connect what they know, and explore the complexity of the past – all things that will produce a truly transformative view of Canadian history. Historic Space is a way of understanding history as a choice between "following prescriptions or having choices" (Freire 2006, 48). Transforming the Canadian history classroom in the service of a more just world does not just mean placing critical histories and critical thinking onto the grand narrative. It means recognizing the grand narrative as a script for the future, a script that can and should be rewritten to reaffirm new possibilities of who "we" are in Canada today and yesterday.

A *historic space* is like a historical period. A *historic space* encapsulates both acknowledged and unacknowledged people, events, and experiences within a set place and time (e.g., post–World War II Canada), and recognizes that some people, events, and experiences *mark* or *guide* significant moments more than others. Unlike the rigidity of a timeline, in a *historic space*, teachers and students can move *marks* and *guides* around to interact with each other and *route* an understanding of the past so that the histories hidden in the shadows can challenge what we know and how we know it, in ways simple additions to a timeline cannot.

A good metaphor for understanding the distinction between the traditional ways we understand history and the way Historic Space presents history is to think of the difference between a book and a magnetic poetry kit. A book can have well-crafted sentences and concise paragraphs, but these groups of words do not encourage a malleable interaction between the student and what s/he is reading. A student can read a book and see a traditional way of telling a story, but they have no way of engaging with that story, to interrupt it or think about alternative endings. In reading the book, they would not be using any organized rhetorical and creative strategies that would democratize the narrative and allow the student to be active in the construction and interpretation of meaning. With a magnetic poetry kit, however, students have the same words, the same punctuation, and, because they are being introduced to these components, they will have a sense of what the story is about. However, with the magnetic poetry kit, students can also *play* with the words, order and reorder them, experiment with punctuation and grammar, and come to alternative interpretations and meanings in ways that make sense to them. With this malleable interaction, students can choose which words they want to use, what they want to say, how they want to say it, and the purpose of what they have written. They are not making up a new vocabulary or resetting the terms of grammar, but rather they are becoming involved with the *construction* of the story, and by becoming involved with the construction of the story, they are able to create greater meaning from what they learn about it.

With Historic Space, students are able to gain the historical literacy needed for understanding the national narrative, but also the critical capabilities needed to explore how hegemonic power functions within those narratives. A timeline can only go one way: forward, marching toward contemporary progress as if that was always the way it was supposed to be. Space invites historical understanding to go forward and backward in time, picking up stories, (re)interpreting them for the present, and thinking about the future as a script waiting to be written.

I have found that the best way to apply these ideas in classroom practice is through concept learning – a set of pedagogical and instructional strategies developed by Hilda Taba (1966) and Jerome Bruner (1990, 1997). Concept learning is based on the idea that everything you see, touch, taste, and feel – the building blocks of knowledge – can be identified as concepts, or the "regularities in objects and events" (Novak 2010, 42). By learning the label placed on these regularities of experiences, our understanding of what an object or event is and how the meaning becomes created and interpreted in reference to other objects, events, or concepts deepens. Historian Claude Bélanger (2000, n.p.) explains that "we might separately learn about tables, chairs, sofas but the process of learning will be facilitated if we arrive at the concept of furniture." Learning through concepts is helpful, according to Hughes (2004, 239), because "long after we have forgotten the details of the events ... there will persist a legacy in the form of the concept."

Concept learning is fundamentally about exploring meanings, assumptions, and relations between and among things, ideas, themes, and classification. It is about defining and laying bare the interwoven components of that which we think we know, but come to find out we know not at all. It is about helping students make sense of large amounts of information by inviting them to lay out the structure of knowledge and then actively negotiate the meanings of that knowledge by testing it against other classifications (Bennett and Rolheiser 2001; Buzan and Buzan 2000; Novak 2010; Taba 1966). Concept learning allows for the transmission of fact and value, but also for an analytical exploration of the ways those facts and values have been constructed, interpreted, and accepted within society.

Concept learning is useful for interpreting poststructuralist ideas because they both draw on the same three assumptions: first, that reality is defined through its linguistic representation and ratified by the majority; second, that the structure of thought defines but also limits one's ability to communicate; and third, that exploring how thoughts are constructed leads to understanding and (re)constructing the world we know. By sharing an interest in coming to know, and challenging, what is known, concept learning can be a way to bring poststructuralist ideas into the classroom. In this way, concept learning can be understood as a form of deconstruction – a way of coming to know what is *not* by understanding what *is*.

Using concept learning, we can instructionally interpret Historic Space in our classrooms (or in our other sites of history teaching, like in an exhibit) with three steps: *mapping, expanding,* and *challenging.* These three steps are based on Hilda Taba's Concept Formation strategy, an inductive thinking model that involves students attaining, interpreting, and applying concepts and conceptual principles as a central focus of their learning (Bennett and Rolheiser 2001; Taba, 1966). In Historic Space, students would *map* the names, dates, and ideas of a historical period (the historical concepts), which would then be *expanded* so that students come to understand more about them. These historical concepts (i.e., the names, dates, and ideas that usually represent the "usual suspects" of a historical period) are then *challenged* by testing how their representation works, or does not work, with histories that are less well known. In doing so, students begin to explore how narratives exclude certain voices and privilege others and how this exclusion or privileging serves our broader understandings of the nation. It is by engaging in all three steps that students gain the historical literacy of a historical period, along with the opportunity to deconstruct and reconstruct elements of this period in a way that reflects the connection and complexity they are looking for.

Historic Space encourages a greater interaction between students and the content *(connection),* greater opportunities to bring in stories that challenge what and how we come to know about history *(complexity),* and a greater impetus to do so in ways driven by a knowledge of students and what they need in their futures *(care).* In this way, Historic Space is a strategy that centres the relationships students build with the content, their teacher, and each other as a key component of their history education. It centres a "we" in thinking with and through history and supports students in understanding their current world within a historical perspective and provides space to do inquiry work driven by students' questions and desires for answers. Novak (2010) writes that for meaningful learning to occur, students need meaningful material as well as the opportunity to negotiate the meaning of that material. Historic Space is a strategy that can do both: provide opportunities for learning content that has greater significance to students' lives as well as opportunities for students to think through and negotiate this content with their class, their teacher, and their prior knowledge.

Historic Space in Practice

Since 2004, I have used Historic Space as a way to teach and learn Canadian history in traditional classrooms, with community groups doing activist work, in lesson plans distributed to expert teachers, in workshops for teacher candidates, and in the curation and interpretation of museum and archival exhibits. In all these experiences, I found that *mapping, expanding,* and *challenging* historic spaces invites greater conversations about the past than traditional teaching, and that it can provide the connection, complexity, and care that students are looking for when learning about the past (Cutrara 2007, 2010).

I now explore the three steps in practice, drawing on my 2011 research in four high-school history classrooms and my 2007 research with individual pairs of students. While not all of the classrooms I worked in focused on Canadian history, the lessons learned from exploring other historic spaces – such as the French Revolution or British imperialism – have augmented the lessons learned from using Historic Space in Canadian history classrooms and further demonstrate how Historic Space creates the space for students to learn history meaningfully, and transformatively, with the past.

Step 1: Mapping

By shifting an understanding of history so that it becomes understood as *space* rather than a line of time, the first step in the Historic Space strategy involves *mapping* a *space*, a historical period, as the basis for students' learning. Like Taba's concept attainment step, *mapping* in Historic Space also involves three sub-steps: gathering, grouping, and labelling. Students *gather* the relevant concepts of a historical period (the names, dates, events, ideas, and themes that are often the focus of a particular time period), *group* them according to themes they see, and then name or *label* these groups to make sense of their relationship. This step is called the *mapping* step, however, because after this grouping, students would take their thematic groups and organize them as a mind map with the time period in the middle and the groups radiating outward. This map would then act as a "note-taking and note-making" tool for the remainder of the unit (Buzan and Buzan 2000).

A good way to start this step is for students to use a resource like a textbook to identify the names, events, and ideas of a historical period.[2] Students would be given a set amount of time, such as fifteen minutes, and flip through the textbook(s) to write down any names, dates, themes, and events they think are important for understanding the period based on how it is presented in the book.[3] They are not reading the book (although some students may), but rather looking for cues of importance based on their understanding of the logic of the textbook. Cues such as bolded terms, photographs, headings, vocabulary lists, and so on, *mark* and *guide* the reader to a particular reading of a historical period. Students instinctively know this even though they do not have knowledge of the period itself. I often have students do this activity by writing the individual concepts (the names, dates, themes, and events) on sticky notes. Writing on and using sticky notes provides a tangible and malleable interaction with the content and, with the notes in front of them, they can move the concepts around into thematic groups, which they would then name. This step often takes a full class, however it is a very active one. Once they have established these groups, students should create a mind map of the historical period; this may take another class. Students should be encouraged to make connections between groups and concepts when they see them.

The intent of this step is to have students build connections with the content before they begin learning it. By going through the chapters in the textbook that cover this period, students become familiar with the main names and dates of the period and make the decision as to which ones are important enough to write down. This step allows students to clarify which concepts belong to which time period and then immediately look for patterns and connections among them, building their own narratives as they make sense of the old. This approach centres students' learning because there is no pressure on the teacher to know, and cover, all the elements of the period. By privileging students' familiarity and comfort with the content at the *beginning* of the unit, there is a democratization of the content, where the teacher is not the one with the knowledge to impart to their students. One teacher I worked with said that this step was "scary" because it was letting "the story" out at the beginning. But by letting the "story" out, we allow that story to morph, change, and develop according to the needs of all the people in the room.

In all four classes, the teachers and I emphasized collaborative learning when gathering and organizing concepts so that students could individually contribute to the whole. Students went through the textbooks and wrote down concepts they thought were important for understanding the period. They then came together in small groups to organize and label them. These steps gave students the independence to determine importance on their own but the collaborative reliance to explore the new content together. In one class, the students had no previous experience with collaborative learning and were shy to work with each other, but once the activity was introduced, students had no problem diving into the activity, and by the time I explained the steps, gave out supplies, and checked in with the teacher, students were busy working with each other and coordinating their individual sticky notes into a series of groupings.

For the students who were unsure about the information they saw in the textbook, this activity provided them with the opportunity to draw on their prior knowledge of the logic of the textbook to organize the information they were seeing in a context that made this information right. In the Canadian history classes, students may not have known who a prime minister was, but by seeing a name in the textbook bolded under a picture, they could determine that this person was significant and write the name down on a sticky note to organize later. During my research, I overheard two students debating whether to write Diefenbaker's name on a sticky note even though they did not know "who he was, what he did." They eventually decided to write his name down and grouped him, and other important figures, in a vague, catch-all category called *Government*. Students could intuit that Diefenbaker would, or could, belong to government and thus they took control of what they did not know by organizing his name in a context that made sense to them. This made students' knowing more important than their not knowing: they knew Diefenbaker was a governmental figure, even if they did not yet know who he was.

In another group, students organized the names/dates/ideas [*Pierre*] *Trudeau, Queen Elizabeth II, Newfoundland becoming a province, potatoes*, and *Diefenbaker* in a category they called *Key People*. When we asked them to explain this seemingly mismatched group, they said that Newfoundland's entrance into Confederation was a politically significant event, equating this with the political significance of [*Pierre*] *Trudeau* and *Queen Elizabeth II*. One student thought of *potatoes* when she thought of Newfoundland and so she combined these concepts together. Later on, students reorganized this category and removed both *potatoes* and *Queen Elizabeth II* from it. Yet neither their first nor their second organization was more "right" than the other. As long as students can articulate the reasons for the connections they are making, there is no "right" in these activities. Maybe the group name should be different than *Key People* if it includes concepts that are not people, but grouping and labelling the concepts of a historic period gives students the power to own their knowledge of the period and organize it according to their own rules. Students can decide if *potatoes* and *Queen Elizabeth II* are equally weighted in terms of importance and organize them accordingly. Although students' broad categories could be interpreted negatively, they allowed students to think about connections and to decide which connections they wanted to make. In a later interview, one student said she liked coming up with concepts and grouping them because it made her realize "how one person can fit into everything."

Because of this step, students start from a place of knowing rather than not knowing when learning about a particular time period. Although students identified "the usual suspects" when generating the concepts, in discussing them together, sharing their personal associations with them, and rationalizing their choices to the teacher, students I have worked with demonstrated their "active pursuit of meaning" with these activities rather than just a rote repetition of fact (Terzian and Yeager 2007, 72). Students in my research also said that generating, grouping, labelling, and mapping historical content at the beginning of the unit helped them understand and invest in the unit in ways they had not previously encountered in a history class. One student recalled: "Picking terms out of the textbook and deciding what's important ... I just had never done that before. And it really helped me, like, memorize things or know what's going on." Another student said that this step resulted in greater class involvement, increased student engagement, and more active thinking. His classmate agreed, calling the activity "a mental hands-on." One of the teachers was so excited about the students' interest and involvement in these activities that she called other teachers into the room to show them students' work and boast about how active the students were in demonstrating their learning.

This *mapping* step serves the important purpose of connecting students to historical content but it also serves the purpose of decentring teachers' narratives for organizing and teaching the period. When students begin a unit by creating a map of a historical period, a *historic space,* according to their understanding and interests, teachers can see where students' interests and connections lie and use this knowledge to organize their teaching in the next, *expanding,* step. Students rarely have the power to choose what they learn in their classes, but the *mapping* step allows both the teacher *and* the students to identify the particular connections in a historical period that the class could focus on.

In one Canadian history class, for example, one student wrote down six different concepts related to post–World War II atomic development. When walking around the classroom I noticed what I saw as repetition in the concepts and commented that he did not have to take so many notes on one subject. He stressed that there were significant differences between the six concepts and that it was important to know them. Standing corrected, I acknowledged the importance of his choices and moved on. By being able to generate the content that he felt was significant, this student provided me, as the educator, with the opportunity to check my own assumptions about the period and to make a greater effort in bringing content into class that was of interest to him. In the following class on the Cold War, I highlighted all six concepts the student had identified in my lecture and indicated that I had done extra research on them because students had added them to their maps. By including this information in my lesson, and by being explicit about why I had included it, I validated students' interests and used their ideas as the foundation for my teaching. The map provided a tool for making students' prior connections visual and, with the visualizing of this knowledge, by actually *seeing* how important certain concepts were for students, I was able to make content decisions that better reflected the students.

Having the mind map as a content organizer also provided opportunities for students to connect their interests to history even if these interests were not explicitly historical. At one of the alternative schools, we focused on the *historic space* of the French Revolution. During my final interview with a student from this class, I asked her if she could fit her experience at a heavy metal concert in with the French Revolution. Without hesitating, she pointed to the concept of *riots* on her map and said that it could connect both the French Revolution and heavy metal. She then said that another connection could be,

> like, rights, like, standing up for something. Because [during the concert] you get really angry and for some reason everyone just has so much energy to, like, live. And it really does feel like you're going to die sometimes and you're just, like, pushing through and everything. So it's like fighting up against something.

Because I am not interested in heavy metal music, this description of the groundswell of emotion based in a desire to "live" provided me with a window into the student's interests outside of class as well as an understanding of how she had been visualizing the French Revolution. Even though I was the educator, the supposed "expert" in the room, I did not have the cultural capital to understand heavy metal concerts and would not have been able to make any connections between such disparate topics. By not allowing these connections to be present in the class, I would have missed a key opportunity for the student to introduce me to different ways of thinking about a time period. This was such a key moment of connection; not just between the student and the content, but between me as teacher and her as student. We found common ground to learn from and with each other. We found common ground for this "we" to result in both of us learning and teaching with and through history and the present. Because *mapping* is a step that enables students to organize and connect their interests to historical content, it provides both teachers and students the chance to explore and negotiate the meaning of historical content in ways that prioritize the personal connections and prior knowledge that students bring to class. This leads to a more meaningful engagement in starting a historical unit.

However, it is important to note that although mapping was received positively by students, it was not a blanket reception across all classes. In the Canadian history class discussed in the preceding chapters, some students said that mapping was boring and "baby work" and they indicated on their surveys that it did not help them learn. During the class where students generated concepts, students actively resisted by refusing to look through the textbook, write down historical concepts, or accept our explanation that this activity would lead to new and more meaningful ways of learning history. When the groups went to organize their concepts in their mind maps, some began running around the class, putting sticky notes on classmates' backs, removing or rearranging concepts on other groups' maps, and generally doing all they could to remove themselves from the learning opportunities we had set up. The failure of the mind mapping lesson in this class was puzzling to me (Ballenger 2009) and prompted me to think about what the students' resistance was telling me about the invisible curricula bound into my instruction (Bernstein 1975).

Upon reflection, I began to appreciate that perhaps because the students felt that they had been subjected to six months of textbook-based Canadian history, starting this activity with the textbook was essentially asking them to validate a version of history that they, rightly, felt excluded them. On top of that, the majority of those previous six months had covered war, something the students were not interested in, and while the post–World War II period took up four chapters in their textbook, the first chapter on the Cold War may have given them the impression that we were going to again cover war, despite our promises that we were going to do something different. Even when they saw pictures, read headings, or skimmed paragraphs that referenced things they were interested in, such as increased multiculturalism or the rise in rock 'n' roll music during the 1950s and 1960s, these students needed encouragement to add these concepts to their maps because their previous experience in that class indicated that their interests would not be privileged.

Thus, another way to introduce this activity would be to start with *connection*. Rather than trying to build relationships with historical content, we could have started with relationships as a way to build history. We could have had students list their interests on the blackboard and then encouraged them to go through the textbook to find names/dates/ideas that aligned with these interests. Because of the logic of the textbook, students would probably have still listed the "usual suspects" in this period, but starting with their interests *first* could have been the signal these students needed to make the choice to learn from us during this activity.

As explored through this book, students in this class were not opposed to learning history, they were just opposed to learning history that had nothing to do with them. In reviewing the list of concepts they did finally generate, prominent concepts such as *cars, Cuban Missile Crisis,* and *bombs* were on students' lists, but also concepts that spoke to the history they wanted; concepts such as *stereotype, tolerance, immigration, Caribbean,* and *boycotting*. While we did this same activity with the same books in two classes, these concepts were unique to this class. Even when students resisted the activity, they still were able to communicate their desire to see and identify the connections they wanted to make during their learning of this historical period. It also provided us, as educators, the opportunity to see how fragile students' perceptions of the content were, and the important role we had to play in validating these connections in the content we covered.

This is the power of the *mapping* step: connection. It gives students the tools and opportunity to create an overview of the period that allows educators to understand students' connections while also giving them a conceptual handle on the main names, dates, and ideas of the period. During the focus groups, students talked about how this step connected them to the content and course in ways that were both unfamiliar and exciting. One student said: "[I like it that] we got to choose what we wanted to talk about, and everyone got to put in their two cents." He then stressed that this was a good strategy for keeping students attentive in a history class because "everyone's going to be involved with it because we all chose it together." This blend of content and connection sets the groundwork for meaningful learning throughout the unit and provides a focus on a new "we" who can learn together.

Step 2: Expanding

The biggest criticism I have heard about Historic Space from people who have not seen it in practice is that it leaves no room to actually learn historical content. I have talked with history educators who interpret Historic Space as being about mapping sticky notes and challenging histories, but not covering the substantive content of a historical period. However, this is not true. Historic Space is a pragmatic strategy designed for students to gain knowledge of a historical period in ways that allow them to *expand* their understanding of a historical period: building out those sticky notes in ways that make *challenging* them more meaningful.

After the initial *mapping* step, three to five class periods should be set aside for *expanding* the historic space by teaching students content from the period. With the historic space *mapped* so that students have an overview of the period, the *expanding* step fills in the blanks of central names, dates, events, or themes. This step is the most like standard teaching practice in that the teacher chooses how and what they are going to teach. However, the *expanding* step deviates from standard practice in that instruction and content should have a keen focus on activating students' learning. Students should understand what is being taught and why, students should not feel that the content being covered is more important than their experiences (something all of us as educators can be guilty of when we are teaching topics we are passionate about), students should be active in articulating their thinking and in making connections with content, and students should trust that their initial conversations related to mapping have been heard and appreciated as part of the lesson(s). By doing so, in this step we keep students' connections at the forefront of how we organize our subsequent lessons and make sure we leave space for students to actively demonstrate their learning by making connections on their mind maps.

Taken together, the four attributes of the *expanding* step – compact instruction, guiding questions, mind maps as note-making tools, and concept maps as summary tools – ensure that the focus is on student learning rather than on teacher teaching and that students are learning a contextualized and connected understanding of the period rather than engaging in simplistic memorization of key names and dates. In this section, I discuss how these four attributes of the *expanding* step worked in practice.

Compact Instruction

We will never be able to teach the full range of experiences and perspectives of any time period. It is impossible. As teachers, we implicitly and explicitly choose elements we want to highlight based on our own interests and understandings, as well as the parameters set by the curriculum. Even when we teach content we find rich and exciting, we often have to teach it in one-dimensional ways because our students do not know the topics well enough to understand the critical details and analyses that have drawn us in. We may feel frustrated by this, but people who have a deep knowledge of a topic can often forget what it is like to not know anything about it; this has been called the "expert blind spot" (Nathan and Petrosino 2003). We often forget that learners have to first understand a basic sketch of a topic before they can go deeper in their understanding.

The compact instruction sub-step of *expanding* a *historic space* involves introducing your students to three to five topics over three to five days in a quick overview of the main elements of a historical period. Students will never learn all the historical details; by using a third of a unit to highlight details, a teacher can provide just enough information for students to learn the main elements of a historic period and to spark potential questions they want to engage in inquiries later on. This approach to teaching the content does simplify the history, but it acknowledges that people come to learn history in simplistic ways before being able to complicate them.

In the two Canadian history classes, we *expanded* students' knowledge of the post–World War II period by focusing on three topics covered over three lessons: the Cold War, the rise of teen culture and rock 'n' roll music, and suburban living. However, because of an unexpected teacher absence, in one class I had to take on the role of primary educator and combine two of these topics into one period. Because we only had one class instead of two, I had to figure out how to connect two topics that are rarely taught together. The result was a lecture entitled "Reds and Rock," which *expanded* students' knowledge of the Cold War and postwar teen culture at the same time.

Because I do not have much interest in, or extensive knowledge of, the Cold War, I created the "Reds" part of the lecture by focusing on concepts that students had identified in the *mapping* step. I used Wikipedia and the students' textbooks to develop this knowledge because, if we had not done the *mapping* step as a way to frame this unit, I probably would not have taught this content at all. While not knowing for teachers "violates a norm" (Loewen 1996, 287), Historic Space encourages teachers to lessen control over the idea that they need to be experts in everything. This perception can preclude them from teaching information they have no knowledge of. Teachers are not (or no longer) gatekeepers of special knowledge.

Students have so much of the world's knowledge on their phones that a teacher's role in the classroom should not be that of expert but as one who faciliates students' learning by telling a story that students can add to themselves. While it was uncomfortable teaching something I did not know about, with students' connections as a guide, I willed myself to be comfortable in ways that validated students' connections as the core focus of that part of the lesson. During the lecture, I highlighted concepts such as *nuclear warheads, atomic bomb,* and *Sputnik,* and pointed them out on the students' mind maps. I found that whenever I began to cover a topic that students had identified during the *mapping* step, students grew more attentive and started asking questions like: "What is the difference between an A-bomb and an H-bomb?" or "How does communism work in daily practice?" I told the students that I could not answer their questions right away, but that I would follow up with answers in the next class. I found that students noticed the attentiveness to their queries more than they noticed my lack of knowledge. Related to that class, one student said in our final group interview: "And then [one student], he asked something and you brought it in. So where people are asking and then they get the information out."

The second, "Rock," part of the lecture was something I knew about, and I focused on race relations and changes to music during the period. While the "Reds" part of the lecture may have isolated students who did not care about war or politics, the socio-cultural emphasis of this part of the lecture ensured all the students heard something that day that they were interested in. One student, a young Black man whose attendance was low, slept through the Reds lecture but woke up and started participating when I introduced the Rock lecture with the top song on the 1951 R&B chart – "Sixty Minute Man" by the Dominos. "Miss, is that a Black man singing?" he asked. "I *know* that is a Black man singing!" The rest of the lecture focused on the appropriation of Black music by white artists in the 1950s, and this student continued to be an active participant by talking about the music he shared with his dad and about how Black folks did "it" (i.e., make music) better. During the lecture, he perked up, moved around in his chair, threw out opinions, and actively engaged in the class. As the students filed out of class, I offered high-fives and he accepted my offer, declaring that I "deserved a high-five" that day.

The dual "Reds" and "Rock" focus was successful for engaging the whole class, albeit at different times, and in creating opportunities for all students to actively learn about the period by connecting to things they were interested in. In the Reds and Rock lesson, I was not concerned with covering every detail of the Cold War or teen culture during the 1950s; I could not have done that if I tried. Rather, the focus was on getting students familiar enough with these topics to build their knowledge, confidence, and relationships with new historical content. They could then build on that content, if they chose, in future assignments. My introduction was simply *expanding* their knowledge of the period.

Students were able to articulate how this *expanding* step was important for them in building their knowledge of the period, negotiating meanings of that knowledge, and developing relationships with the content in ways that held significance to them. During the interviews, one student from this class repeatedly drew on this Reds and Rock lesson to talk about the connections she made between the Cold War, teen culture, and other concepts on her map. She pointed to concepts on her map and explained: "The *music*, like, the '50s music, and how they thought that the Black male singing groups would be, like, a *crisis*. Then there was also a *teen culture*, which was also related to *music* and *pop* and *people*." She took these connections a step further and connected the concept from the period to her own experiences, by saying:

> *A lot of older, more traditional, churchly Black parents, they did not approve [of rock and roll] and so rock was looked down upon, right?*
>
> *And then same like now, hip hop, rap, that kind of music, like, urban music, it was looked down upon when it first came out ...*
>
> *Even now my mom, some artists she does not really like. Let's say Lil Wayne, she'll hear it and then she'll frown upon him, right? And even [though] she was not born during the rock [and roll] age, it still happened before.*

While this student may have been able to make these same linkages after a longer lesson, the connections she articulated demonstrated how we did not need to cover the period in greater depth to understand this historical period as meaningful and connected to her own life. Students never commented about the simplified, shortened teaching of these two topics. Rather, *expanding* their knowledge during these three lessons sparked interest, generated questions, and engendered greater attentiveness to the content that we were able to build on in later classes. When asked about details from this class, the majority of the students were readily able to recall information, make connections, and provide opinions that demonstrated the extent and strength of their learning. We may fear teaching a compact set of history lessons will disadvantage students; but, as I have found, compact instruction gives them the confidence to keep learning, and harnessing this confidence is key to the meaningful connections students want, and need, to make in their history education.

Questions

One of the key components of the *expanding* step involves framing each lesson with questions about how the story functions within the larger structure of the grand narrative. By being asked the question, "What does this new information tell us about the time period and what would we learn about this time period if we did not have this new information?" students are invited to think through new content by actively considering the connections and construction of knowledge. Framing each lesson through questions such as these ensures that students are constantly asked to think about why and how stories come together and how this construction is as important for understanding the period as the individual stories themselves.

The question, "What does this new information tell us about the time period and what would we learn about this time period if we did not have this new information?" may not seem overly complex, but using it to frame the compact instruction of historical topics implicitly prompts other, more complex questions, such as:

- Why are we learning what we're learning? Who does this information serve? Who does this information disadvantage?
- How does this information connect to other things we've been learning?
- What does this information, and these connections, mean to me, my understanding of the past, and my understanding of the present? Does

my history connect to this history? Why or why not? How could it connect?
- What and how does this history show me something I could not see before?

The implicit (or explicit, if one desires) presence of these questions to structure one's lessons works to build and contextualize students' prior knowledge with the new histories as they move through their learning. Thus, by thinking of a history course as a series of questions one poses for, and with, one's students, one can develop a classroom culture that situates students' thinking as the core component of one's practice.

Questions, and the search for answers, make teaching and learning more than simply dropping information into students' heads. It makes teaching and learning a *problem-posing* endeavour that demythologizes the perception of an objective past, present, and future and places students, respectfully, at the middle of interpretation. As Freire (2006, 84) writes, "problem-posing education affirms [students] as beings in the process of *becoming* – as unfinished, uncompleted beings in and with a likewise unfinished reality" (emphasis in the original).

The importance of these questions in contextualizing our teaching in the *expanding* lessons was demonstrated most clearly when the questions were *not* asked rather than when they were. In one Canadian history class, for example, we started *expanding* the post–World War II unit by covering the Cold War. The Cold War was important to this teacher and she was prepared to spend upwards of a week covering it. However, because we were *expanding* our knowledge of the Cold War, we were not supposed to cover this content with as much depth. The plan was to begin the class by posing the question: "What does the Cold War tell us about this period and how does the Cold War link with other concepts and ideas that we previously mapped?" Then, we would only cover the material for a day and use this question to organize our discussion as to how and why the Cold War was important for understanding the period.

However, the teacher started the class by launching into her prepared Cold War lesson and any opportunity for the students to think about a guiding question to recognize that, like all events, the significance of the

Cold War is contingent on (usually unstated) criteria that can be questioned was completely absent. The teacher taught her lesson without an organizing question that drew students into the content and the result was that students received the information like they had done in previous lessons: they half listened, they played on their phones, and they talked to their friends. In other words, because students were not presented with the information differently, there were no opportunities for them to engage with the material differently either and this showed even after the successful *mapping* step.

This class gave me the opportunity to identify how important these guiding questions were for distinguishing between traditional teaching and *expanding* a *historic space*. I wrote in my field notes that "the difference is true versus conceptual" in that, in a standard history lecture, facts are presented, even questioned, but are still meant to be known. In my master's research, however, I found that if I taught history as a series of created concepts, there was more room to bring in complexity and have students negotiate meaning between history and themselves (Cutrara 2007, 2010). While I was prepared for Historic Space to work differently in a class than in my work with individual students, this class presented me with an interesting moment to understand how important these guiding questions were in highlighting the conceptual nature of historical material during the *expanding* step.

Teaching Canadian history so that it is a series of names and dates in a factual chronology that students must unequivocally know makes it difficult for them to learn history in ways that privilege their learning. It makes it impossible to see both connections and complexities of the histories and their relationships with students' lives. When I say complexity, it is not the complexity of the Cold War, for example, that I am emphasizing. Rather, it is the complexity of why something like the Cold War is important to learn, how it fits with a larger understanding of the period, and how it relates (or does not relate) to elements in the present. Framing the complexities of history and the ways it is re-presented as a focal point of learning does not detract from the core information about these histories. Rather it provides scaffolding around that information to support students' investment in the material and ultimately their learning. In this Cold War class, by not inviting students to take up their understanding of history differently, we were not able to have them learn or think through the information differently either, and the result was clear: engagement and investment remained the same, and meaningful learning was precluded.

Mind Mapping

Mapping remains a key element of the *expanding* step. Students start a unit by *mapping* a historic space – creating a visual representation of the people, events, ideas, and themes an overarching resource like a textbook presents as key for the time period. The *expanding* step encourages students to *expand* their map by adding details and connections between and among concepts. This map then serves as a visual organizer for students' learning throughout instruction. Using mind maps as a note-making tool during the unit gives students a safe place to demonstrate and articulate the process and progress of their learning throughout each class.

In the alternative school where we covered the *historic space* of the French Revolution, students created their mind maps of the period by going through the textbook and identifying the main people, dates, events, or ideas they thought were important. To *expand* their knowledge, the teacher showed a documentary over three classes. With the mind maps as an organizing tool, students' individual mind maps became a focal point for watching the documentary. Because students already had a familiarity with the period because of the *mapping* step, when they heard particular names or events mentioned by the documentary narrator they perked up, added them to their map, and asked their teacher more specific questions about them. The teacher occasionally paused the documentary to highlight or provide context for a particular person or event and actively encouraged students to add content to their maps during those moments – not to dictate the connections the students should make, but rather to prompt them for connections they *could* make.

One student found that watching the documentary with her mind map was really helpful, because without it, "it would have gone in the ear and out the other ear ... [but] to have something written on paper was really helpful." Another student said that having the mind map helped him "know the terms [when] making connections and all that stuff." Another student said that with her mind map it "was easier for me to understand things." While pointing to her map, she explained, "there was, like, *hunger*. And then there was ideas of *freedom*. And then there was the *Declaration of the*

Rights of Man. Then there was *Voltaire* in there somewhere, and then something else. And I connected them all." Another student, a student who initially was resistant to creating a mind map because he thought it was childish, added over fifty-five concepts to his map by the time the documentary was over and made complex linkages between concepts and astute observations about their connections, which he shared in later discussions.

This class was particularly impressive in terms of the maps students created to represent their *expanded* knowledge following the documentary, but students across all three schools talked about how the mind maps were helpful for building their understanding of the period during their lessons. As one student said:

> I think that [having the maps] is good because if you have a favourite thing that we learned in history and then there's that map and you do not really like other things, you kind of understand how it led into that thing, even though you do not like it that much.
>
> So you still have an understanding of what went on through that time period. And it keeps linking around so that you understand.

With an emphasis on how things "keep linking around," the maps make students' learning actively present because they have to explore and demonstrate how things can fit together. Students recognized that this type of work was essential for learning. As one student said: "I think a [mind] map would be really important for, like, every unit. Even though it's challenging at points."

While students enjoyed using the mind map as a tool for connecting content during this step, they had different opinions as to how it would work best in future units. I have always envisioned this step taking place individually at the end of all the *expanding* lessons. However, some students said that it should be something to do at the end of each class, others said that it should occur at the end of the week or block of lessons. Some students wanted the maps to be an individual post-lesson review, others wanted to see them used as a teacher-demonstrated pre-lesson introduction. Some students wanted individual maps, others liked the idea of collaborative maps. One student said that working on the map with someone else enabled students to negotiate meaning together, leading to greater connection and understanding; she said: "My opinion and your opinion are two different opinions ... And I'm not saying their opinion was wrong, but if their opinion was wrong, [I could] help them better understand instead of them just trying to learn it." Another student pointed out that with the map, "There is no wrong, really." As long as students are able to explain their connections, the mind map provides a context in which these connections are right. This sense of "right-ness," this sense of being validated in the connections they are making, in sharing and learning from and with others in these connections, is a key element of students' learning. Mind maps help them articulate this learning to themselves as well as to their teachers.

Note that while students' mind maps are designed to be a way for students to have a consistent and personal note-taking and note-making tool to use throughout the unit, in the mainstream Canadian history classes, teachers found that having individual maps was too much to manage. Individual maps worked in one of the smaller alternative schools, but in the Canadian history classes of 30+ students, a class map was better for centring the discussion. To create this class map, the teachers and I showed students the similarities and differences between the individual maps created during the *mapping* step. We then asked students to help us develop one map by voting on the most relevant content to include on the map. The collaboratively created map was then hung in the classroom and printed as a handout for students.

Concept Mapping

The *expanding* step concludes by students demonstrating their learning of the *historic space* by turning their simple mind map into a more complex concept map. Concept maps are graphic organizers that arrange concepts hierarchically with a guiding topic or question at the top of the map. The concepts radiate from this topic/question using linking words and phrases that define the relationships among them – words and phrases like "and," "of," "shows," "is determined by," "may lead to," "implies," or "includes" (Novak 2010). These elements – hierarchy, guiding question, linking words – make concept maps a more sophisticated representation of knowledge than mind maps and thus can help students analytically consolidate their learning following instruction. By transforming their note-making and note-taking mind map into a more sophisticated representation of contextual and networked thinking, students end the *expanding* step by actively interpreting the historical period in ways that are based on their connections.

At the alternative school where we used Historic Space to explore British colonialism and imperialism, we had one large mind map hung in the classroom and, after each lesson, all the students added sticky notes to it to demonstrate their *expanded* understanding of colonialism and imperialism. At the end of the *expanding* step, we then looked at this large mind map and reorganized it as a hierarchical concept map that answered the question, "What are the most important aspects of understanding the political scope of British colonialism and imperialism?" The discussion that followed demonstrated how important this activity was for students to bring together and synthesize the preceding lessons, with everyone weighing in on what was important and how they connected. Students who were laid-back or resistant to the mapping strategy throughout the lessons suddenly grew active and opinionated, contributing to the discussion about placement and priority of the different concepts. It was here where both connection and complexity were able to thrive. If *mapping* deconstructs a historic period, this part of the *expanding* step reconstructs it by drawing on students' learning as a way to define a whole. One student said that with this activity he was able to see "why everything comes together, it's not just like a bunch of little things. It's like everything working as a group, pretty much."

The *expanding* step is the step that teaches the students the foundational content of a historical period and can therefore seem like the most traditional out of all the three Historic Space steps. However, its strength lies in teaching with an eye to students' learning in that teachers should keep their lessons compact, frame their lessons with questions, encourage students to take active notes, and have students synthesize their consolidated learning. By organizing the teaching of content in this way, students are able to learn in ways that allow them to take control of the content, the connections they make with the content, and the complexity within the historical narrative. With this knowledge, with these connections, and an awareness of complexity, students are in a position to dig deeper in understanding the historical period and to *challenge* the traditional narrative of the period.

Step 3: Challenging

A central element of learning history though Historic Space involves *challenging* official narratives by introducing "counterstories" that add complexity to a seemingly neat and progressive view of the past. The power of any narrative is that it constructs "what is, and, almost simultaneously, what ought to be" (Delgado 1989, 2416). The power of *grand* narratives is that they become "habitual, tempting us to believe that the way things are is inevitable, or the best that can be in an imperfect world." In these grand narratives, alternative views "are not explored, or, if they are, [they are] rejected as extreme or implausible" (Delgado 1989, 2417). Thus, *counterstories* are needed to provide alternative views to our grand narratives and in doing so "open new windows into reality, showing us that there are possibilities for life other than the ones we live" (Delgado 1989, 2414).

To open these new windows, however, counterstories cannot just be thought of as new stories added to a solid grand narrative. Research has shown that even if teachers bring in alternative histories to their classes, they often rein in discussion and fail to allow these stories to challenge and complicate what students think about themselves, the past, and the future (Dion 2009; T. Epstein 2009). Thus, counterstories need to be understood, and taught as, stories that actively challenge "what is, and, almost simultaneously, what ought to be" (Delgado 1989, 2416). This *challenge* can be done in two ways. The most obvious is by bringing in histories that are *counter* to the grand narrative, but finding these stories can often be labour-intensive and teachers may not feel like they know enough to teach them. The other way is by looking at the traditional resources one has available (textbooks, Wikipedia, *The Canadian Encyclopedia*), finding the elements of these standard stories that can *counter* the mainstream narrative, and then augmenting these new, challenging elements of the story with primary sources, oral histories, guest speakers, and/or field trips. This approach gives more of a starting point for deconstructing the grand narrative and can allow for more discussion about the inclusions and exclusions hidden in the stories we are taught. It is this *deconstruction* – the witnessing of the instability of the grand narrative and seeing the ways the Other is purposefully absent – that is the key element of this step.

With the Historic Space strategy, half of the classes in a unit should be devoted to this *challenging* step. Students should explore, talk about, research, and demonstrate their learning of counterstories and how they *challenge* standard tellings of the period. This is where inquiry is most helpful. Students can use a variety of primary and secondary resources to ask and explore questions that challenge their ideas of the past. Students are looking for interesting material that connects to them and acknowledges the complexities of life in the past and the present. The *challenge* step can explicitly provide these activities and content by centring the exploration of histories about race, gender, and class missing from many discussions in a Canadian history class. This integration allows students to talk about the power and privilege that keeps these stories sidelined, but also the power and privileges that remain *because* these stories are sidelined. It is the acknowledgment of race, gender, class, power, and privilege that results in challenge, complexity, and counterstory to our study of history, not just the integration of hard-to-find histories. With the redeveloped concept map completed at the end of the *expanding* step, students can be invited to fit the challenges onto their maps and reconstruct the historic spaces to be inclusive of the stories that challenge the way we traditionally understand them.

In each of the classes in which I worked, I suggested two challenges per class, with one challenge as a one or two-class lesson and the second challenge as the basis for a larger cumulative assignment or class project. Because I was the second educator in the class, I was able to conduct primary and secondary research outside class and to identify new resources to support these challenges. However, all the topics we identified were found in the class textbooks, usually as a footnote or in a special section, and could be easily augmented with primary and secondary sources found in public-domain internet searches. For example, in the alternative school where we covered the French Revolution, we used Théroigne de Méricourt as a one-day challenge and the Haitian Revolution as a multi-day challenge. Méricourt was mentioned in a call-out box in the textbook and the Haitian Revolution was the next chapter in the textbook. I was surprised by the connections the French and Haitian Revolutions shared – because we learn histories as separate *spaces* with distinct narratives – and so this challenge started with my surprise and we were able to bring in rich discussions by getting students to articulate the similarities and connections between these revolutions.

In the Canadian history classes at the mainstream school, our two challenges were the West Indian Domestic Scheme as a one-day lesson and Africville as a two-day lesson/class project. I brought these suggestions to class based on my interest and experiences with these histories in my 2007 research. I was specifically interested in covering the West Indian Domestic Scheme as a history that could challenge the dominant narrative of domesticity in the post–World War II period. As a government policy enacted between 1955 and 1965 to bring Caribbean women to Canada on a short visa for domestic work, this challenge would feature stories of working women of colour – stories that are often absent from the grand narrative. I saw this history as demonstrating *complexity* in three ways: first, we could teach about the history of twentieth-century Canadian immigration policy and the rarity of ethnically diverse immigration prior to the 1960s; second, as a policy that attracted single, British-educated women from the West Indies to immigrate to Canada, we could teach about the imperial connections between Canada and Caribbean countries under British rule; third, the similarities between this immigration arrangement and the current Live-in Caregiver Program could demonstrate the changes of Canadian legislation over time. With these complex narrative strands coming from one piece of history, students who were interested in histories of immigration, settlement, struggle, self-determination, transnational identities, and "hidden" stories marked by racial and gendered injustice could find a connection, even if their ethno-cultural background was not the same as that of the West Indian women featured.

Because of the timing of the class and my familiarity with this topic, I took the lead in both Canadian history classes. I gave an overview of the changes to Canadian immigration policies in the post–World War II period, I explained the goals of the West Indian Domestic Scheme, and I used primary sources to narrate the women's experiences. I created a worksheet to frame students' listening and an exit sheet for them to summarize their learning. These tools gave students the opportunity to demonstrate their connections with the content and provide opinions on the complexity of the history they were learning. We used these tools for students' learning and engagement, rather than for evaluation.

In the students' worksheets and exit summaries following class, students wrote that they found the class interesting because "I learned about what my ancestors went through back then" and that the class reminded them of "the days when my grandma was alive." One student wrote that they found class interesting "because I'm Black." Other students wrote that they found the class was important because "I never knew anything about this content. + It's about Caribbean background. That makes it interesting." Students were able to articulate the complexity of state-to-human relationships that I had hoped was conveyed during the lesson by writing things on their worksheets like: "[the government] probably thought the women did not have a plan but they worked there for a year so they could better their life and also travel." In their exit paragraphs, students demonstrated that they were able to connect that day's lesson with the present, by saying they found the history "interesting because the old immigration policies appeared to be racist and today Canada is mainly composed of immigrants."

The levels of understanding students demonstrated in a simple one-page exit sheet indicated how much they were interested in and able to connect with complex material when given the opportunity. They were students with low literacy levels who did not hand in assignments and who were close to failing. These were the same students, however, who asked for more Black history every day and who demonstrated their cultural capital by talking about their familial countries of origin. These were students who wanted to learn history, but these were also students who acted out their frustration that the history they were taught in their history class held no meaning for them.

This class on the West Indian Domestic Scheme was not perfect – there were still students who talked through the class, who had difficulty finishing the worksheet, or who completed it with rote comprehension. On their exit surveys, students were honest in saying that I could have done better: "Sometimes slow down and give more examples that relate to us now in our day to day lives so we can have a better understanding of the lesson." However, the level of invested thought demonstrated by many of the students in their work supports the premise that students like the opportunity to be presented with a challenge that could connect them to the complexities of their identities. As one student said, she enjoyed learning about immigrant women from the West Indies because "I'm from the West Indies, it kind of, like, relates to me."

Like with the other two steps, students' concept maps should be used during and following the *challenging* lessons to make and demonstrate their connections with and between the content. I had envisioned that this element of mapping the *challenges* would give students the opportunity to see the difficulties of fitting challenges into a dominant historical narrative. This would then serve the purpose of students being able to see the ways the grand narrative is constructed to keep some stories out and others in. Thus, it was both my expectation – and my goal – that these challenges *would not* fit into their maps, and it was in this lack of fit where students' learning would lie.

However, in this expectation I underestimated how much students would grow to see their concept maps as the representation of their thinking and thus the depth of their commitment to ensure this complexity was part of their map. In other words, I underestimated students' ability and desire to learn and construct historical knowledge that *challenged* them and the grand narrative. But by listening and watching students and how they were able to construct their meaningful learning through Historic Space, I was humbled to see the ways they demonstrated the connections and complexities of what they had learned about the historical period through their concept maps.

In my 2007 research, I had also used Africville as a *challenge* to the post–World War II period. After watching film footage of residents being removed from their homes and bulldozers destroying public buildings, I asked students to identify where Africville could fit on their maps. Again, I had not expected students to fit this onto their map. However, I found that, in comparison to other concepts, students took greater care in thinking of how to add Africville to their concept map of the period.

During the *mapping* step, students often expressed difficulties as to where or how certain concepts should be placed. They constantly asked each other and me to validate their choices when organizing their concepts. However, when asked to place Africville, students demonstrated a respectful and deliberate demeanour and acted with reverence about where Africville could fit. To reconcile the difficulties they were facing, students added new concepts to their maps, such as *racism*, and/or broadened their definition of other concepts, such as *land issues*, to link *Africville* to something that they felt better demonstrated the importance of this history. Many students had an emotional response to the difficulties and responsibility they felt in adding this history to their maps. One student who was white said that she was "broken inside" for not adding any concepts related to Black history on her initial mind map, even though she remembered seeing concepts about Black history in the textbook. She said it was "so sad" that she did not think of this moment in history as being important enough to add to her initial mind map, repeating: "[I feel] so broken now. I feel so broken inside that I did not mention this."

The concept maps also provided a talking point for students to consider historical exclusion. They often gestured toward their maps and used descriptors like "offside" or "to the side" to demonstrate how Africville was not part of the mainstream narrative of the period. One student, who was Black, highlighted how racism was not part of the mind map he and his partner had created from concepts in the textbook. Gesturing to the side where they had added *racism* following the film about Africville, the student angrily said:

> *We are not learning enough about this in school because the first things we think about were things like this, and all of these other things on this side, and whereas, we only have two small points on racism.*
>
> *And, like, the whole mind map is, like, taken up by things we learned, when really, some of the most important things ... would be more to this side, like with racism.*

With the map as a tool to visualize the separation of Africville from the dominant narratives of the period, the student was able to see and articulate his anger as to how the stories and experiences of racism were sidelined from dominant history. He may have felt or seen this before the activity, but the concept map allowed this exclusion to be visual so that we could talk about it in ways we may not have been able to before. Thus, concept mapping during and following the challenges provided greater opportunities for the students to talk about the inequity in mainstream history because "everything is laid out for you," as one student said. In comparison to a chronological timeline, *challenging* mainstream history by using maps of historic spaces made it easier for students to discuss and learn about/from inequity because, as one student commented: "In a timeline it would be hard to see [racism] because [a timeline] is just the plain things that happened, but like how did they *relate?* It's just all random." Her classmate followed up by saying, "Also because racism is an ongoing thing not just one moment."

By *challenging* the maps they made of *historic space,* students begin to see and work with the dominant structures of power that left these stories out. They also get to learn counterstories and view them as part of, and important to, the Canadian story. In this step, students learn new stories, learn the complexity of these stories, in ways that force their interruption of mainstream narratives. In this way, the *challenge* step moves beyond the add-and-stir approach to histories of racial, gendered, or classed minorities, because these stories challenge what is known and can be known in the mainstream narrative and in doing so, demand new ways of seeing, believing, and accounting for the possible in the past, present, and future.

Teaching is difficult work. The demands on one's day, adhering to the curriculum, communicating to multiple learners with multiple needs, maintaining standards of good practice, and meeting administrative demands all influence what happens in the classroom. As every good educator knows, even with the best of intentions, class does not always go the way you want it to go. There are so many variables that it is humorous to ever plan for perfection. And in a subject like history, fraught with popular demands about what should be taught and how, teachers face even greater pressure to get it "right": to hit that sweet spot of content and instruction that enables the building of proud citizens and critical thinkers.

Fetishizing "right" methods of teaching is especially appealing when teaching students who challenge one's vision of good practice (Bartolomé 1994); however, the last thing I want this book to be is a handbook that prescribes the "right" combination of content and instruction for teachers to teach Canadian history "right." It is not better or more evidence-based instruction that is needed in our classrooms, but a value-driven approach that is more holistic and inclusive of who we are, *together*, in our classrooms (Biesta 2010) – who we can be in learning from and with each other in exploring the Canadian past; how our classrooms can be set up to privilege greater connections, complexity, and care in how we activate meaningful learning for our students; and how we can hold space for transformative teaching practices when institutional structures often do not grant us adequate time, space, or place to do this work as effectively as we want to.

If anything, I hope this book suggests that one needs to *lessen* one's control over one's teaching if one wants to teach in the service of meaningful learning. One does not need to pathologize students or try to save them; one does not need to scour archives and libraries to find the most obscure histories to teach (something one will not have the time to do anyway); one does not have to take a workshop to learn the newest method of ensuring student success (whatever "success" means at that moment). One just has to believe in students' inherent ability and desire to learn Canadian history in ways that makes the most sense to their futures. But we do not need to know or predict what those futures will be or what sense can be made of them. It is just our job to create a learning environment that privileges connection, complexity, and care in how students are able to take up our unconditional invitations to learn meaningfully from and with the Canadian past.

I end this book with the Historic Space model because it has been an instructional and narrative tool that has engendered meaningful learning in many traditional and non-traditional sites of education. Admittedly, however, Historic Space is also a model that will not work for all teachers. The teachers at the alternative schools, for example, found it too restrictive for their classroom environment – but their classroom environments were *already* set up to privilege connection, complexity, and care. This is what happens in *alternative* teaching and learning spaces. Whether or not Historic Space is an instructional model that would work for your own classroom practice, it demonstrates how one can introduce connection, complexities, and care into the history classrooms in ways that centre students' learning and take into account the limitations on a teacher's time, space, and place. This is a transformative vision of what the Canadian history classroom could look like.

Thus, to move forward with our teaching, I ask: What would your practice look like if you entered your history class believing that all the students were interested and willing to explore the national narratives of the past and present in order to use this knowledge for the future? What if you believed that all students held connections to Canada and that they wanted these connections acknowledged and explored in the classroom? What if you walked into class wanting to understand how complex your students were and how this complexity could be connected to national narratives? What if you privileged learning in your classroom, not teaching? This book is about thinking of those possibilities, believing in those possibilities, *creating* those possibilities for imagining a new "we" in facilitating learning in our Canadian history classrooms. It is with this belief in mind that we can transform the Canadian history classroom to be one that speaks to the transnational and (post/neo)colonial youth of the future.

This project has multiple layers to it. On the one hand, it is advocating for a critical and poststructuralist approach to history education that challenges and deconstructs the discourses and structures that frame our lives. On the other hand, it is about classroom practice and how it can support or curtail possibilities for meaningful learning in the Canadian history classroom. However, underlying this work is a concern for students and the ways that we, as educators, can better recognize and be responsive to what they need and want from history, education, and the educators who can facilitate their learning.

The significance of this work is thus: if time is spent fixing history teaching, then time is not spent on thinking about history *learning* and what can best facilitate the meaningful learning that students need for moving forward in their lives. I recognize that this conception of meaningful learning with national history seems to be of particular importance for students who have been marginalized in the nation, but meaningful learning is important for *all* students – important for them to come together and connect their presents as a product of the complex past.

Meaningful learning with historical narratives is based on a relational, political, and affective interaction with historical content and the teachers and students in the room. Meaningful learning can be facilitated regardless of the curriculum, textbook, or political climate because it involves the choice of both the student *and* the teacher to recognize the special place they share in negotiating meaning with and for each other when learning and teaching history. Meaningful learning is based on connection, complexity, and care of the students and the histories they carry, the histories they want to know, and the histories that connect them with their classmates. Meaningful learning is also based on care for the teacher and a commitment to creating institutional structures that give teachers the time, space, and place to do the work they need to do to explore Canada's past and present with their students. Transforming the Canadian history classroom requires imagining us, together, learning meaningfully with the narratives that shape our lives in Canada.

As educators, historians, as adults in Canada, we do not have to convince young people that history is important. We have to make history important enough for them to learn. This is our challenge, not theirs, because, as one student told me: "We come to class to get educated and you're going to have to bring it to the table."

Notes

Chapter 1: Meaningful Learning

1 "Postcolonialism" is a body of theory that signifies the literary and cultural "subaltern" conditions after the formal conditions of coloniality have passed (Loomba 2002). However, the "post" in "postcolonialism" may seem to signify the complete absence of colonialism and coloniality in the present. In Canada, as elsewhere, the ongoing effects of colonialism, the new forms of colonial control, and the continued presence of colonialism in shaping the conditions of our lives as settlers and as Indigenous peoples is ongoing. Thus, in this book, I refer to these conditions as "(post/neo)colonial" to signify the after-effects, new experiences, and ongoing relationships with colonialism and coloniality that still shape our lives.

2 This quote is commonly attributed to Duncan Campbell Scott, deputy superintendent of the Department of Indian Affairs from 1913 to 1932, who was anxious to find a solution to Canada's "Indian problem." It has become a popular quote to use when describing the Indian Residential School system in Canada. See for example the "Historical Overview" from the Truth and Reconciliation Commission, http://www.trc.ca/websites/trcinstitution/index.php?p=39.

3 See Ann L. Brown (1992) and Allan Collins (1992) for early work on "teaching experiments."

Chapter 2: The Present of Today's Past

1 See the debates between Granatstein (1998) and Stanley (2000).

2 For more on the lack of peacekeeping under Harper's leadership, see Dorn (2005), Koring (2012), and Shephard (2014).

3 Many described the tactics under Stephen Harper's government, especially in the last four years of his reign, as an "abuse of power." For more see Beers (2015).
4 See for example, the experiences of Indigenous vendors during the 2015 Pan Am Games hosted in Toronto (Battersby 2015; CBC News 2015).
5 In particular, I am referring to Harper's repeated refusal to establish an inquiry on missing and murdered Indigenous women despite calls from the general public, lobby groups, provincial leaders, Amnesty International, and even the United Nations.
6 Both Alberta and Manitoba also pledged to make residential schools a mandatory topic of study following the recommendations from the Truth and Reconciliation Commission, however neither province's announcement gained the same amount of national attention in the press.
7 This summary is based on a discursive review of mandatory history and social studies curricula across all the provinces conducted in July 2015. It includes elementary school and secondary school curricula, but not elective secondary school courses. My review focused on history curricula within the social studies course lists; however, I also reviewed large-scale objectives for social studies writ large. If there were multiple revisions of the curricula or curricula that were under review or consideration, I reviewed each one.
8 The most noticeable difference was Quebec secondary school curricula that emphasized time periods from pre-contact to Quebec's current populations.
9 For more information about this study see Lee and Ashby (2000), Ashby, Lee, and Dickinson (1997), and Lee (1991, 1998, 2003, 2004).
10 As Justice Murray Sinclair said at the Truth and Reconciliation Commission's closing ceremony, these questions are precisely the questions that cannot be answered for generations of Indigenous peoples affected by the colonial policies and practices of residential schools (Sinclair, Wilson, and Littlechild 2015). As will be discussed later, the objectivity argument of the discipline of history is untrue when it comes to peoples and experiences deemed irrelevant for history, including the histories of Indigenous peoples, women, and other minorities, making skills-based learning as pedagogy and praxis unhelpful and potential harmful for student learning.
11 No theorists are directly cited in the Alberta curriculum documents, however, the curriculum links to thirty-seven teacher resources created by scholars who have worked closely with Seixas, including Alberta scholars Amy von Heyking and Carla Peck.

Chapter 3: Students Speak

1 You can learn about pirates in twentieth-century Canada, however; see Colin (2009). Also see Dalby (2016) to learn about Canada's seventeenth-century "pirate queen."
2 See Warikoo (2011) for similarities between these youth and other youth of colour in large cities such as New York and London.

Chapter 4: Teaching the Others in the Room

1 One teacher at an alternative school said that she agreed to participate in my research specifically because I did not converse in edu-speak when talking to her.
2 Ellipses represent pauses in Erin's speech.
3 Erin was reflecting on her practices before the prominence of the historical thinking concept related to "historical significance." This comment should not be read in the context of doing explicitly historical thinking work.
4 One student told me in our focus group that she did not complete the assignment because: "I called my grandma back home [in Trinidad], but she told me she doesn't want to tell me about it, I don't know why. Probably she had a horrible experience or something, but, she don't want to tell me." The student attempted the assignment but was met with resistance and was unable complete it; however, with an unfinished assignment, if it was graded, the student would have been given a zero, which would not have reflected her attempt at completion. With personal assignments such as these, educators have to be cognizant of ways to accommodate silences as well as stories in order to respect the diversity of experiences that students' histories will represent.
5 Citation not provided in order to protect the anonymity of research participants.
6 Granatstein's book, along with Michael Bliss's 1991–92 article, "Privatizing the Mind: The Sundering of Canadian History, the Sundering of Canada," caused an uproar in the Canadian history community in the 1990s. Both authors lamented the "killing" or "sundering" of Canadian history on behalf of "politically correct" multicultural and gender-focused histories and called for a return to a straightforward, unquestionable national history. It was unclear if Erin appreciated or even knew about the history and conservative legacy of this book, but my feeling is that she did not. She said that she read the book when she began teaching and that she did not think that even Granatstein knew "whose histories [you should] teach." When I challenged her that indeed he did know and that was the thesis of his book, she agreed he did know, but she did not know, and that this

was her challenge as a twenty-first century teacher. Again, I think she found usefulness in the question, but without knowledge of the politics behind it.
7 It is important to note that this rationale also vanished when faced with a "who" who were not white. While the school had a significant Black student population, Erin talked about teachers being "uncomfortable" teaching about Black history in her schools because of the "controversial climate of having 70% [of the students] representing the school being Black and that kind of backlash they might get around that." While unable to fully articulate what her fear was with these inclusions – for example, who would get backlash, for what, by whom – Erin acknowledged the tensions, controversies, and discomfort she felt when a "who" who did not represent mainstream Canadian history was "spotlighted." For more on how Erin centred whiteness in her approach to teaching Canadian history see Cutrara (2020).

Chapter 6: Historic Space

1 See Cherryholmes (1988) for an exploration of Foucault's and Derrida's work interpreted for education.
2 While many teachers want to do away with the textbook when engaging in transformative teaching and learning work in a history classroom, there is a familiarity and stability of the textbook that works as a foundation for the grand narrative needed to do this work. If teaching online, this can also be done with websites such as Wikipedia and the Canadian Encyclopedia or through Canadian history documentaries such as *Canada: A People's History*.
3 I have also used multiple textbooks in the same class. Multiple textbooks can highlight to students the repetition of the same narrative across resources, as well as potentially introduce them to new stories.

Works Cited

Abu El-Haj, Thea Renda. 2007. "'I Was Born Here, but My Home, It's Not Here': Educating for Democratic Citizenship in an Era of Transnational Migration and Global Conflict." *Harvard Educational Review* 77 (3): 285–316.

Ahmad Ali, Mehrunnisa. 2008. "Second-Generation Youth's Belief in the Myth of Canadian Multiculturalism." *Canadian Ethnic Studies* 40 (2): 89–107.

Almarza, Dario J. 2001. "Contexts Shaping Minority Language Students' Perceptions of American History." *Journal of Social Studies Research* 25 (2): 4–22.

An, Sohyun. 2009. "Learning US History in an Age of Globalization and Transnational Migration." *Journal of Curriculum Studies* 41 (6): 763–87.

Andersen, Rachel J., Ian M. Evans, and Shane T. Harvey. 2012. "Insider Views of the Emotional Climate of the Classroom: What New Zealand Children Tell Us about Their Teachers' Feelings." *Journal of Research in Childhood Education* 26 (2): 199–220.

Anderson, Benedict. 2003. *Imagined Communities: Reflections on the Origin and Spread of Nationalism*. Rev. ed. London: Verso.

Anderson, Morgan. 2015. "The Case against 'Critical Thinking Skills': In Pursuit of a Humanizing Pedagogy." *Philosophical Studies in Education* 46: 83–89.

Andrew-Gee, Eric. 2015. "How Canadians Celebrate Their Identity – It's All in the Hyphen." *Toronto Star*. Last modified May 2, 2015, accessed July 2, 2015. http://www.thestar.com/news/gta/2015/05/02/how-canadians-celebrate-their-identity-its-all-in-the-hyphen.html.

Andrews, Rhys, Catherine McGlynn, and Andrew Mycock. 2009. "Students' Attitudes towards History: Does Self-Identity Matter?" *Educational Research* 51 (3): 365–77.

Angus, Lawrence. 2012. "Teaching within and against the Circle of Privilege: Reforming Teachers, Reforming Schools." *Journal of Education Policy* 27 (2): 231–51.

Antrop-González, René, and Anthony De Jesús. 2006. "Toward a Theory of Critical Care in Urban Small School Reform: Examining Structures and Pedagogies of Caring in Two Latino Community-Based Schools." *International Journal of Qualitative Studies in Education* 19 (4): 409–33.

Ares, Nancy, and Jeffrey Gorrell. 2002. "Middle School Students' Understanding of Meaningful Learning and Engaging Classroom Activities." *Journal of Research in Childhood Education* 16 (2): 263–77. doi: 10.1080/02568540209594989.

Ashby, Rosalyn, Peter Lee, and Alaric Dickinson. 1997. "How Children Explain the 'Why' of History: The *Chata* Research Project on Teaching History." *Social Education* 61 (1): 17–21.

Audlaluk, Larry. 2005. "Q & A with Larry Audlaluk." In *Naniiliqpita*, edited by Maria Quqsuut. Nunavut: Nunavut Tunngavik Inc.

Aultman, Lori Price, Meca R. Williams-Johnson, and Paul A. Schutz. 2009. "Boundary Dilemmas in Teacher-Student Relationships: Struggling with 'The Line.'" *Teaching and Teacher Education* 25 (5): 636–46. doi: 10.1016/j.tate.2008.10.002.

Austin, David. 2010. "Narratives of Power: Historical Mythologies in Contemporary Québec and Canada." *Race and Class* 52 (1): 19–32. doi: 10.1177/0306396810371759.

Ausubel, David P., Joseph Novak, and Helen Hanesian. 1978. *Educational Psychology: A Cognitive View*. 2nd ed. New York: Holt, Rinehart, and Winston.

Ballenger, Cynthia. 2009. *Puzzling Moments, Teachable Moments: Practicing Teacher Research in Urban Classrooms*. New York: Teachers College Press.

Ballingall, Alex. 2020. "'Reconciliation Is Dead and We Will Shut Down Canada,' Wet'suwet'en Supporters Say." *Toronto Star*. Last modified February 11, 2020, accessed February 15, 2020. https://www.thestar.com/politics/federal/2020/02/11/reconciliation-is-dead-and-we-will-shut-down-canada-wetsuweten-supporters-say.html.

Bannerji, Himani. 2000. *On the Dark Side of the Nation: Essays on Multiculturalism, Nationalism, and Gender*. Toronto: Canadian Scholars' Press.

Barab, Sasha, and Kurt Squire. 2004. "Design-Based Research: Putting a Stake in the Ground." *Journal of the Learning Sciences* 13 (1): 1–14.

Bartolomé, Lilia. 1994. "Beyond the Methods Fetish: Toward a Humanizing Pedagogy." *Harvard Educational Review* 64 (2): 173–95. doi: 10.17763/haer.64.2.58q5m5744t325730.

Barton, Keith C. 2006. "After the Essays Are Ripped Out, What? The Limits of a Reflective Encounter." In *Social Studies – The New Generation: Re-searching in the Postmodern*, edited by Avner Segall, Elizabeth E. Heilman, and Cleo H. Cherryholmes, 241–44. New York: Peter Lang.

Battersby, Sarah-Joyce. 2015. "Pan Am First Nations Festival Too 'Tucked Away,' Say Exhibitors." *The Star*. Last modified July 22, 2015, accessed July 22, 2015. http://www.thestar.com/news/gta/2015/07/22/pan-am-first-nations-festival-too-tucked-away-say-exhibitors.html.

Battiste, Marie. 2004. "Animating Sites of Postcolonial Education: Indigenous Knowledge and the Humanities." CSSE Plenary Address, Winnipeg, Manitoba, May 29, 2004.

Beauboeuf-Lafontant, Tamara. 2002. "A Womanist Experience of Caring: Understanding the Pedagogy of Exemplary Black Women Teachers." *Urban Review* 34 (1): 71–86.

–. 2005. "Womanist Lessons for Reinventing Teaching." *Journal of Teacher Education* 56 (5): 436–45.

Beck, Mitchell, and James Malley. 1998. "A Pedagogy of Belonging." *Reclaiming Children and Youth* 7 (3): 133–37.

Beers, David. 2015. "Harper, Serial Abuser of Power: The Evidence Compiled." *The Tyee*. Last modified August 10, 2015, accessed August 14, 2015. http://thetyee.ca/Opinion/2015/08/10/Harper-Abuses-of-Power-Final.

Bélanger, Claude. 2000. "Concepts in Social Science and History." Events, Issues and Concepts of Quebec History. Marianopolis College. Last modified August 23. http://faculty.marianopolis.edu/c.belanger/quebechistory/events/concepts.htm.

Bell, Derrick A. 1980. "Brown v. Board of Education and the Interest-Convergence Dilemma." *Harvard Law Review* 93 (3): 518–33.

–. 1987. *And We Are Not Saved: The Elusive Quest for Racial Justice*. New York: Basic Books.

Bell, Lee Anne. 2003. "Telling Tales: What Stories Can Teach Us about Racism." *Race Ethnicity and Education* 6 (1): 3–28. doi: 10.1080/1361332032000044567.

Bennett, Barrie, and Carol Rolheiser. 2001. *Beyond Monet: The Artful Science of Instructional Integration*. Toronto: Bookation.

Berg, Maggie, and Barbara K. Seeber. 2016. *The Slow Professor: Challenging the Culture of Speed in the Academy*. Toronto: University of Toronto Press.

Bernstein, Basil. 1975. "Class and Pedagogies: Visible and Invisible." *Educational Studies* 1 (1): 23–41. doi: 10.1080/0305569750010105.

Biesta, Gert. 2001. "'Preparing for the Incalculable': Deconstruction, Justice, and the Question of Education." In *Derrida and Education*, edited by Gert Biesta and Denise Egéa-Kuehne, 32–53. London: Routledge. Original edition, *Zeitschrift für Erziehungswissenschaft* (1998).

–. 2009. "Deconstruction, Justice, and the Vocation of Education." In *Derrida, Deconstruction, and the Politics of Pedagogy*, edited by Michael A. Peters and Gert Biesta, 15–38. New York: Peter Lang.

–. 2010. "Why 'What Works' Still Won't Work: From Evidence-Based Education to Value-Based Education." *Studies in Philosophy and Education* 29 (5): 491–503. doi: 10.1007/s11217-010-9191-x.

Bliss, Michael. 1991–92. "Privatizing the Mind: The Sundering of Canadian History, the Sundering of Canada." *Journal of Canadian Studies* 26 (4): 5–17.

Booker, Keonya C. 2006. "School Belonging and the African American Adolescent: What Do We Know and Where Should We Go?" *High School Journal* 89 (4): 1–7.

Bosworth, Kris. 1995. "Caring for Others and Being Cared For: Students Talk Caring in School." *Phi Delta Kappan* 76 (9): 686–93.

Brighton, Kenneth L. 2007. *Coming of Age: The Education and Development of Young Adolescents*. Westerville, OH: National Middle School Association.

Brisson, Geneviève. 2018. "Plurilingualism and Transnational Identities in a Francophone Minority Classroom." *Jeunesse: Young People, Texts, Cultures* 10 (2): 73–99.

Brock, André. 2012. "From the Blackhand Side: Twitter as a Cultural Conversation." *Journal of Broadcasting and Electronic Media* 56 (4): 529–49.

Brock, Rochelle. 2014. "Speaking Truth on and about Critical Pedagogy." In *Interrogating Critical Pedagogy: The Voices of Educators of Color in the Movement*, edited by Pierre Wilbert Orelus and Rochelle Brock, 281–93. London: Routledge.

Brown, Ann L. 1992. "Design Experiments: Theoretical and Methodological Challenges in Creating Complex Interventions in Classroom Settings." *Journal of the Learning Sciences* 2 (2): 141–78.

Brown, Tara M., and Kevin Galeas. 2011. "Confronting 'Limit Situations' in a Youth/Adult Educational Research Collaborative." In *Listening to and Learning from Students*, edited by Brian D. Schultz, 13–26. Charlotte, NC: Information Age Publishing.

Brown, Tara M., and Louis F. Rodriguez. 2008. "School and the Co-construction of the Drop-Out." *International Journal of Qualitative Studies in Education* 15 (6): 221–42.

Bruner, Jerome. 1990. *Acts of Meaning*. Cambridge, MA: Harvard University Press.

–. 1997. *The Culture of Education*. Cambridge, MA: Harvard University Press.

Bullough, Robert V., and Stefinee Pinnegar. 2009. "The Happiness of Teaching (as Eudaimonia): Disciplinary Knowledge and the Threat of Performativity." *Teachers and Teaching: Theory and Practice* 15 (2): 241–56.

Burchard, Brendon. 2001. "'Venting' in the Workplace: An Ethnographic Study among Resident Assistants." Annual Meeting of the Western States Communication Association, Coeur d'Alene, ID, February 23–27, 2001.

Burton, Antoinette. 1992. "'History' Is Now: Feminist Theory and the Production of Historical Feminisms." *Women's History Review* 1 (1): 25–39. doi: 10.1080/09612029200200001.

Buzan, Tony, and Barry Buzan. 2000. *The Mind Map Book*. London: BBC Books.

"Canada Day: A Day to Remember All the Good Stuff." 2015. Editorial, *Globe and Mail*. Last modified July 1, 2015, accessed July 6, 2015. https://www.theglobeandmail.com/opinion/editorials/canada-day-a-day-to-remember-all-the-good-stuff/article25207260/.

Canadian Press. 2012. "Few Canadians Aware of War of 1812, Research Suggests." CBC. Last modified August 29, 2012, accessed February 21, 2015. http://www.cbc.ca/news/politics/few-canadians-aware-of-war-of-1812-research-suggests-1.1176690.

Carlson, Kathryn Blaze. 2012. "How Canadian Identity Has Changed and What It Means for Our Future." *National Post*. Last modified December 28, 2012, accessed March 4, 2015. http://news.nationalpost.com/news/canada/year-in-ideas-how-canadian-identity-has-changed-and-what-it-means-for-our-future.

Carney, Nikita. 2016. "All Lives Matter, but So Does Race: Black Lives Matter and the Evolving Role of Social Media." *Humanity and Society* 40 (2): 180–99.

Caron, Daniel. 2012. "Improving Access – Official Response from Daniel Caron." *Canada's History*. Last modified June 12, 2012, accessed July 3, 2012. http://www.canadashistory.ca/community/future-of-archives/articles/improving-access-official-reponse-from-daniel-caron.

Carroll, Berenice A., ed. 1976. *Liberating Women's History: Theoretical and Critical Essays*. Chicago: University of Illinois Press.

Carty, Linda. 1994. "African Canadian Women and the State: 'Labour Only, Please.'" In *We're Rooted Here and They Can't Pull Us Up: Essays in African Canadian Women's History*, edited by Peggy Bristow, Dionne Brand, Linda Carty, Afua Cooper, Sylvia Hamilton, and Adrienne Shadd, 193–228. Toronto:

University of Toronto Press.

Case, Kim A., and Annette Hemmings. 2005. "Distancing Strategies: White Women Preservice Teachers and Antiracist Curriculum." *Urban Education* 40 (6): 606–26.

CBC News. 2013. "Nanos Number: Canadians Would Fete Charter over War of 1812." Last modified February 21, 2013, accessed February 21, 2013. http://www.cbc.ca/news/politics/nanos-number-canadians-would-fete-charter-over-war-of-1812-1.1325819.

–. 2015. "Aboriginal Artists Shut Out of Nathan Phillips Square during Pan Am Games." Last modified July 21, 2015, accessed July 22, 2015. http://www.cbc.ca/news/canada/toronto/aboriginal-artists-shut-out-of-nathan-phillips-square-during-pan-am-games-1.3162478.

Chambers, Iain. 1997. "Migrancy, Culture, Identity." In *The Postmodern History Reader*, edited by Keith Jenkins, 77–81. London: Routledge.

Chan, Anthony B. 2019. "Chinese Canadians." *Canadian Encyclopedia*. Last modified May 22, 2019, accessed September 23, 2019. https://www.thecanadianencyclopedia.ca/en/article/chinese-canadians.

Chapra, A., and S. Chatterjee. 2009. "Talking Race, Talking Colour: Racialized Women, Their Home and Belongingness in Multicultural Canada." *Canadian Woman Studies* 27 (2/3): 14.

Charmaz, Kathy. 2006. *Constructing Grounded Theory: A Practical Guide through Qualitative Analysis*. Thousand Oaks, CA: Sage.

Cherryholmes, Cleo H. 1987. "A Social Project for Curriculum: Post-Structural Perspectives." *Journal of Curriculum Studies* 19 (4): 295–316.

–. 1988. *Power and Criticism: Poststructural Investigations in Education*. Advances in Contemporary Educational Thought, Volume 2, edited by Jonas F. Soltis. New York: Teachers College Press.

Childs, Ann, and Jane McNicholl. 2007. "Investigating the Relationship between Subject Content Knowledge and Pedagogical Practice through the Analysis of Classroom Discourse." *International Journal of Science Education* 29 (13): 1629–653. doi: 10.1080/09500690601180817.

Cho, Seehwa. 2012. *Critical Pedagogy and Social Change: Critical Analysis on the Language of Possibility*. London: Routledge.

Claessens, Luce C.A., Jan van Tartwijk, Anna C. van der Want, Helena J.M. Pennings, Nico Verloop, Perry J. den Brok, and Theo Wubbels. 2017. "Positive Teacher-Student Relationships Go Beyond the Classroom, Problematic Ones

Stay Inside." *Journal of Educational Research* 110 (5): 478–93. doi: 10.1080/00220671.2015.1129595.

Clark, Anna. 2008. *History's Children: History Wars in the Classroom*. Sydney, NSW: New South Publishers.

–. 2009. "Teaching the Nation's Story: Comparing Public Debates and Classroom Perspectives on History Education in Australia and Canada." *Journal of Curriculum Studies* 41 (6): 745–62.

Clark, Penney. 2018. "History Education Debates: Canadian Identity, Historical Thinking and Historical Consciousness." *Arbor: Ciencia, Pensamiento y Cultura* 194 (788): 1–12.

Cole, Alana. 2015. "Winnipeg General Strike Exhibit Removed from National Museum." CBC. Last modified May 26, 2015, accessed June 15, 2015. http://www.cbc.ca/news/canada/manitoba/winnipeg-general-strike-exhibit-removed-from-national-museum-1.3088372.

Cole, Josh. 2016. "Neoliberalism as Historical Narrative: Some Reflections." *Our Schools/Our Selves* (Fall): 41–58.

Collins, Allan. 1992. "Toward a Design Science of Education." In *New Directions in Educational Technology*, edited by E. Scanlon and T. O'Shea. Berlin: Springer-Verlag.

Conlin, Dan. 2009. *Pirates of the Atlantic: Robbery, Murder and Mayhem off the Canadian East Coast*. Halifax, NS: Formac.

Conrad, Margaret, Kadriye Ercikan, Gerald Friesen, Jocelyn Létourneau, Delphin Muise, David Northrup, and Peter Seixas. 2013. *Canadians and Their Pasts*. Toronto: University of Toronto Press.

Cormack, Patricia, and James F. Cosgrave. 2013. *Desiring Canada: CBC Contests, Hockey Violence and Other Stately Pleasures*. Toronto: University of Toronto Press.

Cornelius-White, Jeffrey. 2007. "Learner-Centered Teacher-Student Relationships Are Effective: A Meta-Analysis." *Review of Educational Research* 77 (1): 113–43. doi: 10.1111/1467-8624.00406.

Cotler, Irwin. 2012. "Myopic Government Ignores Charter Anniversary." *The Star*. Last modified April 12, 2012, accessed July 10, 2012. http://www.thestar.com/opinion/editorialopinion/2012/04/12/myopic_government_ignores_charter_anniversary.html.

Coyne, Andrew. 2014. "Stephen Harper's Canada Day Speech the Latest Volley in Pointless History Wars." *National Post*. Last modified July 2, 2014, accessed July

10, 2014. http://news.nationalpost.com/full-comment/andrew-coyne-stephen-harpers-canada-day-speech-the-latest-volley-in-pointless-history-wars.

Crenshaw, Kimberlé Williams. 1988. "Race, Reform, and Retrenchment: Transformation and Legitimation in Antidiscrimination Law." *Harvard Law Review* 101 (7): 1331–387.

–. 1995. "Mapping the Margins: Intersectionality, Identity Politics, and Violence against Women of Color." In *Critical Race Theory: The Key Writings That Formed the Movement*, edited by K.W. Crenshaw, N. Gotanda, G. Peller and K. Thomas, 357–83. New York: New Press.

Crowley, Ryan. 2016. "White Teachers, Racial Privilege, and the Sociological Imagination." *Urban Education* 54 (10): 1462–488. doi: 10.1177/0042085916656901.

Crowley, Ryan, and William Smith. 2015. "Whiteness and Social Studies Teacher Education: Tensions in the Pedagogical Task." *Teaching Education* 26 (2): 160–78.

Cunningham, Deborah L. 2007. "Understanding Pedagogical Reasoning in History Teaching through the Case of Cultivating Historical Empathy." *Theory and Research in Social Education* 35 (4): 592–630. doi: 10.1080/00933104.2007.10473352.

Cutrara, Samantha. 2007. "Historic Space: A Transformative Model of History Education." MA thesis, Ontario Institute for the Studies in Education, University of Toronto.

–. 2009. "To Placate or Provoke? A Critical Review of the Disciplines Approach to History Curriculum." *Journal of the Canadian Association for Curriculum Studies* 7 (2): 86–109.

–. 2010. "Transformative History: The Possibilities of Historic Space." *Canadian Social Studies*, 44 (1): 4–16.

–. 2012. "Ethical Responsibility in Curricular Encounters: The Dilemmas of Teaching History in a Transnational World; A Focus on Canada." American Association for the Advancement of Curriculum Studies, University of British Columbia, April 10–13.

–. 2016a. "Using Primary Sources as a Form of Social Justice." In *Visual History Webinar Series*, edited by Canada's History. https://www.canadashistory.ca/explore/webinars/using-primary-sources-as-a-form-of-social-justice.

–. 2016b. "Young People's Desires for Connection and Complexity in Teaching and Learning Canadian History: Thoughts on the 'Drag and Drop Approach' to Black Canadian History." Canadian History of Education Association, Waterloo, Ontario, October 27–30.

–. 2017. "Curricular Roles: Neoliberal Interactions in/of Education." Canadian Society for the Study in Education, Toronto, Canada, May 27–31.

–. 2018. "The Settler Grammar of Canadian History Curriculum: Why Historical Thinking Is Unable to Respond to the TRC's Calls to Action." *Canadian Journal of Education/Revue canadienne de l'éducation* 41 (1): 250–75.

–. 2019. "The Subjectivity of Archives: Learning from, with, and Resisting Archives and Archival Sources in Teaching and Learning History." *Historical Encounters* 6 (1): 117–32.

–. 2020. "'It Is Hard to Admit your Own Group Did Wrong': Centering Whiteness and Controlling Diversity in the Canadian Social Studies Classroom." In *Marking the Invisible: Articulating Whiteness in Social Studies Education*, edited by Andrea Hawkman and Sarah B. Shear, 477–507. Charlotte, NC: Information Age Publishing.

Dalby, Paul. 2016. "Canada's Pirate Queen." *Canada's History*. Last modified January 9, 2016, accessed November 13, 2019. https://www.canadashistory.ca/explore/women/canada-s-pirate-queen.

Dann, Moira. 2009. "Where Were the Mothers of Confederation?" *Globe and Mail*. Last modified August 23, 2012, accessed August 3, 2015. http://www.theglobeandmail.com/globe-debate/where-were-the-mothers-of-confederation/article4284401.

Darder, Antonia, Marta Baltodano, and Rodolfo D. Torres. 2017. "Critical Pedagogy: An Introduction." In *The Critical Pedagogy Reader*, edited by Antonia Darder, Rodolfo D. Torres, and Marta Baltodano, 1–23. New York: Routledge.

Darder, Antonia, and Rodolfo D. Torres. 2003. "Shattering the 'Race' Lens: Toward a Critical Theory of Racism." In *The Critical Pedagogy Reader*, edited by Antonia Darder, Marta Baltodano, and Rodolfo D. Torres, 245–61. New York: Routledge.

Daro, Ishmael N. 2015. "24 Per Cent of Canadians Think There's No Such Thing as a 'Unique Canadian Culture,' According to Survey." *National Post*. Last modified March 11, 2015, accessed March 20, 2015. http://news.nationalpost.com/news/canada/canadian-culture-survey.

Davis, Bob. 1995. *Whatever Happened to High School History? Burying the Political Memory of Youth*. Toronto: James Lorimer.

Davis, O.L., Jr. 2001. "In Pursuit of Historical Empathy." In *Historical Empathy and Perspective Taking in the Social Studies*, edited by O.L. Davis Jr., Elizabeth Anne Yeager, and Stuart J. Foster, 1–12. Lanham, MD: Rowman and Littlefield.

Dei, George J. Sefa. 1997. *Reconstructing "Dropout": A Critical Ethnography of the Dynamics of Black Students' Disengagement from School.* Toronto: University of Toronto Press.

Delacourt, Susan. 2013. "Canada Day: Is Canadian Identity Tied to Our Stomachs?" *Toronto Star.* Last modified June 28, 2013, accessed July 14, 2015. http://www.thestar.com/news/insight/2013/06/28/canada_day_is_canadian_identity_tied_to_our_stomachs.html.

Delgado, Richard. 1988. "Review: Derrick Bell and the Ideology of Racial Reform: Will We Ever Be Saved?" *Yale Law Journal* 97 (5): 923–47.

–. 1989. "Storytelling for Oppositionists and Others: A Plea for Narrative." *Michigan Law Review* 87 (8): 2411–441.

–. 1990. "When a Story Is Just a Story: Does Voice Really Matter?" *Virginia Law Review* 76 (1): 95–111.

den Heyer, Kent, and Laurence Abbott. 2011. "Reverberating Echoes: Challenging Teacher Candidates to Tell and Learn from Entwined Narrations of Canadian History." *Curriculum Inquiry* 41 (5): 610–35. doi: 10.1111/j.1467-873X.2011.00567.x.

Depaepe, Fien, Erik De Corte, and Lieven Verschaffel. 2012. "Who Is Granted Authority in the Mathematics Classroom? An Analysis of the Observed and Perceived Distribution of Authority." *Educational Studies* 38 (2): 223–34. doi: 10.1080/03055698.2011.598676.

Derrida, Jacques. 1978. *Writing and Difference.* Translated by Alan Bass. Chicago: University of Chicago Press.

–. 1997. *Of Grammatology.* Translated by Gayatri C. Spivak. Baltimore: Johns Hopkins University Press.

Dewey, John. 1933. *How We Think: A Restatement of the Relation of Reflective Thinking to the Educative Process.* Rev. ed. Boston: D.C. Heath.

Diamond, Jared. 1997. *Guns, Germs, and Steel: The Fates of Human Societies.* New York: W.W. Norton.

Diamond, John B., Antonia Randolph, and James P. Spillane. 2004. "Teachers' Expectations and Sense of Responsibility for Student Learning: The Importance of Race, Class, and Organizational Habitus." *Anthropology and Education Quarterly* 35 (1): 75–98. doi: 10.1525/aeq.2004.35.1.75.

Dion, Susan D. 2005. "Aboriginal People and Stories of Canadian History: Investigating Barriers to Transforming Relationships." In *Possibilities and Limitations: Multicultural Policies and Programs in Canada,* edited by Carl E. James, 34–57. Black Point, NS: Fernwood.

—. 2009. *Braiding Histories: Learning from Aboriginal Peoples' Experiences and Perspectives.* Vancouver: UBC Press.

Doharty, Nadena. 2019. "'I Felt Dead': Applying a Racial Microaggressions Framework to Black Students' Experiences of Black History Month and Black History." *Race Ethnicity and Education* 22 (1): 110–29. doi: 10.1080/13613324.2017.1417253.

Doherty, Catherine. 2018. "Keeping Doors Open: Transnational Families and Curricular Nationalism." *International Studies in Sociology of Education* 27 (2–3): 200–16. doi: 10.1080/09620214.2017.1415162.

Donald, Dwayne. 2012. "Indigenous Métissage: A Decolonizing Research Sensibility." *International Journal of Qualitative Studies in Education* 25 (5): 533–23. doi: 10.1080/09518398.2011.554449.

Dorn, A. Walter. 2005. "Canadian Peacekeeping: Proud Tradition, Strong Future?" *Canadian Foreign Policy* 12 (2): 7–32.

Drexler, Wendy. 2010. "The Networked Student Model for Construction of Personal Learning Environments: Balancing Teacher Control and Student Autonomy." *Australasian Journal of Educational Technology* 26 (3): 369–85.

Duff, Wendy M., and Verne Harris. 2002. "Stories and Names: Archival Description as Narrating Records and Constructing Meanings." *Archival Science* 2 (3–4): 263–85. doi: https://doi.org/10.1007/BF02435625.

Earl, Jennifer, Thomas V. Maher, and Thomas Elliott. 2017. "Youth, Activism, and Social Movements." *Sociology Compass* 11 (4): e12465. doi: 10.1111/soc4.12465.

Egéa-Kuehne, Denise, and Gert Biesta. 2001. "Opening: Derrida and Education." In *Derrida and Education*, edited by Gert Biesta and Denise Egéa-Kuehne, 1–10. London: Routledge.

Eley, Geoff. 2000. "Culture, Nation and Gender." In *Gendered Nations: Nationalisms and Gender Order in the Long Nineteenth Century*, edited by Ida Blom, Karen Hagemann, and Catherine Hall, 27–40. New York: Berg.

Emdin, Christopher. 2016. *For White Folks Who Teach in the Hood... And the Rest of Y'all Too: Reality Pedagogy and Urban Education.* Boston: Beacon Press.

Epstein, Shira Eve, and Melissa Schieble. 2019. "Exploring Racial Literacy When Teaching 'Other People's Children.'" *Whiteness and Education* 4 (2): 109–27. doi: 10.1080/23793406.2019.1654909.

Epstein, Terrie. 1998. "Deconstructing Differences in African-American and European-American Adolescents' Perspectives on U.S. History." *Curriculum Inquiry* 28 (4): 397–422.

—. 2009. *Interpreting National History: Race, Identity and Pedagogy in Classrooms and Communities*. New York: Routledge.

Epstein, Terrie, Edwin Mayorga, and Joseph Nelson. 2011. "Teaching about Race in an Urban History Class: The Effects of Culturally Responsive Teaching." *Journal of Social Studies Research* 35 (1): 2–21.

Éthier, Marc-André, and David Lefrançois. 2013. "Teaching History by Thinking about the Concept of Nation." *Canadian Issues* (Summer 2013): 51–53.

Farley, Lisa. 2009. "Radical Hope: Or, the Problem of Uncertainty in History Education." *Curriculum Inquiry* 39 (4): 537–54.

Ferro, Marc. 2003. *The Use and Abuse of History: Or How the Past Is Taught to Children*. London: Routledge.

Foucault, Michel. 1980a. "History of Systems of Thought." In *Language, Counter-Memory, Practice: Selected Essays and Interviews*, edited by Donald F. Bouchard, 199–204. New York: Cornell University Press. Original edition, *Hommage à Jean Hyppolite* (1971).

—. 1980b. "Intellectuals and Power." In *Language, Counter-Memory, Practice: Selected Essays and Interviews*, edited by Donald F. Bouchard, 205–17. New York: Cornell University Press. Original edition, *Hommage à Jean Hyppolite* (1971).

—. 1980c. "Nietzsche, Genealogy, History." In *Language, Counter-Memory, Practice: Selected Essays and Interviews*, edited by Donald F. Bouchard, 139–64. New York: Cornell University Press. Original edition, *Hommage à Jean Hyppolite* (1971).

—. 1995. *Discipline and Punish: The Birth of the Prison*. New York: Vintage Books.

Fredricks, Jennifer A., Alyssa K. Parr, Jamie L. Amemiya, Ming-Te Wang, and Scott Brauer. 2019. "What Matters for Urban Adolescents' Engagement and Disengagement in School: A Mixed-Methods Study." *Journal of Adolescent Research* 34 (5): 491–527. doi: 10.1177/0743558419830638.

Freire, Paulo. 2004. *Pedagogy of Indignation*. Boulder, CO: Paradigm Publishers.

—. 2006. *Pedagogy of the Oppressed*. Translated by Myra Bergman Ramos. 30th anniversary edition. New York: Continuum.

Friedman, Isaac A. 1991. "High- and Low-Burnout Schools: School Culture Aspects of Teacher Burnout." *Journal of Educational Research* 84 (6): 325–33.

Fusani, David S. 1994. "'Extra-class' Communication: Frequency, Immediacy, Self-disclosure, and Satisfaction in Student-Faculty Interaction Outside the Classroom." *Journal of Applied Communication Research* 22 (3): 232–55. doi: 10.1080/00909889409365400.

Gardner, Katy. 2012. "Transnational Migration and the Study of Children: An Introduction." *Journal of Ethnic and Migration Studies* 38 (6): 889–912. doi: 10.1080/1369183X.2012.677170.

Garza, Rubén. 2009. "Latino and White High School Students' Perceptions of Caring Behaviors: Are We Culturally Responsive to Our Students?" *Urban Education* 44 (3): 297–321.

Gay, Geneva. 2010. *Culturally Responsive Teaching: Theory, Research, and Practice*. Edited by James A. Banks. 2nd ed. Multicultural Education Series. New York: Teachers College Press.

Gehlbach, Hunter, Maureen E. Brinkworth, and Anna D. Harris. 2011. 2nd ed. "Social Motivation in the Secondary Classroom: Assessing Teacher-Student Relationships and Student Outcomes." April. American Educational Research Association, New Orleans, LA. https://files.eric.ed.gov/fulltext/ED525284.pdf.

Gholami, Khalil. 2011. "Moral Care and Caring Pedagogy: Two Dimensions of Teachers' 'Praxis.'" *Pedagogy, Culture and Society* 19 (1): 133–51.

Giles, David. 2011. "'Who We Are' and 'How We Are' Are Integral to Relational Experiences: Exploring Comportment in Teacher Education." *Australian Journal of Teacher Education* 36 (1): 60–72.

Gillborn, David. 1995. "Racism and Schooling." In *Racism and Antiracism in Real School: Theory Policy Practice*, 1–13. Buckingham, UK: Open University Press.

Gilmore, Scott. 2015. "A Real Nation Would Not Let This Happen." *Maclean's*. October 12, 25.

Giroux, Henry A. 1984. *Ideology, Culture, and the Process of Schooling*. Philadelphia: Temple University Press.

–. 2001. *Theory and Resistance in Education*. Revised and expanded edition. Westport, CT: Bergin and Garvey.

Glaser, Barney, and Anselm Strauss. 1967. *The Discovery of Grounded Theory: Strategies for Qualitative Research*. Chicago: Aldine.

Glazer, Jeremy. 2018. "Learning from Those Who No Longer Teach: Viewing Teacher Attrition through a Resistance Lens." *Teaching and Teacher Education* 74: 62–71. doi: https://doi.org/10.1016/j.tate.2018.04.011.

Goldstein, Lisa S., and Vickie E. Lake. 2000. "'Love, Love, and More Love for Children': Exploring Preservice Teachers' Understandings of Caring." *Teaching and Teacher Education* 16: 861–72.

Gosselin, Viviane, and Phaedra Livingstone, eds. 2016. *Museums as Sites of Historical Consciousness: Perspectives on Museum Theory and Practice in Canada*. Edited by Penney Clark. THEN/HiER Book Series. Vancouver: UBC Press.

Granatstein, J.L. 1998. *Who Killed Canadian History?* Toronto: HarperCollins Publishers.

Grant, Peter R. 2016. "'Canadian, eh?' An Examination of the Multidimensional Structure and Functions of the National Identity of Immigrants and of Those Raised in Canada." *Canadian Ethnic Studies Journal* 48: 45–75.

Grever, Maria, Ben Pelzer, and Terry Haydn. 2011. "High School Students' Views on History." *Journal of Curriculum Studies* 43 (2): 207–29.

Griffith, Debbie. 2014. "Linking Literacy, Language, and Culture." *Education Matters: The Journal of Teaching and Learning* 2 (1): 101–11.

Gudmundsdottir, Sigrun. 1990. "Values in Pedagogical Content Knowledge." *Journal of Teacher Education* 41 (3): 44–52. doi: 10.1177/002248719004100306.

Gulwadi, Gowri Betrabet. 2006. "Seeking Restorative Experiences: Elementary School Teachers' Choices for Places that Enable Coping with Stress." *Environment and Behavior* 38 (4): 503–20. doi: 10.1177/0013916505283420.

Habermas, Jürgen. 2015. *Knowledge and Human Interests*. Hoboken, NJ: John Wiley and Sons.

Halagao, Patricia Espiritu. 2004. "Holding Up the Mirror: The Complexity of Seeing Your Ethnic Self in History." *Theory and Research in Social Education* 32 (4): 459–83. doi: 10.1080/00933104.2004.10473265.

Harjunen, Elina. 2012. "Patterns of Control over the Teaching-Studying-Learning Process and Classrooms as Complex Dynamic Environments: A Theoretical Framework." *European Journal of Teacher Education* 35 (2): 139–61. doi: 10.1080/02619768.2011.643465.

Harper, Stephen. 2014. "Statement by the Prime Minister of Canada on Canada Day." Prime Minister of Canada. Accessed July 10, 2015. http://pm.gc.ca/eng/news/2014/07/01/statement-prime-minister-canada-canada-day-0.

Harris, Cheryl I. 1993. "Whiteness as Property." *Harvard Law Review* 106 (8): 1707–791.

Harris, Lauren McArthur, Anne-Lise Halvorsen, and Gerardo J. Aponte-Martínez. 2016. "'[My] Family Has Gone through That': How High School Students Determine the Trustworthiness of Historical Documents." *Journal of Social Studies Research* 40 (2): 109–21. doi: https://doi.org/10.1016/j.jssr.2015.06.007.

Harris, Richard, and Rosemary Reynolds. 2014. "The History Curriculum and Its Personal Connection to Students from Minority Ethnic Backgrounds." *Journal of Curriculum Studies* 46 (4): 464–86. doi: 10.1080/00220272.2014.881925.

–. 2018. "Exploring Teachers' Curriculum Decision Making: Insights from History Education." *Oxford Review of Education* 44 (2): 139–55.

Harris, Richard, and Terry Haydn. 2006. "Pupils' Enjoyment of History: What Lessons Can Teachers Learn from Their Pupils?" *Curriculum Journal* 17 (4): 315–33.

Hawley, Todd S., and Gretchen M. Whitman. 2019. "Fear and Learning in Student Teaching: Accountability as Gatekeeper in Social Studies." *Journal of Social Studies Research*. doi: https://doi.org/10.1016/j.jssr.2019.04.003.

Hayes, Cleveland, and Brenda G. Juárez. 2009. "You Showed Your Whiteness: You Don't Get a 'Good' White People's Medal." *International Journal of Qualitative Studies in Education* 22 (6): 729–44.

Hayes, Lynda Fender, and Dorene Doerre Ross. 1989. "Trust versus Control: The Impact of School Leadership on Teacher Reflection." *International Journal of Qualitative Studies in Education* 2 (4): 335–50.

Henry, Frances. 1968. "The West Indian Domestic Scheme in Canada." *Social and Economic Studies* 17 (1): 83–91.

Hensley, Laura. 2015. "Residential School System Was 'Cultural Genocide,' Most Canadians Believe According to Poll." *National Post*. Last modified July 9, 2015, accessed July 10, 2015. http://news.nationalpost.com/news/canada/residential-school-system-was-cultural-genocide-most-canadians-believe-according-to-poll.

Hess, Diana E. 2010. "Discussion in Social Studies: Is It Worth the Trouble?" In *Social Studies Today: Research and Practice*, edited by Walter C. Parker, 205–14. New York: Routledge.

Higton, John, Sarah Leonardi, Arifa Choudhoury, Neil Richards, David Owen, and Nicholas Sofroniou. 2017. *Teacher Workload Survey 2016*. Edited by Department of Education. London: Government Printing Office.

Hobsbawm, Eric. 1992. "Inventing Traditions." In *The Invention of Tradition*, edited by Eric Hobsbawm and Terence Ronger, 1–14. Cambridge: Cambridge University Press.

hooks, bell. 2010. *Teaching Critical Thinking: Practical Wisdom*. New York: Routledge.

Houpt, Simon. 2010. "Tim Hortons: Where Commerce, Culture Intersect." *Globe and Mail*. Last modified August 23, 2012, accessed July 14, 2015. http://www.theglobeandmail.com/report-on-business/industry-news/marketing/tim-hortons-where-commerce-culture-intersect/article4318874.

Hughes, Andrew S. 2004. "Getting the Idea: An Introduction to Concept Learning and Teaching in Social Studies." In *Challenges and Prospects for Canadian Social Studies*, edited by Alan Sears and Ian Wright, 236–46. Vancouver: Pacific Educational Press.

Husbands, Chris, Alison Kitson, and Anna Pendry. 2003. *Understanding History Teaching: Teaching and Learning about the Past in Secondary Schools*. London: McGraw-Hill Education.

Hyland, Nora E. 2005. "Being a Good Teacher of Black Students? White Teachers and Unintentional Racism." *Curriculum Inquiry* 35 (4): 429–59.

"Immigration Act Amendment, 1919." n.d. Canadian Museum of Immigration at Pier 21. Accessed May 26, 2019. https://pier21.ca/research/immigration-history/immigration-act-amendment-1919.

Jacobsen, Rebecca, Anne-Lise Halvorsen, Amanda Slaten Frasier, Adam Schmitt, Margaret Crocco, and Avner Segall. 2018. "Thinking Deeply, Thinking Emotionally: How High School Students Make Sense of Evidence." *Theory and Research in Social Education* 46 (2): 232–76. doi: 10.1080/00933104.2018.1425170.

James, Jennifer H. 2008. "Teachers as Protectors: Making Sense of Preservice Teachers' Resistance to Interpretation in Elementary History Teaching." *Theory and Research in Social Education* 36 (3): 172–205. doi: 10.1080/00933104.2008.10473372.

–. 2012. "Caring for 'Others': Examining the Interplay of Mothering and Deficit Discourses in Teaching." *Teaching and Teacher Education* 28 (2): 165–73.

Jenkins, Keith, ed. 1997. *The Postmodern History Reader*. London: Routledge.

Jewell, Eva, and Ian Mosby. 2019. "Calls to Action Accountability: A Status Update on Reconciliation." Yellowhead Institute. Last modified December 17, 2019, accessed December 20, 2019. https://yellowheadinstitute.org/2019/12/17/calls-to-action-accountability-a-status-update-on-reconciliation.

Joseph, Bob. 2018. *21 Things You May Not Know about the Indian Act: Helping Canadians Make Reconciliation with Indigenous Peoples a Reality*. Port Coquitlam, BC: Indigenous Relations Press.

Kahne, Joseph, and Ellen Middaugh. 2008. "Democracy for Some: The Civic Opportunity Gap in High School. Circle Working Paper 59." Center for Information and Research on Civic Learning and Engagement.

Kaye, Harvey J. 1991. *The Powers of the Past: Reflections on the Crisis and the Promise of History*. Minneapolis: University of Minnesota Press.

Kee, Kevin, ed. 2014. *Pastplay: Teaching and Learning History with Technology*. Ann Arbor, MI: University of Michigan Press.

Kee, Kevin, and Nicki Darbyson. 2011. "Creating and Using Virtual Environments to Promote Historical Thinking." In *New Possibilities for the Past: Shaping History Education in Canada*, edited by Penney Clark, 264–81. Vancouver: UBC Press.

Keinan, A. 1996. *The Teachers' Lounge: Teachers' Professional Culture*. Beer Sheba: Ben Gurion University Press.

Keller, J. David. 2000. "Caring in the Teacher Lounge: The Teacher's TLC." *Education Digest* 65 (6): 49–51.

Kelley, Ninette, and Michael Trebilcock. 1998. *The Making of the Mosaic: A History of Canadian Immigration Policy*. Toronto: University of Toronto Press.

Kelly, A.V. 2003. "Eduspeak and the Thought Police – Reclaiming the Discourse." *Education 3–13* 31 (1): 4–12. doi: 10.1080/03004270385200021.

Khan, Momina, and Michael Cottrell. 2017. "Oh Canada, Whose Home and Native Land? Negotiating Multicultural, Aboriginal and Canadian Identity Narratives." *Education Matters: The Journal of Teaching and Learning* 5 (1): 1–34

Kheraj, Sean. 2013. "More Canadian History, More Better." ActiveHistory.ca. Last modified February 13, 2013, accessed August 2, 2015. http://activehistory.ca/2013/02/more-canadian-history-more-better.

Kim, Eun-mee, and Soeun Yang. 2016. "Internet Literacy and Digital Natives' Civic Engagement: Internet Skill Literacy or Internet Information Literacy?" *Journal of Youth Studies* 19 (4): 438–56. doi: 10.1080/13676261.2015.1083961.

Kinchin, Ian. 2004. "Investigating Students' Beliefs about Their Preferred Role as Learners." *Educational Research* 46 (3): 301–12. doi: 10.1080/0013188042 00277359.

Kinew, Wab. 2015. *The Reason You Walk: A Memoir*. Toronto: Viking.

Kohl, Herbert. 1994. *"I Won't Learn from You" and Other Forms of Creative Maladjustment*. New York: New Press.

Kohn, Alfie. 2005. "Unconditional Teaching." *Educational Leadership* 63 (1): 20–24.

Koring, Paul. 2012. "Blue Helmets Cast Aside, Canada Keeps the Peace No More." *Globe and Mail*. Last modified June 8, 2012, accessed July 8, 2015. http://www.theglobeandmail.com/news/politics/blue-helmets-cast-aside-canada-keeps-the-peace-no-more/article4240950.

Kutsyuruba, Benjamin, Keith Walker, Maha Al Makhamreh, and Rebecca Stroud Stasel. 2018. "Attrition, Retention, and Development of Early Career Teachers: Pan-Canadian Narratives." *In Education* 24 (1): 43–71.

Ladson-Billings, Gloria. 1995. "Toward a Theory of Culturally Relevant Pedagogy." *American Educational Research Journal* 32 (3): 465–91.

–. 1998. "Just What Is Critical Race Theory and What's It Doing in a *Nice* Field Like Education?" *Qualitative Studies in Education* 11 (1): 7–24.

Ladson-Billings, Gloria, and William Tate. 1995. "Toward a Critical Race Theory of Education." *Teachers College Record* 97 (1): 47–68.

Lahelma, Elina, and Tuula Gordon. 1997. "First Day in Secondary School: Learning to Be a 'Professional Pupil.'" *Educational Research and Evaluation* 3 (2): 119–39.

Lamming, George. 1961. "The West Indians: Our Loneliest Immigrants." *Maclean's*. Last modified November 4, 1961, accessed November 5, 2012. https://archive.macleans.ca/article/1961/11/4/the-west-indians-our-loneliest-immigrants.

Landrum, Timothy J., Terrance M. Scott, and Amy S. Lingo. 2011. "Classroom Misbehavior Is Predictable and Preventable." *Phi Delta Kappan* 93 (2): 30–34.

Lawrence, Bonita. 2003. "Gender, Race, and the Regulation of Native Identity in Canada and the United States: An Overview." *Hypatia* 18 (2): 3–31.

Lazare, Gerald. 2005. "A Feeling for the Past: Adolescents' Personal Responses to Studying History." PhD diss., Ontario Institute for the Studies in Education.

Lee, Peter. 1991. "Historical Knowledge and the National Curriculum." In *History in the National Curriculum*, edited by Richard Aldrich, 35–65. Great Britain: Institute of Education.

–. 1998. "'A Lot of Guess Work Goes On': Children's Understanding of Historical Accounts." *Teaching History* 92 (August): 29–32.

–. 2003. "A Scaffold, Not a Cage: Progression and Progression Models in History." *Teaching History* 113: 13–23.

–. 2004. "Understanding History." In *Theorizing Historical Consciousness*, edited by Peter Seixas, 129–64. Toronto: University of Toronto Press.

Lee, Peter, and Rosalyn Ashby. 2000. "Progression in Historical Understanding among Students Ages 7–14." In *Knowing, Teaching, and Learning History: National and International Perspectives*, edited by Peter N. Stearns, Peter Seixas, and Samuel Wineburg, 199–222. New York: New York University Press.

Létourneau, Jocelyn. 2000. *Passer à l'avenir: Histoire, mémoire, identité dans le Québec d'aujourd'hui*. Montreal: Boréal.

–. 2004. *A History for the Future: Rewriting Memory in Identity in Quebec*. Translated by Phyllis Aronoff and Howard Scott. Edited by John Dickenson and Brian Young. Montreal and Kingston: McGill-Queen's University Press.

Létourneau, Jocelyn, and Sabrina Moisan. 2004. "Young People's Assimilation of a Collective Historical Memory: A Case Study of Quebeckers of French-Canadian Heritage." In *Theorizing Historical Consciousness*, edited by Peter Seixas, 103–28. Toronto: University of Toronto Press.

Lévesque, Stéphane. 2003. "Becoming Citizens: High School Students and Citizenship in British Columbia and Québec." *Encounters on Education* 4: 107–26.

Levstik, Linda S. 2000. "Articulating the Silences: Teachers' and Adolescents' Conceptions of Historical Significance." In *Knowing, Teaching, and Learning History: National and International Perspectives.*, edited by Peter N. Stearns, Peter Seixas, and Samuel Wineburg, 284–305. New York: New York University Press.

lisahunter, Tony Rossi, Richard Tinning, Erin Flanagan, and Doune Macdonald. 2011. "Professional Learning Places and Spaces: The Staffroom as a Site of Beginning Teacher Induction and Transition." *Asia-Pacific Journal of Teacher Education* 39 (1): 33–46. doi: 10.1080/1359866X.2010.542234.

Loewen, James W. 1996. *Lies My Teacher Told Me: Everything Your American History Textbook Got Wrong*. New York: Touchstone.

Logan, Tricia. 2014. "National Memory and Museums: Remembering Settler Colonial Genocide of Indigenous Peoples in Canada." In *Remembering Genocide*, edited by Nigel Eltringham and Pam Maclean, 112–30. London: Routledge.

Loomba, Ania. 2002. *Colonialism/Postcolonialism*. Edited by John Drakakis. London: Routledge.

Louws, Monika L., Jacobiene A. Meirink, Klaas van Veen, and Jan H. van Driel. 2017. "Teachers' Self-Directed Learning and Teaching Experience: What, How, and Why Teachers Want to Learn." *Teaching and Teacher Education* 66: 171–183. doi: https://doi.org/10.1016/j.tate.2017.04.004.

Lowenthal, David. 2015. *The Past Is a Foreign Country – Revisited*. Cambridge: Cambridge University Press.

Lyotard, Jean-François. 1997. "The Postmodern Condition." In *The Postmodern History Reader*, edited by Keith Jenkins, 36–38. London: Routledge. Original edition, *The Postmodern Condition* (1984).

Ma, Liping. 1999. *Knowing and Teaching Elementary Mathematics: Teachers' Understanding of Fundamental Mathematics in China and the United States*. Mahwah, N.J.: Lawrence Erlbaum Associates.

MacDonald, Nancy. 2015. "A Deafening Silence." *Maclean's*, October 12, 22–24.

MacDonald, William A. 2015. "To Be a Global Role Model, Canada Must Realize What Sets It Apart." *Globe and Mail*. Last modified June 19, 2015, accessed June 22, 2015. http://www.theglobeandmail.com/news/national/to

-be-a-global-role-model-canada-must-realize-what-sets-it-apart/article 25041223.

Mackey, Eva. 2005. *House of Difference: Cultural Politics and National Identity in Canada*. Toronto: University of Toronto Press.

Mahtani, Minelle. 2002. "Interrogating the Hyphen-Nation: Canadian Multicultural Policy and 'Mixed Race' Identities." *Social Identities* 81 (1): 67–90. doi: 10.1080/13504630220132026.

Main, Shiho. 2012. "'The Other Half' of Education: Unconscious Education of Children." *Educational Philosophy and Theory* 44 (1): 82–95.

Majors, Richard. 2001. *Educating Our Black Children*. London: Routledge.

Malenfant, Jayne. 2018. "Anarchist Youth in Rural Canada: Technology, Resistance, and the Navigation of Space." *Jeunesse: Young People, Texts, Cultures* 10 (2): 126–51.

Manuel, Jackie, Don Carter, and Janet Dutton. 2018. "'As Much as I Love Being in the Classroom ...': Understanding Secondary English Teachers' Workload." *English in Australia* 53 (3): 5–22.

Marker, Michael. 2011. "Teaching History from an Indigenous Perspective: Four Winding Paths Up the Mountain." In *New Possibilities for the Past: Shaping History Education in Canada*, edited by Penney Clark, 97–112. Vancouver: UBC Press.

Martell, Christopher C. 2013. "Race and Histories: Examining Culturally Relevant Teaching in the U.S. History Classroom." *Theory and Research in Social Education* 41 (1): 65–88.

Martell, Christopher C., and Kaylene M. Stevens. 2019. "Culturally Sustaining Social Studies Teachers: Understanding Models of Practice." *Teaching and Teacher Education* 86: 1–11.

Martin, Nick. 2015. "Teacher Unhappy with My Heritage Moment." *Winnipeg Free Press*. Last modified May 7, 2015, accessed June 1, 2015. http://www.winnipegfreepress.com/opinion/blogs/martin/302951642.html.

Massey, Doreen. 1994. *Space, Place, and Gender*. Minneapolis: University of Minnesota Press.

Mawhinney, Lynnette. 2008. "Laugh So You Don't Cry: Teachers Combating Isolation in Schools through Humour and Social Support." *Ethnography and Education* 3 (2): 195–209. doi: 10.1080/17457820802062466.

–. 2010. "Let's Lunch and Learn: Professional Knowledge Sharing in Teachers' Lounges and Other Congregational Spaces." *Teaching and Teacher Education* 26 (4): 972–78.

–. 2012. "The Creation of Restorative Places for Teachers in an Urban School." *Journal of Contemporary Ethnography* 41 (5): 554–80. doi: 10.1177/0891241 612451128.

McCaughtry, Nate. 2005. "Elaborating Pedagogical Content Knowledge: What It Means to Know Students and Think about Teaching." *Teachers and Teaching* 11 (4): 379–95. doi: 10.1080/13450600500137158.

McCutcheon, Gail. 1982. "What in the World Is Curriculum Theory?" *Theory into Practice* 21 (1): 18–22.

McGregor, Jane. 2003. "Making Spaces: Teacher Workplace Topologies." *Pedagogy, Culture and Society* 11 (3): 353–77. doi: 10.1080/14681360300200179.

McIntyre, Alice. 1997. "Constructing an Image of a White Teacher." *Teachers College Record* 98 (4): 653–81.

McKittrick, Katherine. 2006. *Demonic Grounds: Black Women and the Cartographies of Struggle*. Minneapolis: University of Minnesota Press.

McLaren, Peter. 2003. "Critical Pedagogy: A Look at the Major Concepts." In *The Critical Pedagogy Reader*, edited by Antonia Darder, Marta Baltodano, and Rodolfo D. Torres, 69–96. New York: Routledge.

McNeil, Linda M. 1988. *Contradictions of Control: School Structure and School Knowledge*. New York: Routledge.

Meissner, Dirk. 2015. "New B.C. School Curriculum Will Have Aboriginal Focus." *Globe and Mail*. Last modified July 17, 2015, accessed July 17, 2015. http://www.theglobeandmail.com/news/british-columbia/new-bc-school-curriculum-will-have-aboriginal-focus/article25003962.

Middaugh, Ellen, Lynn Schofield Clark, and Parissa J. Ballard. 2017. "Digital Media, Participatory Politics, and Positive Youth Development." *Pediatrics* 140 (Supplement 2): S127–S131.

Miller, John P., and Wayne Seller. 1990. *Curriculum: Perspectives and Practice*. Toronto: Copp Clark Pitman.

Misco, T., and N. Patterson. 2009. "An Old Fad of Great Promise: Reverse Chronology History Teaching in Social Studies Classes." *Journal of Social Studies Research* 33 (1): 71–91.

Molson Coors Brewing Company. 2015. "Molson Canadian's Latest Beer Fridge Opens When 'I Am Canadian' Is Spoken in Six Different Languages." Last modified June 26, 2015, accessed July 14, 2015. http://www.molsoncoors.com/en/news/canada/brands/2015/june/26/molson-canadian-s-latest-beer-fridge.

Montgomery, Ken. 2005. "Banal Race-Thinking: Ties of Blood, Canadian History Textbooks and Ethnic Nationalism." *Paedagogica Historica* 41 (3): 313–36.

Morton, Desmond. 2000. "Teaching and Learning History in Canada." In *Knowing, Teaching, and Learning History: National and International Perspectives*, edited by Peter N. Stearns, Peter Seixas, and Samuel Wineburg, 51–61. New York: New York University Press.

Nathan, Mitchell J., and Anthony Petrosino. 2003. "Expert Blind Spot among Preservice Teachers." *American Educational Research Journal* 40 (4): 905–28. doi: 10.3102/00028312040004905.

Nelson, Jennifer. 2009. *Razing Africville: A Geography of Racism*. Toronto: University of Toronto Press.

Noddings, Nel. 1984. *Caring: A Feminine Approach to Ethics and Moral Education*. Berkeley: University of California Press.

–. 2005. *Challenge of Care to Schools: An Alternative Approach to Education*. New York: Teachers College Press.

Nordgren, Kenneth, and Maria Johansson. 2015. "Intercultural Historical Learning: A Conceptual Framework." *Journal of Curriculum Studies* 47 (1): 1–25. doi: 10.1080/00220272.2014.956795.

Nourie, Meredith C. 2011. "A First-Year Teacher's Top 10 Mistakes." *The Clearing House: A Journal of Educational Strategies, Issues and Ideas* 84 (6): 231–32. doi: 10.1080/00098655.2011.575418.

Novak, Joseph. 2002. "Meaningful Learning: The Essential Factor for Conceptual Change in Limited or Inappropriate Propositional Hierarchies Leading to Empowerment of Learners." *Science Education* 86 (4): 548–71.

–. 2010. *Learning, Creating, and Using Knowledge: Concept Maps as Facilitating Tools in Schools and Corporations*. 2nd ed. New Jersey: Lawrence Erlaum Associates.

Ong, Aihwa. 1996. "Cultural Citizenship as Subject-Making: Immigrants Negotiate Racial and Cultural Boundaries in the United States." *Current Anthropology* 37 (5): 737–62. doi: 10.1086/204560.

Orelus, Pierre Wilbert. 2014. "Critical Pedagogy at the Race and Gender Crossroads." In *Interrogating Critical Pedagogy: The Voices of Educators of Color in the Movement*, edited by Pierre Wilbert Orelus and Rochelle Brock, 1–14. London: Routledge.

Ormond, Barbara Mary. 2017. "Curriculum Decisions – The Challenges of Teacher Autonomy over Knowledge Selection for History." *Journal of Curriculum Studies* 49 (5): 599–619. doi: 10.1080/00220272.2016.1149225.

Osborne, Ken. 2000. "'Our History Syllabus Has Us Gasping': History in Canadian Schools – Past, Present, and Future." *Canadian Historical Review* 81 (3): 1–19.

–. 2002. "Canadian History in the Schools: A Brief History." Historica. Accessed November 20, 2006. http://www.histori.ca/prodev/article.do?id=11630.

–. 2003. "Teaching History in Schools: A Canadian Debate." *Curriculum Studies* 35 (5): 585–626.

–. 2006. "'To the Past': Why We Need to Teach and Study History." In *To the Past: History Education, Public Memory, and Citizenship in Canada*, edited by Ruth Sandwell, 103–31. Toronto: University of Toronto Press.

–. 2011. "Teaching Canadian History: A Century of Debate." In *New Possibilities for the Past: Shaping History Education in Canada*, edited by Penney Clark, 55–80. Vancouver: UBC Press.

Ostashewski, Marcia, Heather Fitzsimmons Frey, and Shaylene Johnson. 2018. "Youth-Engaged Art-Based Research in Cape Breton: Transcending Nations, Boundaries and Identities." *Jeunesse: Young People, Texts, Cultures* 10 (2): 100–25.

Palmer, Parker J. 1998. *The Courage to Teach: Exploring the Inner Landscape of a Teacher's Life*. San Francisco: Jossey-Bass.

Pang, Valerie Ooka, John Rivera, and Jill Kerper Mora. 2000. "The Ethic of Caring: Clarifying the Foundation of Multicultural Education." *Educational Forum* 64 (1): 25–32. doi: 10.1080/00131729908984722.

Paragg, Jillian. 2015. "'What Are You?': Mixed Race Responses to the Racial Gaze." *Ethnicities* 17 (3): 277–98. doi: 10.1177/1468796815621938.

Peace, Tom. 2013. "2013: It's Time to Commemorate the 1763 Royal Proclamation." ActiveHistory.ca. Last modified February 4, 2013, accessed August 3, 2015. http://activehistory.ca/2013/02/2013-its-time-to-commemorate-the-1763-royal-proclamation.

Peck, Carla. 2009. "Multi-Ethnic High School Students' Conceptions of Historical Significance: Implications for Canadian History Education." Unpublished doctoral dissertation. Vancouver: University of British Columbia.

–. 2010. "'It's Not Like [I'm] Chinese and Canadian. I Am in Between': Ethnicity and Students' Conceptions of Historical Significance." *Theory and Research in Social Education* 38 (4): 574–617.

–. 2011. "Ethnicity and Students' Historical Understanding." In *New Possibilities for the Past: Shaping History Education in Canada*, edited by Penney Clark, 305–23. Vancouver: UBC Press.

Perumal, Juliet. 2008. "Student Resistance and Teacher Authority: The Demands and Dynamics of Collaborative Learning." *Journal of Curriculum Studies* 40 (3): 381–98. doi: 10.1080/00220270701724570.

Philip, Marlene Nourbese. 1994. "Immigrants: A Label That Sticks for Life." *Toronto Star*, June 27, A17.

Picower, Bree. 2009. "The Unexamined Whiteness of Teaching: How White Teachers Maintain and Enact Dominant Racial Ideologies." *Race Ethnicity and Education* 12 (2): 197–215.

Pinter, Jacob. 2018. "Young Activists Can Sue Government over Climate Change, Supreme Court Says." NPR. Last modified November 3, 2018, accessed November 3, 2018. https://www.npr.org/2018/11/03/663887560/young-activists-can-sue-government-over-climate-change-supreme-court-says.

Pires, Candice. 2018. "'Young People Are Angry': The Teenage Activists Shaping Our Future." *Guardian* (international edition). Last modified May 13, 2018, accessed October 20, 2018. https://www.theguardian.com/society/2018/may/13/young-people-are-angry-meet-the-teenage-activists-shaping-our-future.

Pomson, Alex D.M., and Hoz Ron. 1998. "Sought and Found: Adolescents' 'Ideal' Historical Conceptions as Unveiled by Concept Mapping." *Journal of Curriculum Studies* 30 (3): 319–37.

Popkewitz, Thomas S. 1998. *Struggling for the Soul: The Politics of Schooling and the Construction of the Teacher*. New York: Teachers' College Press.

Portelli, John P. 1993. "Exposing the Hidden Curriculum." *Journal of Curriculum Studies* 25 (4): 343–58.

Purkey, William Watson, and John N. Novak. 1984. *Inviting School Success: A Self-Concept Approach to Teaching and Learning*. 2nd ed. Belmont, CA: Wadsworth.

Rabson, Mia. 2015. "Winnipeg General Strike Is Out: Federal Museum Dumps Exhibit of Seminal Event." *Winnipeg Free Press*. Last modified May 26, 2015. https://www.winnipegfreepress.com/local/winnipeg-general-strike-is-out-304963481.html.

Ralston Saul, John. 2008. *A Fair Country: Telling Truths about Canada*. Canada: Penguin.

–. 2011. "Canada as an Immigrant Nation: Implications for Educators – Excerpts from an Interview with John Ralston Saul." EdCan Network. Last modified September 12, 2011. https://www.edcan.ca/articles/canada-as-an-immigrant-nation-implications-for-educators-excerpts-from-an-interview-with-john-ralston-saul.

Rankin, Jenny Grant. 2016. *First Aid for Teacher Burnout: How You Can Find Peace and Success*. London: Routledge.

"Reconciliation Is Dead. Revolution Is Alive." 2020. *Unist'ot'en – Heal the People, Heal the Land.* Last modified February 29, 2020, accessed March 15, 2020. https://unistoten.camp/reconciliationisdead/.

Rheingold, Howard. 2008. "Using Participatory Media and Public Voice to Encourage Civic Engagement." In *Civic Life Online: Learning How Digital Media Can Engage Youth*, edited by W. Lance Bennett, 97–118. Cambridge, MA: MIT Press.

Ritchie, Scott. 2012. "Incubating and Sustaining: How Teacher Networks Enable and Support Social Justice Education." *Journal of Teacher Education* 63 (2): 120–31. doi: 10.1177/0022487111428327.

Rolón-Dow, Rosalie. 2005. "Critical Care: A Color(full) Analysis of Care Narratives in the Schooling Experiences of Puerto Rican Girls." *American Educational Research Journal* 42 (1): 77–111.

Rooney, Eilish. 2006. "Women's Equality in Northern Ireland's Transition: Intersectionality in Theory and Place." *Feminist Legal Studies* 14 (3): 353–75. doi: 10.1007/s10691-006-9032-z.

Rose, Steven, and Hilary Rose. 2005. "Why We Should Give Up on Race: As Geneticists and Biologists Know, the Term No Longer Has Meaning." *Guardian*. Last modifed April 9, 2005, accessed September 14, 2015. http://www.guardian.co.uk/world/2005/apr/09/race.science.

Ross, Sabrina. 2009. "Critical Race Theory, Democratization, and the Public Good: Deploying Postmodern Understandings of Racial Identity in the Social Justice Classroom to Contest Academic Capitalism." *Teaching in Higher Education* 14 (5): 517–28.

Salinas, Cinthia, and Jeannette D. Alarcón. 2016. "Exploring the Civic Identities of Latina/o High School Students: Reframing the Historical Narrative." *International Journal of Multicultural Education* 18 (1): 68–87.

Sandwell, Ruth. 2006. "Introduction: History Education, Public Memory, and Citizenship in Canada." In *To the Past: History Education, Public Memory, and Citizenship in Canada*, edited by Ruth Sandwell, 3–10. Toronto: University of Toronto Press.

Sandwell, Ruth, and Amy Von Heyking, eds. 2014. *Becoming a History Teacher: Sustaining Practices in Historical Thinking and Knowing*. Edited by Penney Clark. THEN/HiER Book Series. Toronto: University of Toronto Press.

Saye, John W., and Thomas Brush. 2004. "Scaffolding Problem-Based Teaching in a Traditional Social Studies Classroom." *Theory and Research in Social Education* 32 (3): 349–78. doi: 10.1080/00933104.2004.10473259.

Schultz, Brian D. 2011. "Curricular Possibilities: Listening to, Hearing, and Learning from Students." In *Listening to and Learning from Students*, edited by Brian D. Schultz, 1–8. Charlotte, NC: Information Age Publishing.

Schultz, Brian D., and Paris Banks. 2011. "A Shorty Teaching Teachers: Student Insights and Perspective on 'Keepin' It Real' in the Classroom." In *Listening to and Learning from Students*, edited by Brian D. Schultz, 45–57. Charlotte, NC: Information Age Publishing.

Schultz, Mynn Hickey, Dennis J. Barr, and Robert L. Selman. 2001. "The Value of a Developmental Approach to Evaluating Character Development Programmes: An Outcome Study of *Facing History and Ourselves*." *Journal of Moral Education* 30 (1): 3–27.

Scott, Joan W. 1988. "Deconstructing Equality-versus-Difference: Or, the Uses of Poststructuralist Theory for Feminism." *Feminist Studies* 14 (1): 33–50.

–. 2001. "Fantasy Echo: History and the Construction of Identity." *Critical Inquiry* 27 (2): 284–304.

Sears, Alan. 2011. "Historical Thinking and Citizenship Education: Is It Time to End the War?" In *New Possibilities for the Past: Shaping History Education in Canada*, edited by Penney Clark, 344–63. Vancouver: UBC Press.

Sears, Alan, and Andrew Hughes. 1996. "Citizenship Education and Current Educational Reform." *Canadian Journal of Education* 21 (2): 123–42.

Segall, Avner. 2013. "Revitalizing Critical Discourses in Social Education: Opportunities for a More Complexified (Un)Knowing." *Theory and Research in Social Education* 41 (4): 476–93. doi: 10.1080/00933104.2013.836382.

Seixas, Peter. 1993. "The Community of Inquiry as a Basis for Knowledge and Learning: The Case of History." *American Educational Research Journal* 30 (2): 305–24.

–. 1994. "Students' Understanding of Historical Significance." *Theory and Research in Social Education* 22 (3): 281–304.

–. 1999. "Beyond 'Content' and 'Pedagogy': In Search of a Way to Talk about History Education." *Journal of Curriculum Studies* 31 (3): 317–37. doi: 10.1080/002202799183151.

–. 2000. "Schweigen! Die Kinder! or, Does Postmodern History Have a Place in the Schools?" In *Knowing, Teaching, and Learning History*, edited by Peter N. Stearns, Peter Seixas, and Samuel Wineburg, 19–37. New York: New York University Press.

–. 2002a. "Lessons from the U.K., the U.S. and Australia in History Education Reform." Historica. Last modified October 25–27, accessed November 20,

2006. http://www.histori.ca/prodev/article.do;jsessionid=F30B0FD030B718D 090615BC67354DB18.tomcat1?id=11656.

–. 2002b. "The Purposes of Teaching Canadian History." *Canadian Social Studies* 36 (2): 1–7.

–, ed. 2004. *Theorizing Historical Consciousness*. Toronto: University of Toronto Press.

–. 2006a. "Doing History with Wah Chong's Washing and Ironing." *Canadian Issues* (Fall): 58–60.

–. 2006b. "What Is Historical Consciousness?" In *To the Past: History Education, Public Memory, and Citizenship in Canada*, edited by Ruth Sandwell, 11–22. Toronto: University of Toronto Press.

–. 2009. "National History and Beyond." *Journal of Curriculum Studies* 41 (6): 719–22.

–. 2012. "Indigenous Historical Consciousness: An Oxymoron or a Dialogue?" In *History Education and the Construction of National Identities*, edited by Mario Carretero, Mikel Asensio, and María Rodríguez-Moneo, 125–38. Charlotte, NC: Information Age Publishing.

Seixas, Peter, and Carla Peck. 2004. "Teaching Historical Thinking." In *Challenges and Prospects for Canadian Social Studies*, edited by Alan Sears and Ian Wright, 109–17. Vancouver: Pacific Educational Press.

Septor, Leslie M. 2019. "Culture Matters: Professional Development and the Implementation of Culturally Responsive Pedagogy." PhD diss., Rowan University.

Shadd, Adrienne. 2001. "'Where Are You Really From?' Notes of an 'Immigrant' from North Buxton, Ontario." In *Talking about Identity: Encounters in Race, Ethnicity, and Language*, edited by Carl E. James and Adrienne Shadd, 10–16. Toronto: Between the Lines.

Shapiro, Shawna. 2010. "Revisiting the Teachers' Lounge: Reflections on Emotional Experience and Teacher Identity." *Teaching and Teacher Education* 26 (3): 616–21. doi: https://doi.org/10.1016/j.tate.2009.09.009.

Shephard, Michelle. 2014. "How Canada Has Abandoned Its Role as Peacekeeper." *Toronto Star*. Last modified October 31, 2014, accessed July 8, 2015. http://www.thestar.com/news/world/2014/10/31/how_canada_has_ abandoned_its_role_as_a_peacekeeper.html.

Shkedi, Asher. 1997. "The Tension Between 'Ought' and 'Is': Teachers' Conceptions of the Encounter between Students and Culturally Valued Texts." *Educational Research* 39 (1): 65–76. doi: 10.1080/0013188970390104.

Shulman, Lee S. 1987. "Knowledge and Teaching: Foundations of the New Reform." *Harvard Educational Review* 57 (1): 1–23.

Sinclair, Murray, Marie Wilson, and Wilton Littlechild. 2015. "For the Record: Justice Murray Sinclair on Residential Schools." *Maclean's*. Last modified June 2, 2015, accessed on June 8, 2015. https://www.macleans.ca/politics/for-the-record-justice-murray-sinclair-on-residential-schools.

Smith, A.D. 1999. *Myths and Memories of the Nation*. Oxford: Oxford University Press.

Smith, Kari, and Marit Ulvik. 2017. "Leaving Teaching: Lack of Resilience or Sign of Agency?" *Teachers and Teaching* 23 (8): 928–45. doi: 10.1080/13540602.2017.1358706.

St. Denis, Verna. 2011. "Silencing Aboriginal Curricular Content and Perspectives through Multiculturalism: 'There Are Other Children Here.'" *Review of Education, Pedagogy, and Cultural Studies* 33 (4): 306–17. doi: 10.1080/10714413.2011.597638.

Stanley, Timothy. 2000. "Why I Killed Canadian History: Conditions for an Anti-Racist History in Canada." *Histoire sociale/Social History* 33 (36): 79–103.

Statistics Canada. 2010. "The Ethnocultural Diversity of the Canadian Population." Last modified March 9, 2010, accessed June 4, 2019. http://www.statcan.gc.ca/pub/91-551-x/2010001/hl-fs-eng.htm.

–. 2013. "Immigration and Ethnocultural Diversity in Canada." Edited by Ministry of Industry, Ottawa. Accessed December 11, 2016. https://www12.statcan.gc.ca/nhs-enm/2011/as-sa/99-010-x/99-010-x2011001-eng.cfm.

–. 2017a. *Aboriginal Peoples in Canada: Key Results from the 2016 Census*. Edited by Ministry of Industry, Ottawa. Accessed December 11, 2016. https://www150.statcan.gc.ca/n1/daily-quotidien/171025/dq171025a-eng.htm.

–. 2017b. "Canada Goes Urban." *The Daily*. Accessed March 17, 2017. http://www.statcan.gc.ca/pub/11-630-x/11-630-x2015004-eng.htm.

–. 2017c. "Population Growth: Migratory Increase Overtakes Natural Increase." *The Daily*. Accessed March 17, 2017. http://www.statcan.gc.ca/pub/11-630-x/11-630-x2014001-eng.htm.

Stearns, Peter N., Peter Seixas, and Samuel Wineburg, eds. 2000. *Knowing, Teaching, and Learning History: National and International Perspectives*. New York: New York University Press.

Steffe, Leslie P., and Patrick W. Thompson. 2000. "Teaching Experiment Methodology: Underlying Principles and Essential Elements." In *Research*

Design in Mathematics and Science Education, edited by A.E. Kelly and R.A. Lesh, 267–307. Hillsdale, NJ: Erlbaum.

Stovall, David. 2006. "Forging Community in Race and Class: Critical Race Theory and the Quest for Social Justice in Education." *Race Ethnicity and Education* 9 (3): 243–59.

Strauss, Anselm, and Juliet Corbin, eds. 1997. *Grounded Theory in Practice*. Thousand Oaks, CA: Sage.

Style, Emily. 1996. "Curriculum as Window and Mirror." *Social Science Record* (Fall): 1–5.

Subedi, Binaya. 2019. "Narrating Loss, Anxiety and Hope: Immigrant Youth's Narratives of Belonging and Citizenship." *Journal of Social Studies Research* 43 (2): 109–21. doi: https://doi.org/10.1016/j.jssr.2018.09.008.

Taba, Hilda. 1966. *Teaching Strategies and Cognitive Functioning in Elementary School Children*. San Francisco: San Francisco State College.

Talaga, Tanya. 2020. "Reconciliation Isn't Dead. It Never Truly Existed." *The Globe and Mail*. Last modified February 29, 2020, accessed February 29, 2020. https://www.theglobeandmail.com/opinion/article-reconciliation-isnt-dead-it-never-truly-existed/.

Tastsoglou, Evangelia, and Sandy Petrinioti. 2011. "Multiculturalism as Part of the Lived Experience of the 'Second Generation'? Forging Identities by Lebanese-Origin Youth in Halifax." *Canadian Ethnic Studies* 43 (1): 175–96.

Tattrie, Jon. 2019. "Africville." *Canadian Encyclopedia*. Last modified November 20, 2019, accessed December 1, 2019. https://www.thecanadianencyclopedia.ca/en/article/africville.

Teotonio, Isabel. 2018. "Tens of Thousands of High School Students Walk Out En Masse to Protest Out-of-Date Sex-Ed Curriculum." *Toronto Star*. Last modified September 21, 2018, accessed September 22, 2018. https://www.thestar.com/news/gta/2018/09/21/tens-of-thousands-of-high-school-students-walk-out-en-masse-to-protest-out-of-date-sex-ed-curriculum.html.

Terzian, Sevan G., and Elizabeth Anne Yeager. 2007. "'That's When We Became a Nation': Urban Latino Adolescents and Designation of Historical Significance." *Urban Education* 42 (1): 52–81.

THEN/HiER. 2011. "THEN/HiER Goals and Background." History Education Network/Histoire et éducation en réseau. Accessed July 5, 2015. http://thenhier.ca/en/content/thenhier-goals-and-background.

–. 2015. "Small Project Grants Reports." History Education Network/Histoire et éducation en réseau. Accessed May 4, 2016. http://thenhier.ca/en/content/small-project-grants-reports.html.

Thomas, Christa Zeller. 2015. "Birthing a Dominion." ActiveHistory.ca. Last modified January 8, 2015, accessed February 21, 2015. http://activehistory.ca/2015/01/birthing-a-dominion.

Thomas, Matthew Krehl Edward, and Benjamin Jay Whitburn. 2019. "Time for Inclusion?" *British Journal of Sociology of Education* 40 (2): 159–73. doi: 10.1080/01425692.2018.1512848.

Thompson, Greg, and James Bell. 2005. "School Connectedness: Student Voices Examine Power and Subjectivity." *International Journal on School Disaffection* 3 (1): 1–28.

Todd, Douglas. 2015. "Is Canada a Blank Slate, with No Culture?" *Vancouver Sun*. Last modified March 14, 2015, accessed March 30, 2015. https://vancouversun.com/news/staff-blogs/is-canada-a-blank-slate-with-no-culture-many-beg-to-differ.

Toshalis, Eric. 2012. "The Rhetoric of Care: Preservice Teacher Discourses that Depoliticize, Deflect, and Deceive." *Urban Review* 44 (1): 1–35. doi: 10.1007/s11256-011-0177-y.

TRC (Truth and Reconciliation Commission of Canada). 2015a. "Canada's Residential Schools: Reconciliation." In *Final Report of the Truth and Reconciliation Commission of Canada*. Toronto: James Lorimer.

–. 2015b. "Volume One: Summary – Honouring the Truth, Reconciling for the Future." In *Final Report of the Truth and Reconciliation Commission of Canada*. Toronto: James Lorimer.

Tremonti, Anna Maria. 2015. "History of Residential Schools Ignored in Canadian Curriculum." CBC. Last modified June 12, 2015, accessed June 29, 2015. http://www.cbc.ca/radio/thecurrent/the-current-for-june-10-2015-1.3107341/history-of-residential-schools-ignored-in-canadian-curriculum-1.3107389.

Trouillot, Michel-Rolph. 1995. *Silencing the Past: Power and the Production of History*: Boston: Beacon Press.

Tuhiwai Smith, Linda 2008. *Decolonizing Methodologies: Research and Indigenous Peoples*. London: Zed Books.

Tye, Barbara Benham, and Lisa O'Brien. 2002. "Why Are Experienced Teachers Leaving the Profession?" *Phi Delta Kappan* 84 (1): 24–32.

Valenzuela, Angela. 1999. *Subtractive Schooling: US-Mexican Youth and the Politics of Caring*. Albany: SUNY Press.

Valli, Linda. 1997. "Listening to Other Voices: A Description of Teacher Reflection in the United States." *Peabody Journal of Education* 72 (1): 67–88. doi: 10.1207/s15327930pje7201_4.

van Hover, Stephanie, and Elizabeth Yeager. 2007. "'I Want to Use My Subject Matter to..': The Role of Purpose in One U.S. Secondary History Teacher's Instructional Decision Making." *Canadian Journal of Education* 30 (3): 670–90.

van Kan, Carlos A., Petra Ponte, and Nico Verloop. 2013. "How Do Teachers Legitimize Their Classroom Interactions in Terms of Educational Values and Ideals?" *Teachers and Teaching* 19 (6): 610–33. doi: 10.1080/13540602.2013.827452.

Vandermaas-Peeler, Alex, Daniel Cox, Molly Fisch-Friedman, and Adam C. Jones. 2018. "Diversity, Division, Discrimination: The State of Young America." Public Religion Research Institute. Last modified January 10, 2018, accessed October 20, 2018. https://www.prri.org/research/mtv-culture-and-religion.

Vangrieken, Katrien, Ilke Grosemans, Filip Dochy, and Eva Kyndt. 2017. "Teacher Autonomy and Collaboration: A Paradox? Conceptualising and Measuring Teachers' Autonomy and Collaborative Attitude." *Teaching and Teacher Education* 67: 302–15.

VanSledright, Bruce A. 2008. "Narratives of Nation-State, Historical Knowledge, and School History Education." *Review of Research in Education* 32 (1): 109–46. https://journals.sagepub.com/doi/abs/10.3102/0091732X07311065.

Vaught, Sabina E., and Angelina E. Castagno. 2008. "'I Don't Think I'm a Racist': Critical Race Theory, Teacher Attitudes, and Structural Racism." *Race Ethnicity and Education* 11 (2): 95–113.

Vaz, Kim Marie. 1995. "Racial Aliteracy: White Appropriation of Black Presences." *Women and Therapy* 16 (4): 31–49.

Vickery, Amanda E. 2016. "'I Worry about My Community': African American Women Utilizing Communal Notions of Citizenship in the Social Studies Classroom." *International Journal of Multicultural Education* 18 (1): 28–44.

Vogt, Franziska. 2002. "A Caring Teacher: Explorations into Primary School Teachers' Professional Identity and Ethic of Care." *Gender and Education* 14 (3): 251–64.

Wah, Fred. 1996. "Half-Bred Poetics." *absinthe* 9 (2): 60–66.

Wane, Njoki Nathani. 2007. "African Women and Candian History: Demanding Our Place in the Curriculum." In *Theorising Empowerment: Canadian Perspectives on Black Feminist Thought*, edited by Notisha Massaquoi and Njoki Nathani Wane, 129–53. Toronto: Inanna Publications and Education.

Warikoo, Natasha. 2011. *Balancing Acts: Youth Culture in the Global City*. Berkeley: University of California Press.

Warren, John T. 2011. "Reflexive Teaching: Toward Critical Autoethnographic Practices of/in/on Pedagogy." *Cultural Studies – Critical Methodologies* 11 (2): 139–44. doi: 10.1177/1532708611401332.

Waters, Tony. 2005. "Why Students Think There Are Two Kinds of American History." *History Teacher* 39 (1): 1–7.

Welch, Mary Agnes. 2015. "CMHR 'Model of Complacency.'" *Winnipeg Free Press*. Last modified May 6, 2015, accessed July 17, 2015. http://www.winnipegfreepress.com/local/Former-curator-of-CMHR-says-she-was-ordered-to-limit-aboriginal-content-302847231.html.

Wenk, Silke. 2000. "Gendered Representations of the Nation's Past and Future." In *Gendered Nations: Nationalisms and Gender Order in the Long Nineteenth Century*, edited by Ida Blom, Karen Hagemann, and Catherine Hall, 63–77. New York: Berg.

Wenshya Lee, Jennifer, and Yvonne M. Hébert. 2006. "The Meaning of Being Canadian: A Comparison between Youth of Immigrant and Non-Immigrant Origins." *Canadian Journal of Education* 29 (2): 497–520.

Wertsch, James V. 2000. "Is It Possible to Teach Beliefs, as Well as Knowledge about History?" In *Knowing, Teaching, and Learning History: National and International Perspectives*, edited by Peter N. Stearns, Peter Seixas, and Samuel Wineburg, 38–62. New York: New York University Press.

Westwood, Rosemary. 2013. "Canada's Greatest Gift." *Maclean's*. Last modified June 30, 2013, accessed July 10, 2015. http://www.macleans.ca/general/canadas-greatest-gift.

Wheeler, Schaun. 2007. "History Is Written by the Learners: How Student Views Trump United States History Curricula." *History Teacher* 41 (1): 9–24.

Winn, Ira J. 2004. "The High Cost of Uncritical Teaching." *Phi Delta Kappan* 85 (7): 496–500.

Wright, Cecile. 2010. "Othering Difference: Framing Identities and Representation in Black Children's Schooling in the British Context." *Irish Educational Studies* 29 (3): 305–20. doi: 10.1080/03323315.2010.498569.

Yilmaz, Kaya. 2008. "Social Studies Teachers' Views of Learner-Centered Instruction." *European Journal of Teacher Education* 31 (1): 35–53. doi: 10.1080/02619760701845008.

Yon, Daniel. 2000. *Elusive Culture: Schooling, Race, and Identity in Global Times*. Edited by Deborah Britzman. Albany: SUNY Press.

Young, D'bi. 2016. "Evening Celebrating Black Women in Canada." Historica Canada. Last modified February 29, 2016, accessed September 30, 2017. https://www.youtube.com/watch?v=iefJu_9EqPI.

Yuval-Davis, Nira. 2007. "Intersectionality, Citizenship and Contemporary Politics of Belonging." *Critical Review of International Social and Political Philosophy* 10 (4): 561–74. doi: 10.1080/13698230701660220.

Zanazanian, Paul, and Sabrina Moisan. 2012. "Harmonizing Two of History Teaching's Main Social Functions: Franco-Québécois History Teachers and Their Predispositions to Catering to Narrative Diversity." *Education Sciences* 2 (4): 255–75.

Zhang, Yan, and Yan Guo. 2015. "Becoming Transnational: Exploring Multiple Identities of Students in a Mandarin-English Bilingual Programme in Canada." *Globalisation, Societies and Education* 13 (2): 210–29. doi: 10.1080/14767724.2014.934071.

Index

active democratic citizenship, 51
active learning, 26, 52, 63–64, 71, 75, 111, 177–78, 182
add-and-stir histories, 15, 91, 138, 199
affective learning, 77–78, 94, 99
Africville, 19–20, 35, 99, 109–10, 150–51, 195, 197–98
Alberta, 57, 204n6, 204n11
alternative schools, 33–34, 96, 145–46, 150, 155–56, 162–64, 178–79, 189–90, 192, 194, 200, 205n1
Anderson, Benedict, 43
anger in learning history, 61, 72, 85–86, 198
archives, 45, 58–59, 148, 174, 200
Asian students, 131
assent to learn, 10, 29–32, 99–100, 107, 117–18
assessment or evaluation, 34, 51, 147
"at risk" students, 76–77, 107
Audlaluk, Larry, 87–88

banking model, 9, 27

belonging in Canada, 129–30, 139
belonging in school, 5–6, 72, 73, 75, 127
Benchmarks of Historical Thinking, 12–13, 54–55
"the big six," 54–55
Black history, 5, 61, 81–83, 90–94, 99–100, 124, 131, 133–35, 137, 184–85, 196; Black History Month, 91–92, 121–22
Black students, 5–6, 76–77, 81–83, 89–100, 114–17, 121–22, 131–35, 158, 184, 196, 197–98, 205n7
British colonialism, learning about, 35, 174, 192
Bruner, Jerome, 107, 172
burnout, teacher, 162, 165

Canada-first narrative, 104, 139, 143
#Canada150, 50
Canadian Charter of Rights and Freedoms, 45
Canadian identity, 4, 20, 38–39, 43–47, 50, 65

Canadian identity, youth, 67–68, 73, 89–91, 94, 101, 128–29, 135–36
"*Canadian*-Canadian" identity, 138–40, 143
Caribbean history, 181, 195, 205n4
Caribbean students, 67, 132, 134, 158, 197
causation, 139
cause and consequence, historical thinking concepts, 55, 59–60, 63
Chinese Canadians, 18, 60–62
Chinese Exclusion Act (1923) (formerly Chinese Immigration Act), 18, 169
chronology or timeline, 138–43, 168–69, 170–71, 199
citizenship or civics education, 5, 51, 63
class community, 10
Coastal GasLink, 48
Cold War, 125, 178, 183–85, 187–88
collaborative learning, 176
colonialism, 203n1; history, 5, 8, 123–24; policies, 17, 50; postcolonialism, definition, 203n1; practices, 49, 50; structures, 17, 48, 50, 63
commemoration, 43–46, 50
community, classroom, 109–10, 133, 135–36, 200
complexity, definition, 83–84, 91
concept formation strategy, 173–74
concept learning, 32–33, 172–74
concept map, 191–92, 197–98
Concepts of History and Teaching Approaches (CHATA), 53–54, 204n7
Confederation, 43, 45, 175–76
connection, definition, 70–72, 80

Conservative government, 44–45
continuity and change, as historical thinking concepts, 55, 59–60, 63
controversial histories, avoiding or limiting when teaching, 6, 26, 75, 82–83, 90, 96–97, 111, 193, 205nn6–7
counterstories, 15, 84–86, 91, 93, 133–35, 149–50, 193–94, 199
critical care, 28–29, 32, 125
critical literacy, 27–28, 115
critical pedagogy, 26–32, 139, 151, 156
critical race theory (CRT), 14–16, 20–21, 25, 84, 167, 201
culturally responsive education, 30–32
curricular roles, 34, 147

decolonizing, education for, 11–12, 50
deconstruction, 8, 24–25, 63, 166, 168–69, 192–94
democracy, education for, 11, 51, 27–28, 54–55, 75–77, 124–25, 175
Derrida, Jacques, 23–25, 169–70, 206n1
design-based research (DBR), 34, 36–37
Dewey, John, 59, 159
difficult histories, 12, 97, 126
digital engagement, youth, 7
discipline-based history education, 12–13, 52–63, 167
discussion, instructional, 75–77, 86–87, 97–98, 109–10, 117, 124–25, 136
documentaries, learning histories, 78, 147, 189–90, 206n2

educational rhetoric. *See* edu-speak
edu-speak, 34, 107–12, 205*n*1
emotion, learning history, 59, 61, 62, 72, 78–79, 198
engaged pedagogy, 11, 28, 127
ethical dimension, historical thinking concepts, 55, 59–60, 63
ethical relationality, 12
ethics of care, 28–29
evidence, historical thinking concepts, 55, 59–60, 63
expectations of students, 80
"expert blind spot," 183

failing, students, 5–6, 69–70, 98–99, 117–18, 196
fantasy echo, 22, 62
feminist theory, 15, 21–22, 25, 167–68, 201
Filipino students, 132
Foucault, Michel, 9, 25, 170, 206*n*1
Foundation for the Atlantic Canada Social Studies Curriculum, 56–57
founders, Canada or story or nation, 8, 17, 45, 47
Freire, Paulo, 9, 11, 27, 64, 70, 170, 187
French revolution, 35, 71, 174, 178–79, 189–90, 194

gang violence, 82, 93–94
geography, 51
Granatstein, Jack, 130–31, 203*n*1 [chap. 2], 205*n*6
grand narrative, Canada, 5, 7, 14, 38, 65, 67, 83, 84–86, 89–92, 118, 119, 129, 133–35, 143, 168–70

grand narrative, concept, 7, 22–25, 124, 139, 193, 197–98
Grise Fiord relocation, 87–88

Haitian revolution, 35, 194
Harper, Stephen, 44–48, 203*n*2, 204*n*5
hating Canadian history, 14, 66, 74, 85–86, 88
heritage sites, 32, 45, 48, 58–59, 168, 174
higher education, 6, 116, 152
Historic Space, 32–38, 168–200
historical consciousness, 12–13, 54–55
historical empathy, 78–79
historical perspective, historical thinking concepts, 55, 59–60, 62, 63
historical significance, historical thinking concepts, 59–60, 63, 205*n*3
historical thinking, 12–13, 52–63
history curriculum, 5, 12–13, 49, 51–53, 90, 147, 167, 182
history of education, 3, 42, 53
history wars, 44, 203*n*1
Hobsbawm, Eric, 43
home lives, students', 106, 116–18, 143
home-school split, 7–8, 73–74, 114–15, 117, 119, 185
hooks, bell, 11, 27–28, 75
hyphenated identity, 46

identity, youth, 71–73, 89–91, 94, 97, 101, 116, 166

"imagined communities," 43
Immigration Act (1919), 18, 61
immigration policies, history, 8, 17–19, 60–61
Indian Act (1876), 17
Indigenous epistemologies, 8, 47, 48, 49, 50, 59
Indigenous youth, 13–14
infantilizing students, 29, 179–80
inquiry, as educational method, 51, 53, 56–57, 63–64, 88, 103, 147, 152, 168, 173
intersectional analysis, 5, 21–22
Inuit, 49, 87–88
invitational education, 31–32, 99–100, 107, 164

justice, education for, 22, 24–25, 50, 58, 62–63, 84

knowledge packages, teaching from, 137–38, 140–41, 146, 149
Kohl, Herbert, 29–30

learning science, 10–11
learning styles, 34, 106, 108–12, 143
Liberal government, 45
liberalism, 20, 92, 131, 136–37
Library and Archives Canada, 45
local history, 81–83, 92–93
logic of the textbook, 175, 180
love, 11, 28

Macdonald, John A., 17, 18, 60–62
mainstream schools, 33, 145–46, 150–51, 153–55, 161, 163, 195

Manitoba, 204n6
McClung, Nellie, 169
meaningful learning, definition, 173
Métis, 49
mind map, 174–75, 181–82, 189–90, 198
mirror and window learning, 74–75, 193
misbehaviour in classroom, 31–32, 83, 106–7, 111–14, 118, 157–58
mothering students, 29, 116–17, 200
movies, learning history, 78–79, 87
multiculturalism, false promise, 11, 16, 20–21, 44, 131, 137, 140; idealized, 138, 139, 142; policy, 20
museums. *See* heritage sites

New Brunswick, 56–57
Noddings, Nel, 28–29
Novak, Joseph, 10, 57, 66, 70–71, 77, 173, 191

oral histories, 59, 125–26, 193, 205n4
Other/Others/Othering, 7, 23, 24–25, 46, 48, 59–60, 90, 104, 106–7, 118–19, 122, 127, 132, 135, 136, 138, 194

pedagogy of belonging, 72, 75; of connectedness, 72; of the oppressed, 11, 27
personal histories, 120–22, 126–27, 196
places for teacher-student interaction, 160–64, 166
positive emotional climate, 10, 66, 95, 98–99, 124–25, 152

postcolonialism, definition, 203n1
postmodernism, 9, 15, 22–25, 32–33, 59, 167–72, 201
poststructuralism, 9, 15, 22–25, 32–33, 59, 167–72, 201
post–World War II, 35, 43, 61, 71, 87–88, 113–14, 125, 141, 170, 176–78, 180–81, 183, 187, 195, 197
power plays by teachers, 98–99
presentations, instructional strategy, 109–11
primary sources, learning with/teaching with, 52–53, 58–59, 87–88, 103, 109–11, 113–14, 133, 148–49, 193–94
prior knowledge, students', 10, 30–31, 66, 71, 73–74, 81–82, 94, 173, 187
problem-posing approach, 11, 27, 64, 187
professional development, 148–50, 200
"proper teachers," according to students, 95–96
public history. *See* heritage sites

quasquicentennial, 138–40
Quebec, 204n8

racialized Canadians, not belonging, 19
racialized students, 14, 62, 65–70, 77, 89–98, 107, 114–17, 120–23, 128–38, 141–42, 201
racism in Canadian history, 8, 15–21, 60–62, 110
racist policies, 169, 196
Ralston Saul, John, 47

reconciliation, 48
reflection, 149–60, 164, 167
research, by teachers, 131–32, 147–53, 164, 200
residential schools, 17, 48, 49, 203n2, 204n10
resistance or rejections, students, 31–32, 69–70, 83, 85, 97, 99, 100, 106–7, 108, 111–12, 120, 122–24, 179–80
#Resistance150, 50
reverse racism, 133
role play, instructional strategy, 78, 109–11, 114

"school knowledge," 70, 83
schooling, structure and system of, 102, 107, 145, 149–52, 163–65, 200, 202
Seixas, Peter, 12–13, 52–63, 204n11
semiotics, 23–25
sesquicentennial, 45, 50
Seven Sacred Teachings, 50
Sinclair, Justice Murray, 13, 49, 204n10
skills-based history education, 12–13, 52–63
social media, 112–13
social science, 51
social studies curriculum, 51, 56
spaces for student-teacher interaction, 153–59, 164, 166
staff room, 154–58, 161–62
sticky notes, 175–76, 180–81
student success, 34, 200
students' age, 106, 111–16, 143
subtractive education, 29–32, 107
supportive agency, 149

Taba, Hilda, 172–74
Taiwanese Canadians, 18
teacher-student relationship, 11, 29–30, 37, 105, 107, 127, 147, 152, 162, 173
teachers: bitching, 153–56, 161; burnout, 162, 165; meditative deliberation, 153, 159–60; not knowing, 126–27, 128, 131, 183–84; venting, 153, 156, 158
technology, in schooling, 52, 112–15
textbooks, 85–88, 90, 100, 133, 168, 175–76, 180, 183, 193–94, 206n3
THEN/HiER, 55–56
time, schooling, 146–53, 164, 166, 200
toxic school culture, 154–58
treaties: treaty rights, 48
Trudeau, Justin, 45, 48
Truth and Reconciliation Commission (TRC), 3, 8, 17, 49, 50, 203n2, 204n6, 204n10; calls to action, 49–50

unconditional education, 31–32, 99–100, 107, 163–64
unsuccessful students, 69–70, 76–77, 98–99
"us" vs "them," 11–12, 20, 136, 163

Wah, Fred, 46
War of 1812, 19, 45, 46
West Indian Immigration Scheme, 18–19, 35, 99, 133, 136, 195
Wet'suwet'en, 48
white students, 90, 133–35
white teachers, 26, 29, 31–32, 116–17, 124, 137, 205n7
whiteness and Canada, 16, 20–21, 81–83, 90–95, 124, 131, 135, 136, 138–40
"Whose histories should you teach?" 90, 130, 135–36, 138, 142, 205n7
Winnipeg General Strike, 45
World War I, 43, 45, 91, 120, 140
World War II, 81–83, 93, 120, 125
writing in role, instructional strategy, 78

Young, D'bi, 6